62

Skepticism and Humanism

Skepticism and Humanism

The New Paradigm

Paul Kurtz

Transaction Publishers
New Brunswick (U.S.A.) and London (U.K.)

Preparation of this volume was partly supported by the Committee for Scientific Research (Komitet Badan Naukowych), Poland

This book is printed on acid-free paper that meets the American National Standard for Permanence of Paper for Printed Library Materials.

Library of Congress Catalog Number: 00-061552
ISBN: 0-7658-0051-9
Printed in the United States of America

Library of Congress Cataloging-in-Publication Data

Kurtz, Paul, 1925-
    Skepticism and humanism : the new paradigm / Paul Kurtz.
        p.cm.
    Includes bibliographical refernces and index.
    ISBN 0-7658-0051-9 (alk. paper)
        1. Humanism. 2. Skepticism. 3. Secularism. I. Title.

BL2747.6 K89 2000
144—dc21

00-061552

Contents

Part Four   Humanism Writ Large

Introduction:
A New Paradigm for the Third Millennium

I

As we begin the third millennium, there are conflicting prognostications of what is likely to occur in the twenty-first century and beyond. There are those who are perennial optimists, forecasting unlimited horizons, exuding enthusiastic expectations of continued unparalleled growth and development. These come from those who have confidence in the advance of the frontiers of scientific research, who believe that our understanding of nature will continue to grow, that new technologies will conquer diseases, extend life, and contribute to rising standards of living, affluence, and cultural freedom on a worldwide basis. Economic forecasters assert that improvements in production and technological innovation will contribute to continued economic expansion over the long range. They point to the great achievements of human ingenuity in the twentieth century—at least in the free-market economies of the democratic world. They think that these trends are likely to continue, barring some unexpected disasters.

Opposing their buoyant optimism are the pessimists in our midst, the Jeremiahs of doom and gloom. Religious prophets predicted "end days" around the year 2000, basing this on biblical sources. Although Armageddon did not occur they continue to decry the loosening of traditional moral values, the growth of personal freedom, and sexual liberation. They moan about the death of outrage by those who do not share their moral revulsion, and they express dire forebodings about our decay from within. Allied with these religious naysayers are secular pessimists who predict other forms of apocalypse, believing that environmental degradations, pollution, global warming, runaway population, nuclear war, terrorism, and weapons of mass destruction will destroy civilization. The fear of the unknown has perennial roots within the human breast; for there have always been constant worries and insecurities of one form or another of the future. "The barbarians threaten to destroy us," the cry goes up, "They are either at the gates" or "within the city."

The onset of a new millennium is a special occasion to reflect on what is likely to happen. Both the extreme optimists and the dismal pessimists are no doubt wrong. Humankind will muddle through, perhaps with two steps forward and one backward. Having been a young American soldier in the European theater of operations in World War II and having viewed first-hand the near total destruction of so many cities and also their almost Phoenix-like resurrection 50 years later, one can only admire the determination and fortitude of humans to overcome adversity; that is, given the right social conditions and attitudes. In certain social climates, such as slave cultures, it is often difficult to succeed (if one is a slave or serf, or lives in a closed authoritarian society), and human beings sometimes seem helpless and resigned to their fate. Nevertheless, I submit that the human prospect as we enter the third millennium is a cause for some measured optimism. There is nothing in the nature of things which dictates that the future must be malevolent or beneficent, and/or that disaster or prosperity will prevail. Whatever will be depends in part on the resolve of human beings in any one period in history to dream up new images of the future to undertake new plans and projects, and to adopt bold and intelligent solutions, and the action necessary to fulfill them. There is, of course, no guarantee that they will be realized. "The best-laid schemes o' mice an' men gang aft agley, an' lea'e us nought but grief and pain," said Robert Burns. Moreover, the audacious Promethean spirit necessary for great achievements of the past has often gone into hibernation or retreat. During the Dark Ages men and women feared to challenge the gods and/or to creatively forge their own destinies. Religious faith, if excessive, can dampen the ardor for living the adventurous life. To intensify one's obedience to God often is to lessen one's lust for living.

In any case, the beginning of the third millennium is an opportunity to reflect on the human condition and to ask where our journeys have taken us thus far and which roads we wish to travel in the future. Yogi Berra, the shortstop, once remarked, "If you see a fork in the road, take it!"—but this is of little help for those who wish to construct new roads. I need, however, to enter an important caveat here, for the beginning or end of a millennium has no special significance *per se* in the nature of things. Nature remains indifferent as to whether our hopes are fulfilled. The year 2000 is an arbitrary point in the Western calendar based upon the alleged birth of Jesus. For the Christian it has special meaning; for the skeptical secularist it is simply a cultural artifact, not an anchor rooted in existential reality. Nevertheless, our Western calendars today can interpret ancient civilization by calculating B.C.E., before the Common Era, and C.E., the Common Era, without any religious significance. The only meaning of the third millennium is as a cultural contrivance. Human history rarely has sharp dividing lines or decisive turning points (there are, of course, exceptions to this generalization, such as the utter destruction of Carthage at the hands of the Romans)—and so the millennium means nothing in the nature of things, nor do years or centuries. They are simply human constructs. Yet this is as good an occasion as any to reflect on likely cultural developments in the future. I should add that humankind has evolved over thousands of millennia on this planet; to focus on the two or three most recent is an encapsulated view.

Another caveat: history is not predetermined, nor are there inexorable trends (beyond the proverbial death and taxes). The fact that we may forget history does not mean that we are condemned to always repeat it. Nor will the trends that are discernible today necessarily mean that they will persist tomorrow. No one could have predicted that a large part of humanity some nineteen centuries later would continue to deify and worship a Galilean Jew of doubtful parentage, allegedly nailed to a cross or to a tree. Nor was it possible to predict that a seventh-century Arab trader managing a caravan business of his older wealthy wife would in his forties claim to receive messages from Gabriel in the caves of Hijra on the outskirts of Mecca, and that these so-called revelations would develop into Islam and rapidly conquer large sections of the world. Could anyone have foretold with confidence in the nineteenth century that the writings of a German émigré working in the British Museum would transform half the globe in the twentieth century and beguile the rest of the world and would just as suddenly fall into disrepute? It is doubtful that the signers of the Declaration of Independence and the authors of the Constitution would have conceived that the three million colonists in the new country would in a century conquer much of the continent and in two become the dominant superpower of the world. Again, who could have predicted in 1900 that the fascists would seize Germany and Italy and bathe Europe in the blood of the Holocaust or that Stalinism would betray socialist ideals and lead to a gulag of murderous repression?

How can we write scenarios for the twenty-first century when those for the twentieth have been so wide of the mark? The twentieth century is surely the century of dramatic scientific and technological achievement. yet the thrill of scientific discovery often has unexpected consequences. Einstein's relativity theory and quantum mechanics modified the Newtonian world view, but the great breakthroughs in subatomic physics led to the splitting of the atom, the development of nuclear energy and the hydrogen bomb. In astronomy, Hubble's discoveries of galaxies beyond the Milky Way and his postulation that the universe was receding at a terrific speed enormously altered our conceptions of the universe. This has opened the imagination to other unanticipated results, such as the discovery of planetary star systems beyond our own, the possibility that forms of extraterrestrial, possibly even intelligent, life may exist. New breakthroughs in science often have unexpected consequences—as Sir Arthur Fleming's discovery of penicillin and the subsequent development of other antibiotics against infectious diseases, or the Crick-Watson discovery of DNA, which expanded our understanding of the human genome. And new computer technologies have radically globalized human civilization and altered economic parameters virtually overnight.

The democratic revolutions and the doctrine of universal human rights have captured the imagination of large sectors of humanity and gained widespread acceptance, so much so that with the growth of democracy there would be, Fukuyama predicted, an "end to history." Paradoxically almost at the same time ancient authoritarian fundamentalist religions have grown in vitriolic intensity along with bizarre New Age media-driven paranormal belief systems. Also surprising is the resurgence of primitive tribal and ethnic loyalties, unleashing wars of intolerance and bitterness.

II

As I write these lines, it is not without some surprise that I have lived almost three quarters of a century (I was born in 1925). I am old enough to have known people who have lived in the nineteenth century. Charlie White who was in his late 80s tended bar at my father's tavern in the 1930s. He fought in the Civil War and came to work in a horse and buggy. My maternal grandfather fought in the Philippines in the Spanish-American War. He and his sons were freethinkers and socialists. Indeed, practically everyone that I knew as an undergraduate at New York University believed that socialism and the nationalization of the means of production would positively transform the world—how these dreams have been shattered, as free-market capitalism has triumphed (for the moment at least) everywhere.

I can also well remember how the Nazis launched the first jet airplane in 1944. I was in an anti-aircraft half-track unit in France. The jets were so fast, or so we thought, that we could hardly see them until they flew beyond us toward the horizon. And I saw the first rockets launched over London and later over Liege during the Battle of the Bulge. How all of these innovations transformed air travel and space technology in later decades is a marvel to behold. Similarly, I can vividly recall the first television sets (seen at the New York World's Fair in 1939) and the first computers, introduced at IBM, and the first cybernetic machines introduced at the AAAS (in 1948) by MIT Professor Norbert Weiner.

Thus in my lifetime, I have witnessed the rise and fall of Nazism, and the rapid decline of socialist ideals, the growth of democratic values (even among conservatives), the Great Depression of the '30s and the post-war boom, the sexual revolution and the women's movement, prognostications of the end of religion and its revival, the withering away of British, French, Dutch, and Belgian colonialism and the emergence of America as the pre-eminent superpower, the sudden appearance of the New Right and the New Left on campuses, and their demise.

Thus, the pace of change is so rapid that one cannot predict with confidence what will come next. Marx and Engels thought that there were laws governing history and that we could analyze the causes of social change ("The Economic or Sociological Interpretation of History"). History surely reveals to some extent similar patterns of human behavior. At the same time, the contingent is real in history. Accidents, anomalies, novelties, and uncertainties are enduring features of the human condition. Heroes and heroines, great benefactors and malefactors, noble geniuses and evil men emerge to turn the tide of events at decisive moments. This is an indelible part of the socio-cultural landscapes of the past, and this will no doubt continue in the future. No one can hope to stop in midstream and/or get off of the roller coaster. There are constant ups and downs, and in rushing and ebbing tides. Although historians can look back and characterize certain epochs—Hellenic civilization, the rise of monotheistic religions, the Renaissance, the Enlightenment, the growth of modern science, the age of democratic revolutions, etc., none of these are at fixed points, but are part of the continuous flow of historical events.

Still, we need to constantly reckon our place in history, or at least get some sense of where we have been and where we are going. There are quarterly, annual, five-, ten-, or thirty-year plans (such as retirement) and constant attempts to make projections. It is vital that we draft plans for the future and these be based on some rational estimate of past trends and future outcomes. I should add another personal note: I have studied and taught the history of ideas (and the history of philosophy and science) during most of my professional university career. I am enamored of the great pagan civilizations of the Greeks and Romans, and I have deplored the "failure of nerve" (as Gilbert Murray characterized it) that overcame them. I have studied with fascination the origins of Christianity and of Islam. I have been a devotee of the Renaissance and the Enlightenment and of modern science and democracy. And I have been intrigued by the rise and fall of civilizations (à la Arnold Toynbee and Oswald Spengler)—viewing history from the broader perspective.

III

An interesting analytical concept that has been introduced is that of "paradigm." This refers to the basic concepts and categories by which a culture interprets the universe and the place of human beings in the scheme of things. Such paradigms provide groundings for explaining events and predicting what is likely to ensue. Thomas Kuhn,[1] the historian of science, used the concept "paradigm shift" to describe the gradual erosion or rapid collapse of a set of key concepts and convictions that prevail during certain historical periods. For example, Aristotelian science gave way to the Newtonian world view, and this in turn was transformed by relativity theory and quantum mechanics. Or again, the Judæo-Christian doctrine of special creation was radically altered by the Darwinian theory of evolution. So there have been large-scale intellectual paradigm shifts that have occurred in the past and are most likely to occur in the future.

There are several questions that can be raised: Does the concept of a paradigm apply only to the intellectual world; or does it include wider aspects of mass society? I think that the answer to this is clearly the latter; for eventually the meaning of a new outlook (for example, the heliocentric conception of astronomy) penetrates to ordinary persons—especially in the contemporary world where education and literacy is widespread and information can be conveyed everywhere by the new infomedia technologies. Thus a paradigm not only applies to sophisticated scientific theories but to religious, economic, and political ideas and other forms of artistic and cultural expression.

One can discern changes in religious beliefs and practices, such as the rise of the Protestant Reformation challenging the hegemony of the Roman Catholic Church, or the conversion to Islam of North Africa, the Middle East, and parts of Eastern Europe. In European music, classical forms (Bach, Mozart, and Beethoven) are challenged by Romanticism (Brahms and Tchaikovsky) and this in turn by contemporary atonal music (Bartok, Schoenberg, and Stravinsky). Twentieth-century abstract modern art transforms the classical forms of earlier generations. There are schools within disciplines, some proclaiming new forms of expression or belief, some adhering to conventional modes.

There is obviously a cross fertilization of the disciplines and an interpretation and overlap of perspectives, with constant processes of revolution and counter-revolution, the appearance of fads and fashions, the avant-garde and old guard; traditions and revolts from them are often made to shock and bemuse opponents or curry favor from patrons—each faction contends for attention or notoriety. In different generations there are bearded gentlemen or clean-shaven faces, long- or short-skirted women, and these processes apply to the entire gamut of human tastes and interests; though in some cultures the traditional habits of thought and conduct are so ingrained that innovation or substitution is frowned upon and forbidden.

A key factor responsible for changing paradigms is the clash of cultures. No society can long endure in splendid isolation. Although the Chinese built a Great Wall to defend it from invading hordes, eventually it could no longer resist Western ideas and values; nor could the Japanese, who were huddled on their island redoubts for so long. In human history the old paradigms, which may dominate an area for a period of time, are eventually challenged by alternative paradigms. One may absorb the others, as in the case of China, or eventually be conquered by them. Often within a socio-cultural context the defenders of an entrenched outlook are not refuted by logic or evidence—as in the case of science or philosophy—they simply die out; for the stalwart proponents of previous generations are not succeeded by young blood that is willing to follow in the old masters' footsteps and assume the mantle of leadership of a school, movement, or outlook. Poets, philosophers, scientists, and artists may find the existing framework irrelevant, boring, confining, restrictive; and they may seek to break out to new forms, liberating them from the old. These in turn may in time be viewed as banal or trivial and there may be new calls for a return to classical structures and values. The lust for fame and glory is a powerful impulse in creative people, who are willing to abandon the temptations of wealth or power that motivates other men and women for intellectual or artistic acclaim and recognition; securing their place in history is what moves them.

A genius is someone who is heralded by society because he or she sees things in a new way (Kant, Freud, and Marx), makes new discoveries (Faraday, Niels Bohr, Marie Curie), introduces new forms of expression (Picasso, Hemingway), or new forms of moral behavior (Confucius, Jesus, Buddha), or are successful inventors or doers (Edison, Carnegie, Ford). There are many creative individuals who introduce daring ideas or forms. Yet they may not be accepted in their own day by their peers (Kierkegaard, Kafka), or never heralded by society for their breakthroughs, and they, along with their gifts, may be buried by the sands of time. They die ignominiously for they are ignored. The dead hand of custom or the tyranny of fashions may have passed them by. His or her ideas may never be incorporated into the existing paradigm; and the new directions that are recommended may never be appreciated or adopted.

Often a new paradigm is proclaimed as a harbinger of the future; in time it may undermine the official doctrines, and what was considered unthinkable and outrageous in one age may be fervently believed in the next. The former dominant paradigms are then labeled as *outdated*, and the old ones are replaced and labeled as *new*. The *ancien regimes* of the aristocracy and all of their prerogatives and values were overthrown by democratic reformists. In later periods in France, republican radicals were overthrown by the restoration of the monarchy, which was in turn abandoned. Of the thousands of religious sects that have sprung up in turn, only a few have survived the test of time. Others eventually vanquished all before them. Traditional religions were in their own day considered to be fringe cults. Those that have endured often are not any the less irrational or fanciful than those that have disappeared.

IV

A key question that has concerned me for most of my adult life, particularly in the past decade, is whether or not a major paradigm shift is now occurring and whether this will transform the modernist outlook. I should qualify the question by pluralizing it—for there are a multiplicity of paradigms in the contemporary world competing for attention and influence, not one. In particular, I have been a defender of skepticism—which has been a powerful factor in modern philosophy and science; and I have helped to energize a new approach to skepticism, which focuses on skeptical *inquiry* rather than simply doubt. I have also been passionately committed to the secular humanist outlook—a viewpoint shared by many modern intellectuals—and I have attempted to take the secular humanist movement in new directions.

There are powerful critics of both skepticism and secular humanism, who insist that we have reached the end of "the secular century" (an anomaly in human history) and that the naturalistic-materialistic world view and/or the rationalistic-scientific methodology it has used have been discredited. In its place they propose a new paradigm for the next millennium, which they claim will be "spiritual-paranormal" in its contours.

Michael Novak, a conservative Roman Catholic theologian-philosopher, says that the twentieth century has been witness to the "butcher's bench," in which the tyrannical gulags of fascism and communism have bathed the world in blood. He says that this is a result of the "secular humanist" outlook, which has dominated the modern world for 500 years. The new paradigm which will replace it, he says, is a religious one. What Novak proposes is a return to the doctrines of the Roman Catholic faith. Perhaps it is unnecessary to point out that Hitler did not accept the rationalist or humanist outlook. Moreover, Mussolini and Hitler had reached Concordats with the Vatican—which never officially condemned fascism. The totalitarian communism of Stalin was hardly humanistic, for it betrayed the basic principles of humanist ethics, democracy, tolerance, and freedom. Surely many of the wars in European history (internal and external) were religiously inspired: the Crusades, the Inquisition, and the protracted battles between Protestants and Catholics. The Spanish Conquistadors' decimation of Native American peoples in North and South America were in the name of God. And American settlers practiced genocide against the Indians at the same time that they professed religious piety. In the modern world there had been an alliance between the church and state in many Catholic countries, such as Spain during Franco, and in Latin American dictatorships. This was broken only when freethinkers in France, Mexico, and throughout the Catholic world demanded an end to ecclesiastical domination and defended secularism and democracy. The contemporary *jihad*, launched by Muslim fundamentalists today, is hardly due to secular humanism; nor are the conflicts between Hindus and Muslims or Orthodox Jews and Muslims due to a lack of faith but rather to an overabundance of it.

Novak's criticisms of modern secular humanism are shared by right-wing conservatives and fundamentalists of many stripes. Protestant fundamentalists demand a return to biblical values and the biblical outlook, as do Muslims and Hindus to their historic traditions. In many parts of the world this has led to barbaric ethnic cleansing and tribal violence. Humanists wish to overcome the chauvinism and nationalism of religious, racial, and ethnic intolerance; and they emphasize the need to develop a new global ethic, overcoming the dogmatic doctrines of the past. They hope that some skeptical examination of absolute theological principles and values will soften fanaticism.

Religion in the best sense has come to share liberal humanistic and democratic values. It is a paradox to observe that theistic religions, if nominally held, may do some good. They are only dangerous when they are taken seriously and seek to dominate society or impose their will on others and/or threaten the values of the pluralistic, open, and tolerant society, in which the freedom to believe or not believe is respected.

There are other similar indictments of modernism today by postmodernists. These criticisms often come from left-wing sources; they are especially prominent in the humanities and social-science faculties. These critics lambaste the *philosophes* of the Enlightenment, often considered to represent the apogee of modernism. They likewise indict humanism and its ideals of individual freedom and autonomy. These postmodernists seem to revert to nihilistic skepticism. They maintain that objective scientific methods do not exist, that science offers its own set of mythic metaphors to explain reality, that it is allied with repressive socio-political structures, and that it represents the views of "dead white males" of Western societies. Postmodernists have little confidence in human progress or in any moral-political ideology of emancipation. Following Heidegger, they are suspicious of the benefits of technology and the superiority of democracy. They declare that we have reached the end of the modern age.

We are thus confronted with four major competing paradigms. The first is premodern, the second is modern, third is postmodern, and the fourth is a *post*-postmodern new paradigm which has emerged because of the information revolution.

The premodern paradigm draws primarily from the religious traditions of the past. This paradigm has its roots in an agricultural and nomadic past. Its cosmic outlook and moral values are taken as divinely inspired, and its sources for truth are the prophets of Christianity, Judaism, Islam, Hinduism, or Buddhism. In these religions the social structure is generally patriarchal and authoritarian, and the priestly class is allied with ruling oligarchies. The highest form of learning is inspirational, poetic, and literary; though in time these traditions sought to accommodate themselves to philosophical learning, and to adapt faith to reason.

The premodern paradigm emerged before the development of modern science, i.e., before the Copernican, Darwinian, and behavioral revolutions expanded our conceptions of the natural universe and the place of the human species in an evolutionary framework. For premoderns, the Earth was the center of the universe and God, the Creator, was clothed in anthropomorphic and anthropocentric terms: He loved us and we were to love Him in return. The chief end of Man was to fear God, submit totally to His omnipotence, and obey

His commandments. The human habitat was often a miserable place, overladen with drudgery, tears, and sorrow. Our only hope of deliverance from suffering was piety. We could by faith alone obtain Paradise as promised in the Bible or Koran. The entire culture, its art and poetry, philosophy and learning, supported this view of the meaning of life and the divine order.

V

What was distinctive about the modern paradigm was the questioning of faith and piety as the be-all and end-all of human existence, along with the emergence of human-centered values. Beginning with the Renaissance, men and women turned from temporal and spiritual pursuits to the building of the secular city, in which human, not divine, happiness was the ultimate good. This ethical outlook was stimulated by the rediscovery of the great classics of pagan literature; and they provided a sharp contrast with religious values. Secularizing forces have attempted to liberate the individual from ecclesiastical control. Out of these emerged the ideas that the methods of science, namely appeals to reason and experience, would be the most effective way to describe and explain nature. Natural, not occult, causes governed the universe. Moreover, as Francis Bacon forecast, such knowledge could be an immense source of power; for scientific understanding could be applied to nature and serve practical aims.

The Industrial Revolution was a product of the scientific outlook. It led to the age of technology, in which machines replaced human labor—windmills, steam engines, electrical and nuclear power. With this transformation of the forces of production, human beings could be liberated from the bane of physical drudgery. By the end of the second millennium, the Green Revolution was in full force in many areas of the world, and by utilizing modern methods of production and fertilization, only two to three percent of the population in advanced nations was required to work the land. European explorations on the high seas put voyagers in touch with diverse cultures, languages, and religions; and this tended to emancipate people from unthinking acceptance of their own sacred doctrines. With the growth of commerce and trade, great urban centers developed. There was widespread migration as new continents were opened up for further exploration and settlement—North and South America, Australia and New Zealand, Africa and the coastal cities of Asia. The world was becoming an international community; no corner was left untouched. With this came all of the problems of rapid population growth, environmental exploitation and exhaustion, as formerly isolated multicultural ethnic enclaves were scattered worldwide to exploit new frontiers.

The modern world would also benefit from scientific medicine and technology. It was able to cure disease, mitigate pain, and extend life spans. The products of manufacturing led to the expansion of a consumer culture to all strata of society and increased levels of affluence and leisure and the possibility of travel. It contributed to the erosion of racial, religious, and ethnic differences. As new ethnic identities and nationalities emerged—Americans, Canadians, Brazilians, Australians, etc.—the great question (posed by both the defenders of the premodern and postmodernist paradigms) is whether the modernist paradigm has failed, and whether challenges to its hegemony would succeed, and if so what this would entail. Is it to be a multicultural paradigm in which separate and distinct religious and cultural traditions persist and compete? Is it to be antiscientific and/or antirationalistic? Will a new spiritualist outlook replace the naturalistic-materialistic secular humanist framework of the modern era?

There were similar declarations in 1900, when many Christians thought that Christianity would in short order vanquish all the other religions in the world; for Western European colonial expansion had by then brought Christian missionaries to all corners of the globe. This process had begun four centuries earlier when Columbus discovered the Americas and successive waves of explorers and immigrants brought their religious creeds to the new continents of North and South America—along with modern science, technology, and democracy. And it happened as vessels landed in Africa, India, Asia, and Australia. These migrants attempted to settle in new areas, where native populations were sparse, and to convert the native people to Catholicism or Protestantism. By 1900 Eurocentric imperialism was everywhere dominant. The religions of the indigenous populations of North and South America had largely been defeated; India lay prostrate, China controlled by Western powers.

In the twentieth century there were great changes as Russia overthrew the Eastern Orthodox church and was communized. Marxism-Leninism and atheism-freethought went hand in hand, challenging both the capitalist system and traditional religious institutions. In the First World War both the Ottoman and the Austro-Hungarian Empires were defeated and forced to abandon large sectors of Eastern Europe, where countries became independent (Yugoslavia, Czechoslovakia, etc.), and Middle Eastern countries were made into French or British protectorates (Syria, Lebanon, Egypt, etc.).

Before the First World War, new developments occurred as minority religions began to develop in American and European countries. Large Russian-Jewish and Irish-Catholic, Polish-Catholic, and Italian-Catholic emigrations to the United States challenged the dominant Anglo-Saxon Protestant establishment. Since the Second World War the influx of foreign workers and refugees implanted significant Muslim, Hindu, and Buddhist minorities in all the major European countries—France, Germany, Britain, the Netherlands, etc. The same thing happened in the United States, where Asian religions—such as Buddhism—appealed to many young persons and intellectuals. Conversely, in many countries of the world Christianity began to take new roots—very strong Protestant or Catholic minorities in Korea and Vietnam, and much weaker minorities in India and China. Moreover, a revivified militant Islam began a new process of conversion, as fundamentalists challenged the democratic or secular conceptions that the Europeans and Americans had brought. Islamic minorities demanded independent states in the former Soviet Union and Yugoslavia, and strong missionary efforts continued elsewhere.

After the Second World War the United Nations was established, and even though the major powers dominated it, the newly emerging nations were given new voices, and indeed formed new blocs, such as the Third World or the Arab States. After the Cold War the division between the Western capitalist and the communist bloc was weakened as plural centers of power began to emerge. Although the United States was considered to be the dominant superpower, the development of new European institutions challenges its hegemony.

Since the breakup of the Soviet Union and its Eastern European empire, evangelical Protestant missionaries have moved in, and, further, they have intensified their activities in Africa, Asia, central and Latin America. At the same time Hindu fundamentalism confronts the Indian secular state and battles the Sikhs and Muslims. In Israel a modern Zionist state has been established (in 1948), with the Orthodox splinter parties playing a role in a struggle for power with secular Jews. The Eastern Orthodox Church emerged anew in Russia and Eastern Europe. And the Vatican, with its conservative theological doctrines, attempts to re-evangelize Europe and abandon much of Vatican II.

What we are thus witnessing on a worldwide basis is a polycentric religious world scene where many of the major religions are in contention—at times this leads to bitter wars in which xenophobic hatred and fanaticism rule the day. Muslims, Hindus, and Sikhs in Kashmir and the Punjab; Hindus and Buddhists in Sri Lanka; Jews and Muslims in Israel; Protestants and Catholics in Northern Ireland; Roman Catholic Croats, Muslims, and Serbian Orthodox in Yugoslavia, etc.

We can ask, Is there any way to overcome the intense multicultural ethnic/religious rivalries? Can secular humanism provide common ethical and political principles by which contending parties of discord can come together? That is the immediate challenge of the twenty-first century. The nineteenth and twentieth centuries have been witness to constant waves of ideological and religious missionaries and subsequent paradigm shifts—from militant communism to free-market capitalism, from evangelical Christianity to Islam, Buddhism, and Hinduism. No doubt similar processes will occur in the twenty-first century. Again, I submit, both skepticism and secular humanism can play a vital role in these confrontations.

I should point out that although European religions were transmitted throughout the world, so were humanist ideals—the Founding Fathers of America were influenced by the Enlightenment, they were fearful of clerical domination and the U.S. Constitution reflected that. Similarly, the ideals of the

French Revolution and the Industrial Revolution were transmitted worldwide. Jürgen Habermas has suggested that the Enlightenment Project has not been fulfilled, even partially. This is not due so much to an intrinsic defect of the modernist paradigm as by the failure to implement and extend it further. Thus we face a new challenge: paradigm shifts do not come into being by themselves; they are the result of human dedication and effort and of passionate commitment to them. What will occur in future decades and centuries depends upon how we respond to the new situations that we encounter, and what we are able to bring into being.

A third postmodern paradigm rejects most of the ideals of the Enlightenment and is skeptical of reason, science, humanism, and human rights. This paradigm, I submit, is self-defeating and suicidal in its prophecies; for it lacks any viable social-moral project of emancipation and realization for humankind.

A fourth *post*-postmodern paradigm today has emerged. This is post-industrial; it draws on the information revolution and the new dramatic realities of the global civilization in which we, all members of the human family, now participate. This new paradigm has gone beyond the eighteenth-century Enlightenment, though it builds on its foundations, especially its faith in human potentialities, and its desire for progress. The information age has defeated or supplanted the New Age postmodern pessimism by its sheer breathtaking leap ahead. It is thoroughly *humanistic* in that it turns from religious matters to a concern with satisfying human desires and needs. Thus it concentrates its energies on ways of realizing human happiness in this world, not the next. It does not wish to "leave unto Cæsar the things that are Cæsar's," but is concerned with the *secular city*; i.e., it wishes to separate the church (or mosque or temple) from the state, politics from religion, the moral domain from the religious. It is *democratic* in that it emphasizes the dignity and worth of every person; it seeks to enhance the dimensions of human freedom; it believes in social justice, equality, and fairness; it wishes to afford to each individual the opportunities to achieve the good life. It is *naturalistic* in that it wishes to extend the methods of science and reason to understanding nature and solving human problems. It is *skeptical* in that it doubts claims for which there are insufficient reasons or evidence. It emphasizes *education* and *critical thinking* as the best means of achieving social change. It is *universal* in that it seeks to rise above the narrow parochial interests of the past in order to build a *world community* based on planetary ethics. And it is *optimistic* and *realistic* in that it has some confidence in the ability of humans to resolve their problems by methods of intelligence. It wishes to cultivate *good will*. It prefers the *arts of negotiation*, compromise, and the peaceful resolution of conflicts to violence or force. It is *melioristic*, believing that it is possible to create a better world. It does not council retreat into a mood of passive acceptance or piety, but wishes to actuate the virtue of *courage*, the courage to overcome and achieve what we believe in. It is not the tragic dimensions of human existence, angst, or despair that are the marks of the humanist, but the quest for the best that we are capable of achieving—in human terms, the *bountiful life* of *excellence and nobility* for ourselves and our fellow human beings.

The secular humanist outlook is the culmination of modernism, but it is a *new* paradigm, for it goes beyond modernism, for it clearly rejects deism in all of its senses and it is integral to the information/space age. It has already had a profound impact on human civilization; but it still has a long way to go if it is to achieve its goals. For we are surrounded by the naysayers—those who wish to look backward to the salvational doctrines of premodern eras, seek to enshrine in stone the ancient doctrines, and wish to block human progress. We are also confronted by new forms of the romantic protest against rationalism by a literary culture which does not understand science, fears reason, and has little or no confidence in the ability of men and women to solve the problems of living. Postmodernist Heideggerian nihilists abhor technology. But to abandon its fruits now or to seek to impede new discoveries is to slip backwards into a more primitive age. Granted that technology can be used negatively, but it also can enhance our understanding of nature and contribute to a more wholesome human civilization. Technology can be used to build gas ovens in order to bake bread, but it also can be used to immolate the innocent in diabolic Holocausts of hatred. Nuclear energy can be tapped for peaceful means, or it can be used by militarists to build weapons of mass destruction. Humanism is vital; for although it appreciates science and technology, it also wishes to focus on ethical values: dignity, tolerance, and peaceful negotiation. We should sit down and reason together, not be enflamed by our differences. Humanism appeals to an ethic of principles. The means we are willing to use to achieve our ends must be constrained by ethical considerations.

The reality of the present world scene is that there are many paradigms competing for ascendancy. The secular humanist perspective is only one among many; though I think that it is the one that still offers the best promise for the future. Why do I say this?

First, because it is science and reason that have provided us with the most effective methods for understanding nature and coping with the problems and conflicts that we encounter. Which paradigms now available can best put food on the table, diagnose and cure illnesses, and give us the means to achieve the fullness of life for the bulk of humanity? I submit that reason and evidence are the best way to test our hypotheses, not mysticism, poetry, intuition, faith, emotion, or tradition? No doubt some will argue that the latter approaches have played important roles in human affairs, and this I do not deny. Indeed, the passionate life of feeling must accompany the arts of intelligence. But surely this does not mean that we should entirely abandon scientific inquiry.

Postmodernism no doubt has made some telling points in criticizing absolutist forms of rationalism of the past; and the unfortunate coöption of science by powerful political and economic interests is to be deplored. We need to use the fruits of science and technology wisely and humanely, not abandon them.

Second, humanism has made it possible for the democratic revolutions of our time to succeed. These are based on the idea of the open society and the basic value is human freedom, including freedom of conscience. Humanism and democracy go hand in hand and the democratic way of life is best justified by its positive benefits for humankind.

Third, human civilization is entering into a new and exciting phase of development. Because of modern technology, and in particular the infomedia revolution, for the first time we have become a global family—for each and every person is able by means of satellites and the Internet to communicate and interact directly with virtually everyone on the global scale. Which paradigm is best able to find common ground for the diverse cultures on the world scene? I submit that it is a planetary humanist civilization that is developing and provides a basis for finding common ground, a new global ethics, which enunciates our responsibilities to the world community over and beyond our narrow ethnic, racial, religious, and national loyalties of the past. I should make it clear that although it is skeptical of theistic claims, it recognizes that liberal religions often share many of the ethical, scientific, and democratic principles of secular humanism. If we are to live together in free societies there does not exist any basis for irreconcilable quarrels between liberal religions and secular humanism. My chief caveats are with repressive orthodox and fundamentalist religions, not open-minded free religious expressions.

VI

As I have said, there are no guarantees in human history, no assurance that the future will be like the past, and no certainty that destructive demonic systems of belief will not again sweep the world. Perhaps virulent forms of racism, fundamentalist religious fanaticism, and terrorism will emerge to poison the wells of human civilization. I submit that those who believe in the modernist project and share secular humanist values need to exert every effort to defend them. Many intellectuals understand the issues at stake; yet they are often reluctant to do anything about them. Many are disillusioned by what they view as excessive attacks on the Enlightenment and the emergence of pre- and postmodernist spiritual/paranormal paradigms.

I have devoted the lion's share of my professional life to these challenges, operating on the assumption that ideas have consequences and that they need to be tested in practice and defended against their critics. The lessons of history are that unless the convictions that we cherish are *institutionalized*, they will lose influence and may fade away. One reason premodern systems have lasted so long is that they have been sustained by institutions that were constructed long ago—synagogues, mosques, temples, and cathedrals have remained with us after those who have built them have died. "Memes" (a term first introduced by Richard Dawkins) refer to ideas that are transmitted throughout a culture by imitation. And these memes are replicated—no matter how false or dysfunctional they may turn out to be—because conveyer belts have been built to transmit their messages and sustain them. Their lore has been conveyed to future generations because they have inculcated the young into their mysteries, by means of rites and rituals and a priestly class. What have secular humanists done to compete with the needs of traditional institutions? All too little explicitly, I fear, largely because of the belief that secular institutions already pervade all aspects of modern cultural life and there is no need to create additional ones. I think that this view is badly mistaken and that unless efforts are made to create alternative sustaining institutions, secular humanist ideas are likely to falter.

I have been personally involved in my lifetime in the task of helping to create alternative institutions. First, by building a viable skeptical movement interested in applying skeptical inquiry to paranormal claims, using the best methods of science. It think that it is vital that we develop the capacity for critical thinking in society at large, and the best way to do this is by means of education and the media. This is not only important in defending the integrity of science, but of the open democratic society itself, which presupposes that the best guarantee of democracy is an educated citizenry. Scientists and scholars have some obligation to explicate the scientific outlook and the methods of scientific inquiry. Hence, Part I of this volume, "Skeptics of the World Unite," consists of working papers concerning not only theoretical philosophical issues but also organized action. I was chiefly responsible for founding the Committee for the Scientific Investigation of Claims of the Paranormal (CSICOP) in 1976. Its journal, the *Skeptical Inquirer*, was launched the following year. CSICOP has become the lead battleship in an Armada of skeptical groups worldwide. Indeed, the contemporary skeptics movement is perhaps the first major institutional organization since the schools of skepticism in the third and fourth centuries C.E.! They have become important voices in the world of science and the media, often presenting in the latter a dissenting viewpoint concerning claims of the paranormal.

Skepticism has been viewed by some as destructive; but this need not be the case. It can play an essential and constructive role in the sciences and in all areas of human inquiry. It is committed to *methodological naturalism*, i.e., seeking for natural and causal explanations that are testable in place of occult ones. But many skeptics are not interested in going beyond intellectual and scientific inquiry. Many of them resist the next step—building a humanist alternative. Like the specialist, they believe that they can investigate in narrow disciplines without drawing any generalizations from their inquiry. "Never the twain shall meet," they say. I think that this is a profound mistake, and that unless scientists, skeptics, philosophers, and other scholars are willing to sum up the results of scientific inquiry (I call this *scientific naturalism*, as an alternative to the spiritual-paranormal paradigm), then the scientific enterprise is in jeopardy and in danger of being undermined. Will skeptics ever marshal the courage to say that they are skeptical of religious claims and that they are agnostics or atheists?

I happen, of course, to hold both positions. I am committed to using the methods of skeptical inquiry in all fields of human interest—including religion. But I am likewise committed to the secular humanist paradigm, because I think it provides a viable alternative to the premodern and postmodern paradigms.

The rest of this volume is devoted to humanist themes. I have been directly involved in building humanist institutions; for I believe that the arena in which ideas are to be examined and carried out is society at large, not the cloistered university. Thus I founded the Council for Secular Humanism in 1980 and have been editor-in-chief of *Free Inquiry*, the leading secular humanist magazine in the world. Part II, "Beyond Religion," is designed to demonstrate that it is possible to lead the good life without religion, whether natural or supernatural. I call this *eupraxsophy*, and I try to spell out in concrete terms what this means. Part III, "Neo-Humanist Politics," argues that although humanism is a scientific, philosophical, and moral point of view, it needs to take part in political action. The religious forces arrayed against secular humanism surely do not shy away from political programs and platforms. Indeed, the historical success of the great religions is that they grew when imposed by the sword. Christianity prevailed when it was proclaimed by Constantine the official religion of Rome, and Islam was carried forward by legions fighting for its hegemony. Today the only method that we wish to use in democratic societies is persuasion, not force, but we will not persuade our fellow citizens unless we organize to do so. Part IV, "Humanism Writ Large," deals with humanism on the world scene, and it includes papers delivered at congresses throughout the world since humanism has become a global movement.

The chapters in the book are adapted from papers that have been published in various journals or talks that I have delivered in recent years. Many of these essays are fugitive for they are not otherwise readily available. Hence, I decided to bring them together in one volume. All of them deal in greater depth with themes raised in this preface. In one sense they may be viewed as preparatory reflections on the third millennium.

Concluding Unspiritual Postscript

The great challenge that we will face in the third millennium is whether we can discover new sources of meaning and enrichment in a naturalistic universe. I am well aware that efforts to replace temples of worship with temples of reason have often failed in the past, and that the bulk of humanity has preferred to worship false prophets such as Jesus (who believed that he died for our sins) or Muhammad (who promised paradise in the hereafter) rather than Socrates, who sacrificed himself for the cause of the free mind, or Galileo, martyred for scientific inquiry. Perhaps naturalism and humanism are meaningful only for an anomalous minority of human beings. Perhaps the rest of humanity will continue to crave spiritual wine to assuage their fears of the unknown and alter their consciousness.

Yet a significant number of brave men and women no longer are willing to submit to the primitive temptation for the transcendental; they seek rather an entirely new enlightenment fulfilling the ideals of reason, ethical wisdom, and humanism. Courageous souls have lit candles in the dark, not to glorify or worship false deities in dank cathedrals, but to find their own ways out of the darkness. With the power of scientific discovery today, we can increase and enhance our ability to illuminate new paths into the future. These at least are the directions taken by inventive men and women who have shed the illusions of the past, and are able and willing to forge their own destinies. The future remains open to human ingenuity. Whether humankind will have the resolve to embark on these new adventures is always an open option.

We have come a long way in human civilization, particularly in the modern age, but we still have exciting new frontiers to forge. And we will succeed in creating a joyful and exciting future only if we are able to defeat and overcome the naysayers in our midst, those who sneer at our efforts or advise retreat. This has always been the counsel of the small-minded—to return to the caves of security and ignorance.

Yet history is the result of audacious heroes and heroines who were willing to explore the planet, build new societies, contribute to the arts and the sciences, and cultivate the arts of intelligence. Thus we should not turn back to a spiritual era of the past. We should not cringe in pessimism, fear, and foreboding. We should resolve to move ahead. "The only thing we have to fear is fear itself," said Franklin D. Roosevelt as a great nation faced economic depression. And, I might add, the one virtue that we will need to cultivate if we are to succeed is the *courage to become* what we want and the intelligence and compassion to work with others to bring it into being.

Skepticism and Humanism: The New Paradigm is a companion volume to *Toward a New Enlightenment: The Philosophy of Paul Kurtz*, edited by Vern L. Bullough and Timothy J. Madigan (New Brunswick, N.J.: Transaction Publishers, 1994), although each volume can be read separately.

---

1. Thomas S. Kuhn, *The Structure of Scientific Revolutions* (Chicago: University of Chicago Press, 1966).

Part One

Skeptics of the World Unite!

1

Antiscience Paradigms

It is paradoxical that today, when the sciences are advancing by leaps and bounds and when the earth is being transformed by scientific discoveries and technological applications, a strong antiscience counter-culture has emerged. Some consider this to represent a paradigm shift to a new spiritual conception of reality. This contrasts markedly with attitudes toward science that existed in the nineteenth and the first half of the twentieth centuries. The popularity of Albert Einstein perhaps best typified the high point of the public appreciation of scientists that prevailed at that time. Paul De Kruif, in his book, *The Microbe Hunters*,[1] described the dramatic results that scientists could now achieve in ameliorating pain and suffering and improving the human condition. John Dewey, perhaps the most influential American philosopher in this century, pointed out the great pragmatic benefits to humankind from the application of scientific methods of thinking to all aspects of human life. But today the mood has radically changed.

This article first appeared in *Skeptical Inquirer* 18, no. 3 (Spring 1994), pp. 255–264. It is based on a talk delivered at the Fifth European Skeptics' Conference at Keele University, United Kingdom, August 1993.

Philosophical Critics

There have always been two cultures existing side by side, as Lord C. P. Snow has shown.[2] There has been a historic debate between those who wish to advance scientific culture and those who claim that there are "two truths." According to the latter, there exists, along with cognitive scientific knowledge, a mystical and spiritual realm and/or æsthetic and subjective aspects of experience. The two cultures do not live side by side in peaceful coexistence any longer; in recent decades there have been overt radical attacks on science that threaten its position in society.

From within philosophy dissent has come from two influential areas. First, many philosophers of science, from Kuhn to Feyerabend, have argued that there is no such thing as scientific method, that scientific knowledge is relative to socio-cultural institutions, that paradigm shifts occur as a result of extrarational causes, and that therefore the earlier confidence that there are objective methods for testing scientific claims is mistaken.

This critique is obviously greatly exaggerated. It is true that science functions in relation to the social and cultural conditions in which it emerges, and it is true that we cannot make absolute statements in science. Nonetheless, there are reliable standards for testing claims and some criteria of objectivity, and these transcend specific social and cultural contexts. How does one explain the vast body of scientific knowledge we possess? A specific claim in science cannot be said to be the same as a poetic metaphor or a religious tenet, for it is tested by its experimental consequences in the real world.

The second philosophical attack comes from the disciples of Heidegger, especially the French postmodernists, such as Derrida, Foucault, Lacan, and Lyotard. They argue that science is only one mythic system or narrative among many others. They maintain that by deconstructing scientific language, we discover that there are no real standards of objectivity. Heidegger complained that science and technology were dehumanizing. Foucault pointed out that science is often dominated by power structures, bureaucracy, and the state, and that the political and economic uses of science have undermined the pretensions of scientific neutrality. Some of these criticisms are no doubt valid, but they are overstated. If the alternative to objectivity is subjectivity, and if there are no warranted claims to truth, then the views of the postmodernists cannot be said to be true either. Surely we can maintain that the principles of mechanics are reliable, that Jupiter is a planet that orbits the sun, that cardiovascular diseases can be explained causally and preventive measures taken to lower the risk, that the structure of DNA is not simply a social artifact, nor insulin a cultural creation.

The postmodern critics of "modernity" are objecting to the rationalist or foundationalist interpretations of science that emerged in the sixteenth and seventeenth centuries, and perhaps rightly so. For the continuous growth and revision of scientific theories demonstrates that any "quest for certainty" or "ultimate first principles" within science is mistaken. Nonetheless, they go too far in abandoning the entire modern scientific enterprise. The scientific approach to understanding nature and human life has been vindicated by its success; and its premises, I submit, are still valid. What are some of the characteristics of this modern scientific outlook as it has evolved today?

First, science presupposes that there are objective methods by which reliable knowledge can be tested. Second, this means that hypotheses and theories can be formulated and that they can be warranted by reference to the evidence, by criteria of rational coherence, and by their predicted experimental consequences. Third, modern scientists find that mathematical quantification is a powerful tool in establishing theories. Fourth, they hold that there are causal regularities and relationships in our interactions with nature that can be discovered. Fifth, although knowledge may not be universal, it is general in the sense that it goes beyond mere subjective or cultural relativity and is rooted in an intersubjective and intercultural community of inquirers. Sixth, as the progressive and fallible character of science is understood, it is seen that it is difficult to reach absolute or final statements, that science is tentative and probabilistic, and that scientific inquiry needs to be open to alternative explanations. Previous theories are therefore amenable to challenge and revision, and selective and constructive skepticism is an essential element in the scientific outlook. Seventh, is the appreciation that knowledge of the probable causes of phenomena as discovered by scientific research can be applied, that powerful technological inventions can be discovered, and that these can be of enormous benefit to human beings.

Ethical Critiques

Yet the scientific approach, which has had such powerful effectiveness in extending the frontiers of knowledge, is now under heavy attack. Of special concern has been the dramatic growth of the occult, the paranormal, and pseudosciences, and particularly the promotion of the irrational and sensational in these areas by the mass media. We allegedly have been living in the New Age. Side by side with astronomy there has been a return to astrology, and concomitant with psychology there was the growth of psychical research and parapsychology. The paranormal imagination soars; science fiction has no bounds. This is the age of space travel, and it includes abductions by extraterrestrial beings and unidentified flying objects from other worlds. The emergence of a paranormal worldview competes with the scientific worldview. Instead of tested causal explanations, the pseudosciences provide alternative explanations that compete in the public mind with genuine science. The huge increase in paranormal beliefs is symptomatic of a profound antiscience attitude, which has not emerged in isolation but is part of a wider spectrum of attitudes and beliefs.

The most vitriolic attacks on science in recent decades have questioned its benefits to society. To a significant extent these criticisms are based on ethical considerations, for they question the value of scientific research and the scientific outlook to humankind. Here are 10 categories of such objections. There are no doubt others.[3]

1. After World War II great anxiety arose about a possible nuclear holocaust. This fear is not without foundation; for there is some danger of fallout from nuclear accidents and testing in the atmosphere, and there is the threat that political or military leaders might embark, consciously or accidentally, upon a devastating nuclear war. Fortunately, for the moment the danger of a thermonuclear holocaust has abated, though it surely has not disappeared. However, such critiques generated the fear of scientific research, and even, in some quarters, the view that physicists were diabolical beings who, in tinkering with the secrets of nature, held within their grasp the power to destroy all forms of life on this planet. The fear of nuclear radiation also applies to nuclear power plants. The accident at Chernobyl magnified the apprehension of large sectors of the world's population that nuclear energy is dangerous and that nuclear power plants should be closed down. In countries like the United States, no nuclear power plants are being built, although France and many other countries continue to construct them. The nuclear age has thus provoked an antinuclear reaction, and the beneficent symbol of the scientist of the past, Albert Einstein, has to some been transmogrified into a Dr. Strangelove. Although some of the apprehensions about nuclear radiation are no doubt warranted, to abandon nuclear fuel entirely, while the burning of fossil fuels pollutes the atmosphere, leaves few alternatives for satisfying the energy needs of the world. This does not deny the need to find renewable resources, such as solar and wind power, but will these be sufficient?

2. The fear of science can also be traced to some excesses of the environmental movement. Although the environmentalists' emphasis on ecological preservation is a valid concern, it has led at times to the fear that human technology has irreparably destroyed the ozone layer and that the greenhouse effect will lead to the degradation of the entire planet. These concerns are reasonable. Yet such fears often lead to hysteria about all technologies.

3. In large sectors of the population, there is a phobia about any kind of chemical additive. From the 1930s to the 1950s, it was widely held that "better things and better living can be achieved through chemistry" and that chemicals would improve the human condition. Today there is, on the contrary, a widespread toxic terror—of PCBs and DDT, plastics and fertilizers, indeed of

any kind of additive—and there is a worldwide movement calling for a return to nature, to organic foods and natural methods. No doubt we need to be cautious about untested chemical additives that may poison the ecosystem, but we should not forget that the skilled use of fertilizers led to the green revolution and a dramatic increase in food production that reduced famine and poverty worldwide. There is widespread fear of genetically altered food crops. Although we need to be cautious, the demands for a moratorium are illustrative of the fear of the unknown.

4. Suspicion of biogenetic engineering is another dimension of the growth of antiscience. From its very inception biogenetic research has met opposition. Many feared that scientists would unleash a new, virulent strain of *E. coli* bacteria into sewer pipes—and then throughout the ecosystem—that would kill large numbers of people. Jeremy Rifkin and others have demanded that all forms of biogenetic engineering research be banned because of its "dehumanizing" effect.[4] A good illustration of this can be seen in the film *Jurassic Park*, produced by Steven Spielberg. Here not only does a Dr. Frankenstein seek to bring back the dead, but we are warned that a new diabolical scientist, in cloning dinosaurs, will unleash ominous forces across the planet. Although there may be some dangers in biogenetic engineering, it offers tremendous potential benefit for humankind—for the cure of genetic diseases as well as the creation of new products. Witness, for example, the production of synthetic insulin. The condemnation of cloning research after the cloning of Dolly unleashed widespread fears that there would be cloning of a master race and/or that cloning was contrary to God's will, overlooking its possible enormous benefits to humankind.

5. Another illustration of the growth of antiscience is the widespread attack on orthodox medicine. Some of these criticisms have some merit. With the advances of the scientific revolution and the growth of medical technology, we have been able to extend human life; yet many people are kept alive against their will and suffer excruciating pain; and the right to die has emerged as a basic ethical concern. Medical ethicists have correctly pointed out that the rights of patients have often been ignored by the medical and legal professions. In the past physicians were considered authoritarian figures, whose wisdom and skills were unquestioned. But to many vociferous critics today, doctors are demons rather than saviors. The widespread revolt against animal research is symptomatic of the attack on science. Granted that animals should not be abused or made to suffer unnecessary pain, but some animal rights advocates would ban all medical research on animals.

6. Another illustration of antiscience is the growing opposition to psychiatry. Thomas Szasz has no doubt played a key role here.[5] Szasz is committed to science; many of his critiques of the excesses of psychiatric intervention are no doubt warranted. But there has been a political and public

outcry against psychiatry. As a result, large numbers of mental patients were deinstitutionalized and many have since been placed in prisons. *One Flew Over the Cuckoo's Nest*, by Ken Kesey, dramatizes the view that it is often the psychiatrist himself who is disturbed rather than the patient.[6] Many, like Szasz, even deny that there are mental illnesses, though there seems to be considerable evidence that some patients do suffer behavioral disorders and exhibit symptoms that can be alleviated by anti-psychotic drugs.

7. Concomitant with the undermining of public confidence in the practice of medicine and psychiatry has been the phenomenal growth in "alternative medicine," from faith healing and Christian Science to the relaxation response, therapeutic touch, iridology, homeopathy, and herbal medicines. This is sometimes labeled as "complementary" medicine. The proponents of scientific medicine insist on double-blind clinical tests of alleged therapies. The development of alternative medicine is paradoxical, because medical science has made heroic progress in the conquering of disease and the development of antibiotics and the highly successful techniques of surgical intervention. These have all been a boon to human health. But now the very viability of scientific medicine itself has been questioned.

8. Another area of concern is the impact of Asian mysticism, particularly since World War II, whereby Yoga meditation, Chinese Qigong, gurus, and spiritualists have come into the Western world arguing that these ancient forms of knowledge and therapy can lead to spiritual growth and health in a way that modern medicine does not. Unfortunately, there are very few reliable clinical tests of these so-called spiritual cures. What we have are largely anecdotal accounts, but they hardly serve as objective tests of alternative therapies.

9. Another form of antiscience is the revival of fundamentalist religion even within advanced scientific and educational societies. Fundamentalists question the very foundation of scientific culture. Indeed, in the modern world, it is religion, not science, that seems to have emerged as the hope of humankind. Far more money is being poured into religion than into scientific research and education. Especially symptomatic is the continued growth of "scientific creationism" and widespread political opposition to the teaching of evolution in the schools, particularly in the United States.

10. A final area of antiscience is the growth of multicultural and feminist critiques of science education, particularly in the universities and colleges. The multiculturist view is that science is not universal or transcultural, but relative to the culture in which it emerges. There are, we are told, non-Western and primitive cultures that are as "true" and "valid" as the scientific culture of the Western world. This movement supports the complete relativization of scientific knowledge. The radical feminist indictment of "masculine bias" in science maintains that science has been the expression of "dead, white Anglo-Saxon males"—from Newton to Faraday, from Laplace to Heisenberg. What we must

do, the extremists of these movements advise, is liberate humanity from cultural, racist, and sexist expressions of knowledge, and this means scientific objectivity as well. The positive contribution of these movements, of course, is that they seek to open science to more women and minorities. The negative dimension is that multiculturalist demands on education tend to weaken an understanding of the rigorous intellectual standards essential for effective scientific inquiry. Clearly we need to appreciate the scientific contribution of many cultures and the role of women in science throughout history; on the other hand, some multicultural critics undermine the very possibility of objective science.

Some Possible Remedies

What I have presented is a kaleidoscope illustration of many current trends that are undermining and threaten the future growth of science. They raise many questions. Why has this occurred? How shall those who believe in the value of scientific methods and the scientific outlook respond?

This is a complex problem, and I can only suggest some possible solutions. But unless the scientific community and those connected with it are willing to take the challenge to science seriously, then I fear that the tide of antiscience may continue to rise. Scientific research surely will not be rejected where there are obvious technological uses to be derived from it, at least insofar as economic, political, and military institutions find these profitable. But the decline in the appreciation of the methods of science and in the scientific outlook can only have deleterious effects upon the long-term role of science in civilization.

One reason for the growth of antiscience is a basic failure to educate the public about the nature of science itself. Of crucial significance is the need for public education in the aims of science. We need to develop an appreciation of the general methods of scientific inquiry, its relationship to skepticism and critical thinking, and its demand for evidence and reason in testing claims to truth. The most difficult task we face is to develop an awareness that the methods of science should not only be used in the narrow domains of the specialized sciences but should also be generalized, as far as possible, to other fields of human interest.

We also need to develop an appreciation for the cosmic outlook of science. Using the techniques of scientific inquiry, scientists have developed theories and generalizations about the universe and the human species. These theories often conflict with theological viewpoints that for the most part go unchallenged. They also often run counter to mystical, romantic, and æsthetic attitudes. Thus it is time for more scientists and interpreters of science to come forward to explain what science tells us about the universe: for example, they should demonstrate the evidence for evolution and point out that creationism does not account for the fossil record, that the evidence points to a biological basis for the mind, and that there is no evidence for reincarnation or immortality. Until the scientific community is willing to explicate openly and defend what science tells us about life and the universe, then I fear it will continue to be undermined by the vast ignorance of those who oppose it.

In this process of education, what is crucial is the development of scientific literacy in the schools and in the communications media. Recent polls have indicated that a very small percentage of the U.S. population has any understanding of scientific principles. The figures are similar for Britain, France, and Germany, where large sectors of the population are abysmally unaware of the nature of the scientific outlook. Thus we need to educate the public about how science works and what it tells us about the world, and we should make sure this understanding is applied to all fields of human knowledge.

The growth of specialization has made this task enormously difficult. Specialization has enabled people to focus on one field, to pour their creative talents into solving specific problems, whether in biology or physics, mathematics or economics. But we need to develop generalists as well as specialists. Much of the fear and opposition to science is due to a failure to understand the nature of scientific inquiry. This understanding should include an appreciation for what we know and do *not* know. This means not only an appreciation of the body of reliable knowledge we now possess, but also an appreciation of the skeptical outlook and attitude. The interpreters of science must go beyond specialization to the general explication of what science tells us about the universe and our place in it. This is unsettling to many within society. In one sense, science is the most radical force in the modern world, because scientists need to be prepared to question everything and to demand verification or validation of any claims.

The broader public welcomes scientific innovation. Every new gadget or product and every new application in technology, where it is positive, is appreciated for its economic and social value. What is not appreciated is the nature of the scientific enterprise itself and the need to extend the critical methods of science further, especially to ethics, politics, and religion. Until those in the scientific community have sufficient courage to extend the methods of science and reason as far as they can to these other fields, then I feel that the growth of antiscience will continue.

Now it is not simply the task of scientists who work in the laboratory, who have a social responsibility to the greater society; it is also the task of philosophers, journalists, and those within the corporate and the political world who appreciate the contribution of science to humankind. For what is at stake in a sense is modernism itself. Unless corporate executives and those who wield political power recognize the central role that science and technology have played in the past four centuries, and can continue to play in the future, and unless science is defended, then I fear that the irrational growth of antiscience may undermine the viability of scientific research and the contributions of science in the future. The key is education—education within the schools, but education also within the media. We need to raise the level of appreciation, not simply among students, from grammar school through the university, but among those who control the mass media. And here, alas, the scientific outlook is often overwhelmed by violence, lurid sex, the paranormal, and religious bias.

The world today is a battlefield of ideas. In this context the partisans of science need to defend courageously the authentic role that science has played and can continue to play in human civilization. The growth of antiscience must be countered by a concomitant growth in advocacy of the virtues of science. Scientists are surely not infallible; they make mistakes. But the invaluable contributions of science need to be reiterated. We need public reenchantment with the ideals expressed by the scientific outlook.

---

1. Paul De Kruif, *The Microbe Hunters* (New York: Harcourt, Brace, 1926).

2. C. P. Snow, *The Two Cultures and the Scientific Revolution* (New York: Cambridge University Press, 1991).

3. For an extreme case of antiscience paranoia, see David Ehrenfeld's *The Arrogance of Humanism* (New York: Oxford University Press, 1975), where the author virtually equates humanism with science and modernism.

4. Jeremy Rifkin, ed., The Green Lifestyle Handbook (New York: Henry Holt, 1990); Biosphere Politics: A New Consciousness for a New Century (New York: Crown, 1959); Ted Howard and Jeremy Rifkin, Who Should Play God? The Artificial Creation of Life and What It Means for the Future of the Human Race (New York: Delacorte Press, 1977).

5. Thomas Szasz, *The Theology of Medicine* (New York: Harper and Row, 1977); *The Myth of Mental Illness,* rev. ed. (New York: Harper and Row, 1984).

6. Ken Kesey, *One Flew Over the Cuckoo's Nest* (New York: New American Library, 1962).

2

Skeptical Inquiry

Skepticism has historic roots in the classical philosophical tradition. The term derives from the Greek word *skeptikos,* which means "to consider, examine." It is akin to the Greek *skepsis,* which means "inquiry" and "doubt." Succinctly stated, a skeptic is one who is willing to question any claim to truth, asking for clarity in definition, consistency in logic, and adequacy of evidence. The use of skepticism is thus an essential part of objective scientific inquiry and the search for reliable knowledge.

Skepticism provides powerful tools of criticism in science, philosophy, religion, morality, politics, and society. It is thought to be exceedingly difficult to apply it to ordinary life or to live consistently with its principles. For human beings seek certitudes to guide them, and the skeptical mode is often viewed with alarm by those who hunger for faith and conviction. Skepticism is the intractable foe of pretentious belief systems. When people demand definite answers to their queries, skepticism always seems to give them further questions to ponder. Yet in a profound sense, skepticism is an essential ingredient of all

This article first appeared in *Skeptical Inquirer* 18, no. 2 (Winter 1993/1994), pp. 134–141. It was adapted from my book, *The New Skepticism: Inquiry and Reliable Knowledge* (Amherst, N.Y.: Prometheus Books, 1992).

reflective conduct and an enduring characteristic of the educated mind. Still, skeptics are considered dangerous because they question the reigning orthodoxies, the shibboleths and hosannas of any age. Although the skeptical attitude is an indelible part of reflective inquiry, can a person get beyond the skeptical orientation to develop positive directions and commitments in belief and behavior, and will skepticism enable one to do so?

Skeptics are viewed as dissenters, heretics, radicals, subversive rogues, or worse, and they are bitterly castigated by the entrenched establishments who fear them. Revolutionary reformers are also wont to turn their wrath on skeptical doubters who question their passionate commitment to ill-conceived programs of social reconstruction. Skeptics wish to examine all sides of a question; and for every argument in favor of a thesis, they usually can find one or more arguments opposed to it. Extreme skepticism cannot consistently serve our practical interests, for insofar as it sires doubt, it inhibits actions. All parties to a controversy may revile skeptics because they usually resist being swept away by the dominant fervor of the day.

Nevertheless, skepticism is *essential* to the quest for knowledge, for it is in the seedbed of puzzlement that genuine inquiry takes root. Without skepticism, we may remain mired in unexamined belief systems that are accepted as sacrosanct yet have no factual basis in reality. With it, we allow for some free play for the generation of new ideas and the growth of knowledge. Although the skeptical outlook may not be sufficient unto itself for any philosophy of the practical life, it provides a necessary condition for the reflective approach to life. Must skepticism leave us floundering in a quagmire of indecision? Or does it permit us to go further, and to discover some probabilities by which we can live? Will it allow us to achieve reliable knowledge? Or must all new discoveries in turn give way to the probing criticisms of the skeptic's scalpel? The answer to these questions depends in part on what one means by skepticism, for there are various kinds that can be distinguished.

Total Negative Skepticism

The first kind of skepticism that may be identified is *nihilism*. Its most extreme form is total negative skepticism. Here I am referring to skepticism as a complete rejection of all claims to truth or value. This kind of skepticism is mired in unlimited doubt, from which it never emerges. Knowledge is not possible, total skeptics aver. There is no certainty, no reliable basis for convictions, no truth at all.

Nihilistic skepticism has also been used in ethics with devastating results. Here the total skeptic is a complete relativist, subjectivist, and emotivist. What is "good" or "bad," "right" or "wrong," varies among individuals and societies. There are no discernible normative standards other than taste and feeling, and there is no basis for objective moral judgment. We cannot discern principles that are universal or obligatory for morality. Complete cultural relativity is the only option for this kind of skepticism. Principles of justice are simply related to power or the social contract; there are no normative standards common to all social systems. In the face of moral controversy, total skeptics may become extreme doubters; all standards are equally untenable. They may thus become conservative traditionalists. If there are no reliable guides to moral conduct, then the only recourse is to follow custom. Ours is not to reason why, ours is but to do or die, for there are no reasons. Or total skeptics may become cynical amoralists for whom "anything goes." Who is to say that one thing is better or worse than anything else? they ask; for if there are no standards of justice discoverable in the nature of things, political morality in the last analysis is a question of force, custom, or passion, not of reason or of evidence.

This kind of total skepticism is self-contradictory; for in affirming that no knowledge is possible, these skeptics have already made an assertion. In denying that we can know reality, they often presuppose a phenomenalistic or subjectivistic metaphysics in which sense impressions or ideas are the constitutive blocks out of which our knowledge of the world, however fragmented, is constructed. In asserting that there are no normative standards of ethics and politics, total skeptics sometimes advise us either to be tolerant of individual idiosyncrasies and respect cultural relativity, or to be courageous and follow our own quest to satisfy ambition or appetite. But this imperceptibly masks underlying value judgments that skeptics cherish. This kind of skepticism may be labeled "dogmatism"; for in resolutely rejecting the very possibility of knowledge or value, such skeptics are themselves introducing their own questionable assertions.

Neutral Skepticism. One form of nihilistic skepticism that seeks to avoid dogmatism does so by assuming a completely neutral stance. Here skeptics will neither affirm nor deny anything. They are unwilling to utter any pronouncements, such as that sense perception or formal reasoning is unreliable. They reject any type of skepticism that masks a theory of knowledge or reality in epistemology, metaphysics, ethics, and politics. Neutralists claim to have no such theory. They simply make personal statements and do not ask anyone to accept or reject them or be convinced or persuaded by their arguments. These are merely their own private expressions they are uttering, and they are not generalizable to others. For every argument in favor of a thesis, they can discover a counterargument. The only option for neutral skeptics is thus to suspend judgment entirely. Here agnosticism rules the roost. They are unable in epistemology to discover any criteria of knowledge; in metaphysics, a theory of reality; in religion, a basis for belief or disbelief in God; in ethics and politics, any standards of virtue, value, or social justice.

The ancient pre-Socratic Greek philosopher Cratylus (fifth–fourth century B.C.E.) was overwhelmed by the fact that everything is changing, including our own phenomenological worlds of experience; and he therefore concluded that it is impossible to communicate knowledge or to fully understand anyone. According to legend, Cratylus refused to discuss anything with anyone and, since it was pointless to reply, only wiggled his finger when asked a question. The neutral state of suspension of belief, now known as Pyrrhonism, was defended by Pyrrho of Elis and had a great impact on the subsequent development of skepticism. It applied primarily to philosophical and metaphysical questions, where one is uncertain about what is ultimately true about reality, but it put aside questions of ordinary life, where convention and custom prevail. This form of skepticism also degenerates into nihilism, for in denying any form of knowledge it can lead to despair.

Mitigated Skepticism

There is a fundamental difficulty with the forms of skepticism outlined above, for they are contrary to the demands of life. We need to function in the world—whatever its ultimate reality—and we need to develop some beliefs by which we may live and act. Perhaps our beliefs rest ultimately upon probabilities; nevertheless we need to develop knowledge as a pragmatic requirement of living and acting in the world. A modified form of skepticism was called *mitigated skepticism* by David Hume, the great eighteenth-century Scottish philosopher. It is a position that was also defended by the Greek philosopher Carneades of the second century B.C.E. Mitigated skeptics have confronted the black hole of nothingness and are skeptical about the ultimate reliability of knowledge claims. They are convinced that the foundations of knowledge and value are ephemeral and that it is impossible to establish ultimate truths about reality with any certainty. Nonetheless, we are forced by the exigencies of practical life to develop viable generalizations and to make choices, even though we can give no ultimate justification for them. One cannot find any secure basis for causal inferences about nature, other than the fact that there are regularities encountered within experience, on the basis of which we make predictions that the future will be like the past. But we have no ultimate foundation for this postulate of induction. Similarly, one cannot deduce what *ought* to be the case from what is. Morality is contingent on the sentiments of men and women who agree to abide by social convention in order to satisfy their multifarious desires as best they can.

Mitigated skepticism is not total, but only partial and limited, forced upon us by the exigencies of living. It would be total if we were to follow philosophy to the end of the trail, to irremediable indecision and doubt. Fortunately, we take detours in life, and thus we live and act *as if* we had knowledge. Our generalizations are based upon experience and practice, and the inferences that we make on the basis of habit and custom serve as our guide.

Unbelief

The term *skepticism* has sometimes been used as synonymous with *unbelief* or *disbelief* in any domain of knowledge. Actually there are two aspects to this—one is the *reflective* conviction that certain claims are unfounded or untrue, and hence not believable, and this seems a reasonable posture to take; the other is the negative *a priori* rejection of a belief without a careful examination of the grounds for that belief. Critics call this latter form of skepticism "dogmatism." The word *unbelief* in both of these senses is usually taken to apply to religion, theology, the paranormal, and the occult.

In religion the unbeliever is usually an atheist—not simply a neutral agnostic—for this kind of skepticism rejects the claims of theists. The atheist denies the basic premises of theism: that God exists, that there is some ultimate purpose to the universe, that men and women have immortal souls, and that they can be saved by divine grace.

Reflective unbelievers find the language of transcendence basically unintelligible, even meaningless, and that is why they say they are skeptics. Or, more pointedly, if they have examined the arguments adduced historically to prove the existence of God, they find them invalid, hence unconvincing. They find the so-called appeals to experience unwarranted: neither mysticism nor the appeal to miracles or revelation establishes the existence of transcendental realities. Moreover, they maintain that morality is possible without a belief in God. Unbelievers are critics of supernaturalistic claims, which they consider superstition. Indeed, they consider the God hypothesis to be without merit, a fanciful creation of human imagination that does not deserve careful examination by emancipated men and women. Many classical atheists (Baron d'Holbach, Diderot, Marx, Engels) fit into this category, for they were materialists first, and their religious skepticism and unbelief followed from their materialistic metaphysics. Such skeptics are dogmatic only if their unbelief is a form of doctrinaire faith and not based on rational grounds.

In the paranormal field, unbelievers similarly deny the reality of psi phenomena. They maintain that ESP, clairvoyance, precognition, psychokinesis, and the existence of discarnate souls are without sufficient evidence and contrary to our knowledge of how the material universe operates. Some skeptics deny paranormal phenomena on *a priori* grounds, i.e., they are to be rejected because they violate well-established physical laws. They can be considered dogmatists only if they refuse to examine the evidence brought by the proponents of the paranormal, or if they consider the level of science that has been reached on any one day to be its final formulation. Insofar as this kind of unbelief masks a closed mind, it is an illegitimate form of skepticism. If those who say that they are skeptics simply mean that they deny the existence of the paranormal realm, they are aparanormalists. The question to be asked of them always is, *Why?* For much as the believers can be judged to hold certain convictions on the basis of inadequate evidence or faith, so the dogmatic unbelievers may reject such new claims because these violate their own preconceptions about the universe. This latter kind of skepticism has many faults and is in my judgment illegitimate. These skeptics are no longer open-minded inquirers, but debunkers. They are convinced that they have the Non-Truth, which they affirm resolutely, and in doing so they may slam shut the door to further discoveries.

Skeptical Inquiry

There is yet another kind of skepticism, which has emerged on the contemporary scene and which differs from the kinds of skepticism encountered above. Indeed, this form of skepticism strongly criticizes nihilism, total and neutral; mitigated skepticism; and dogmatic unbelief—although it has learned something from each of them. This kind of skepticism I label "skeptical inquiry," with inquiry rather than doubt as the motivation. I call it the *new skepticism,* although it has emerged in the contemporary world as an outgrowth of pragmatism. A key difference between this and earlier forms of skepticism is that it is *positive* and *constructive.* It involves the transformation of the negative critical analysis of the claims to knowledge into a positive contribution to the growth and development of skeptical inquiry. It is basically a form of *methodological* skepticism, for here skepticism is an essential phase of the process of inquiry; but it does not and need not lead to unbelief, despair, or hopelessness. This skepticism is not total, but is limited to the context under inquiry. Hence we may call it *selective* or *contextual* skepticism, for one need not doubt everything at the same time, but only certain questions in the limited context of investigation. It is not neutral, because it believes that we do develop knowledge about the world. Accordingly, not only is human knowledge possible, but it can be found to be reliable; and we can in the normative realm act on the best evidence and reasons available. Knowledge is not simply limited to the descriptive or the formal sciences, but is discoverable in the normative fields of ethics and politics. Although this is a modified form of skepticism, it goes far beyond the mitigated skepticism of Hume; for it does not face an abyss of ultimate uncertainty, but is impressed by the ability of the human mind to understand and control nature.

The new skepticism is not dogmatic, for it holds that we should never by *a priori* rejection close the door to any kind of responsible investigation. Thus it is skeptical of dogmatic or narrow-minded atheism and aparanormalism.

Nonetheless, it is willing to assert reflective *unbelief* about some claims that it finds lack adequate justification. It is willing to assert that some claims are unproved, improbable, or false.

Skepticism, as a method of doubt that demands evidence and reasons for hypotheses, is essential to the process of scientific research, philosophical dialogue, and critical intelligence. It is also vital in ordinary life, where the demands of common sense are always a challenge to us to develop and act upon the most reliable hypotheses and beliefs available. It is the foe of absolute certainty and dogmatic finality. It appreciates the snares and pitfalls of all kinds of human knowledge and the importance of the principles of fallibilism and probabilism in regard to the degrees of certainty of our knowledge. This differs sharply from the skepticisms of old, and it can contribute substantially to the advancement of human knowledge and the moral progress of humankind. It has important implications for our knowledge of the universe and our moral and social life. Skepticism in this sense provides a positive and constructive eupraxsophy that can assist us in interpreting the cosmos in which we live and in achieving some wisdom in conduct.

The new skepticism is more in tune with the demands of everyday knowledge than with speculative philosophy. Traditional skepticism has had all too little to say about the evident achievements of constructive skeptical inquiry. And derisive skeptical jabs hurled from the wings of the theater of life are not always appreciated, especially if they inhibit life from proceeding without interruption.

Skeptical inquiry is essential in any quest for knowledge or deliberative valuational judgment. But it is limited and focused, selective, and positive, and it is part and parcel of a genuine process of inquiry. This form of modified skepticism is formulated in the light of the following considerations:

There has already been an impressive advance in the sciences, both theoretically and technologically. This applies to the natural, biological, social, and behavioral sciences. The forms of classical skepticism of the ancient world that re-emerged in the early modern period were unaware of the tremendous potential of scientific research. Pyrrhonistic skepticism is today invalidated, because there now exists a considerable body of reliable knowledge. Accordingly, it is meaningless to cast all claims to truth into a state of utter doubt. The same considerations apply to postmodernist subjectivism and Richard Rorty's pragmatic skepticism, which I believe are likewise mistaken.

Contrary to traditional skeptical doubts, there are methodological criteria by which we are able to test claims to knowledge: empirical tests based upon observation, logical standards of coherence and consistency, and experimental tests in which ideas are judged by their consequences. All of this is related to the proposition that it is possible to develop and use objective methods of inquiry in order to achieve reliable knowledge.

Doubt plays a vital role in the context of ongoing inquiry. It should, however, be selective, not unlimited, and contextual, not universal. The principle of fallibilism is relevant. We should not make absolute assertions, but be willing to admit that we may be mistaken. Our knowledge is based upon probabilities, which are reliable, not ultimate certainties or finalities.

Finally, skeptical inquirers should always be open-minded about new possibilities, unexpected departures in thought. They should always be willing to question or overturn even the most well-established principles in the light of further inquiry. The key principle of skeptical inquiry is to seek, when feasible, adequate evidence and reasonable grounds for any claim to truth in any context.

3

Skepticism and the Paranormal

Scientific Investigations

What is the relevance of skeptical inquiry to investigations of claims of the paranormal? There has been a spirited debate between believers in the paranormal, i.e., those who maintain that there are paranormal aspects of human experience and/or reality that transcend the categories of existing science, and skeptics, who deny these claims. Many pro-paranormal claimants accuse the skeptics of dogmatic unbelief and of having foreclosed the possibility of paranormal phenomena, antecedent to inquiry. Skeptics, on the other hand, maintain that believers often make a leap of faith without adequate evidence or allow their bias in favor of the paranormal to color their interpretations.

The first part of this article is adapted from my article in the *Encyclopedia of the Paranormal*, ed. by Gordon Stein (Amherst, N.Y.: Prometheus Books, 1996), pp. 684–701; the second part from "The New Skepticism: A Worldwide Movement," from *Skeptical Briefs* 8, no. 2 (June 1998), pp. 1–3, 9–11 (which was reprinted in skeptical magazines in Spain, Australia, Germany, the Netherlands, and Italy); and the final part, "Further Retrospective Reflections," is excerpted from remarks delivered at "Science in the Age of (Mis)Information," the First World Skeptics Congress, June 1996, in celebration of the Twentieth Anniversary of CSICOP, which was published as "CSICOP at Twenty" in *Skeptical Inquirer* 20, no. 4 (July/August 1996), pp. 7–8.

Serious skeptical scientific investigations of claims of the paranormal first began to develop in the late eighteenth and early nineteenth centuries. For example, many scientists were skeptical of the work of Franz Mesmer, who maintained that he could cure people by the use of "animal magnetism." Two scientific commissions appointed by the French Academy of Sciences and the Royal Society of Medicine in 1784 found no evidence to support the existence of animal magnetism. Critics of the study defended Mesmer, saying that he had contributed to the development of hypnotism. Another group of scientists were called upon by the French Academy of Sciences, including Antoine Lavoisier, the father of modern chemistry, to examine a stone, which is said to have fallen from the sky. They interpreted the stories about such "thunderstones" as a form of superstition, and they said that these were probably ferrous sandstones struck by lightning. In 1803, however, chemical analysis of such stones concluded that they were indeed meteors from outer space. Paranormal believers have criticized this commission for being "closed minded." What they fail to see, however, was that when sufficient empirical evidence was amassed that they were meteors, the scientific community was willing to modify its views.

The scientific study of anomalous phenomena became especially popular with the emergence of spiritualism in the nineteenth century. Spiritualism may be said to have begun in 1848 in Hydesville, New York, when two young girls, Margaret and Kate Fox, claimed to be able to communicate with dead spirits. It was alleged that they received messages in the form of rappings. Among the first scientists to examine them was a committee of three doctors in 1851 from the newly founded University of Buffalo Medical School. They said that these rappings were most likely a result of the cracking of the toe knuckles by the Fox sisters on a wooden floor or bedstead, and were not due to supernatural intervention. Such skeptical criticisms had little effect on stemming the tide of spiritualism. Thousands of mediums on both sides of the Atlantic appeared, claiming wondrous powers, and they were tested by believers and skeptics alike. Among the spiritualistic anomalies they investigated in addition to rappings were table-top movement, levitation, ectoplasmic emergence, automatic writing, voices heard in a trance state, etc. Perhaps the best known of the early skeptics was the physicist Michael Faraday, who carefully investigated cases of table turnings in 1852 by examining possible causal explanations. This is the phenomenon in which several people sitting around a table and touching its surface result in its movement. He concluded that the table turnings were not due to supernatural causes, but most likely resulted from unconscious muscular movements guided by expectations of the sitters.

A great stimulus to scientific and skeptical inquiry was the founding of the Society for Psychical Research in Britain in 1882 and the American Society for Psychical Research in 1885. Involved in both ventures were a number of important scientific and philosophical figures. These societies at first focused on the question of survival after death, apparitions, and poltergeists, which many hoped could be demonstrated empirically to exist. These inquiries were later broadened to include studies of thought reading, clairvoyance, and hypnotism. Often there was no sharp dividing line between skepticism and belief in the paranormal, and in some cases there was a balancing between belief and doubt.

William James, the eminent American philosopher and psychologist, reported that he and his colleagues expected when they founded the society "that if the material were treated rigorously and, as far as possible, experimentally, objective truth would be elicited, and the subject rescued from sentimentalism on the one side and dogmatic ignorance on the other."[1] According to James both he and Henry Sidgwick had hoped for prompt results. However, after 20 years Sidgwick confessed to James that he was in the same state of doubt and balance that he started with. And James himself revealed that after 25 years he was "theoretically no further" than he was at the beginning. It was not possible to obtain "full corroboration." There were "so many sources of possible deception" that the entire lot of reports, he said, "may be worthless." The same disquietude has been expressed by other inquirers throughout the history of the field.

This skeptical attitude about the paranormal was no doubt precipitated by the considerable body of fraudulent mediums uncovered. Margaret Fox Kane, for example, on October 21, 1888, confessed to a large audience in New York City that she, her sister Kate, and her older sister Leah had been perpetrating fraud for 40 years by cracking their toe knuckles, as earlier scientists had suspected. Douglas Blackburn revealed on September 1, 1911 in a newspaper story that he and G. A. Smith had duped the researchers of the Society for Psychical Research 30 years earlier. The Society had conducted experiments on "thought reading," and had maintained that the Smith-Blackburn experiments provided evidence for telepathy.

The same problem of duplicity emerged with the testing of the Creery sisters, who under the supervision of their father, the Reverend A. M. Creery, had allegedly demonstrated telepathy. They were caught using a secret code to communicate. The extensive testing of the Italian medium Eusapia Palladino by scientific bodies split the scientific community between those who alleged that her powers were genuine and skeptics who, because she was detected cheating several times, doubted that she had any psychic powers. Some members of the Society became extremely skeptical. Frank Podmore, a senior member of the British SPR, who consistently rejected the magical way of viewing the world, gradually became disillusioned. "Is it credible," he asked, "that there is anything of value behind the fifty-year span of quibbling and chicanery?"[2] Among some other leading skeptics of the day were Simon Newcomb, American astronomer and first president of the American Society for Psychical Research, who said that he was, after many years of research, extremely skeptical about "occultism." Another skeptical investigator was Hugo Münsterberg, Harvard psychologist, who on December 18, 1909, caught Eusapia Palladino in the act of cheating. Similarly for the noted magician, Joseph F. Rinn, who has given a full account of fraudulent behavior in a test of Palladino at Columbia University. Notable in the field of exposing quackery was Harry Houdini (who discredited the Boston psychic Margery Crandon and other well-known psychics). Similarly for Amy Tanner, whose book on spiritism exposed Leona Piper, whom James thought was a genuine psychic.[3] Another important skeptical investigator was John E. Coover, a psychologist at Stanford University, who criticized "metapsychism," primarily because it did not satisfy the standards of scientific methodology and admissible evidence.[4]

Another wave of skepticism emerged because of the parapsychological experimental work of J. B. Rhine, who studied with McDougall at Harvard and then established a laboratory at Duke. He claimed that he was able to demonstrate the existence of ESP (clairvoyance, telepathy, precognition) and PK (psychokinesis) by using rigorous statistical laboratory methods. He thought that he had found certain individuals with psychic powers who when tested with the Zener cards were able to make correct guesses, at above or below chance. Many American psychologists attempted to replicate Rhine's experiments, but most received negative results. They noted that a decline effect was apt to set in, and when psychics were brought to other labs they did not manifest their powers. These psychologists criticized the design of the experiment and/or the grading techniques. Moreover, they thought that Rhine's results could be parsimoniously accounted for by prosaic explanations, such as sensory leakage, ill-designed experiments, questionable grading procedures, fraud, and so on Among the critics were J. L. Kennedy (Stanford), Professor W. S. Cox (Princeton), E. T. Adams (Colgate), J. C. Crumbaugh (Southern Methodist University), Raymond Willoughby (Brown), and C. P. and J. H. Heinlein (Johns Hopkins). In September 1938 the American Psychological Association held a symposium on the methods of ESP research and a committee under the chairmanship of S. B. Sells (Columbia) was established to review and report on ESP experiments. Their reports were invariably negative. B. F. Skinner (Harvard), the influential behavioral psychologist, was a strong critic of Rhine's work, as was Donald J. Hebb (McGill). An important review of psychokinesis was published by Edward Girden, who concluded that the results were negative.

Still another wave of skeptical criticism emerged in Great Britain following the Soal-Goldney experiments in London beginning in 1941. Samuel G. Soal for many years attempted to replicate the results of Rhine but was unable to do so. After reviewing his data, he thought that he had uncovered two subjects, Basil Shackleton and Mrs. Gloria Stewart, who manifested psychic powers. Testing them under what seemed to be rigorous conditions, he claimed that he could prove the reality of telepathy and precognition. The odds against chance were astronomical. In a controversial article in *Science* magazine, published in 1955,[5] George R. Price, in the Department of Medicine at the University of Minnesota, raised the question of whether there had been cheating in the experiments. Other researchers raised similar doubts about Soal's work. C. E. M. Hansel emerged as a leading critic of parapsychology. His book, *ESP: A Scientific Evaluation*[6] was very influential in setting forth the skeptics' case against Soal, Rhine, and others. It was only in 1978, however, that Betty Markwick definitively showed that S. G. Soal had cheated in the Soal-Goldney tests and that random-number grading sheets, which he brought to the experiment and took back, were doctored.[7] This scandal in parapsychology led to many people abandoning the field and becoming skeptics, in particular Antony Flew, Christopher Scott, Dennis Parsons, and Eric Dingwall.

The New Skepticism

A significant new factor in the contemporary growth of skeptical inquiry was the founding of the Committee for the Scientific Investigation of Claims of the Paranormal (CSICOP) in 1976. The kind of skepticism which it represents is continuous with what I have called "the new skepticism." This form of skepticism is constructive and positive. It focuses on *inquiry* rather than doubt, and it is based on the realization that skepticism is an intrinsic part of the process of scientific inquiry.

Permit me to say something about the reasons why CSICOP was created. I had long been a critic of paranormal (and supernatural) claims that could not be supported by the evidence. And I was astonished that many or most of the claims continued to enjoy widespread public support, even though they had been refuted. Moreover, the mass media latched onto paranormal claims, and psychic gurus were enjoying a huge following with nary a dissent. This in spite of the case that scientific inquiry, which investigated their claims and rejected them because of a lack of evidence. Astrology is a good case in point, for it was refuted by astronomers, physicists, statisticians, psychologists, and other scientists. There is no empirical basis for horoscopes or sun-sign astrology; its cosmology is based on the discredited Ptolemaic system; moreover, it is possible to test its predictions and forecasts; and the results are invariably negative. Yet very few in the general public are aware of these criticisms, and indeed often confuse astronomy with astrology.

With this in mind, I helped to draft a statement, "Objections to Astrology," with the help of Bart Bok, a noted astronomer, and Lawrence Jerome, a science writer.[8] This statement was issued and endorsed by 186 leading scientists, including 19 Nobel Laureates. It received immediate worldwide attention, especially after the *New York Times* did a front-page story on the statement. It seemed to me that the success of this effort, especially within the scientific community, which welcomed it, called for the need for a more organized response by the academic and scientific community. With this in mind, I called for the organization of a new coalition comprised of scientists, philosophers, skeptics, and others. Hence, I invited several dozen critics of the paranormal to an open conference to explore developing an organized opposition to the uncontested growth of belief in the paranormal. These included some well-known popular critics, such as Martin Gardner, Milbourne Christopher, Marcello Truzzi, Ray Hyman, James Randi, and others. I also invited some distinguished philosophers and scientists, such as Ernest Nagel, Sidney Hook, and W. V. Quine to endorse the statement of purpose which I had drafted.

The conference was held at the new campus of the State University of New York at Buffalo, in Amherst, New York. At that time, I was editor of *The Humanist* magazine, one of the leading journals critical of religion. At the inaugural meeting of CSICOP, in my opening address ("The Scientific Attitude versus Anti-Science and Pseudoscience"), I said that there was a long-standing conflict in the history of culture between religion and science, but that today a new challenge to science has come to the fore because of the growth of pseudoscientific and paranormal claims. The apparent popular belief in exorcism,[9] nouveau witches, and Satanism were symptomatic of the Aquarian consciousness then being proclaimed. The mass media also presented as true and usually without any dissent accounts of Kirlian photography, the wonders of ESP and psychokinesis, UFO sightings, the Bermuda Triangle, Bigfoot, von Däniken's *Chariots of the Gods?*, etc. A great number of quasi-religious irrational cults had emerged at that time, including Hare Krishna, Reverend Moon, and the Scientologists. These were symptomatic of a countercultural opposition to science that had begun to appear, and it needed, in my judgment, to be responded to—for the public had a right to hear the scientific critique of the pseudoscientific and fringe claims.

I raised the following question:

> Should we assume that the scientific revolution, which began in the sixteenth century, is continuous? Or will it be overwhelmed by the forces of unreason?

And I replied:

> We ought not to assume, simply because ours is an advanced scientific-technological society, that irrational thinking will be overcome. The evidence suggests that this is far from being the case. Indeed, there is always the danger that science itself may be engulfed by the forces of unreason.[10]

Since that time, postmodernism has emerged, denying the possibility of scientific objectivity, and considering science one mythic narrative amongst others. And much to everyone's surprise there have been widespread attacks on the Enlightenment and the ideals of the scientific revolution.

Today these antiscientific protests are accompanied by a resurgence of fundamentalist religions. So the challenge to science is not simply from propagandists for the paranormal, but also from the disciples of many religions. I should point out that although I personally believe that skeptics need to deal with religious claims as well as with paranormal claims, I recommended that CSICOP concentrate on paranormal and pseudoscientific claims. The British and the American Societies for Psychical Research were basically made up of those committed to the psychical point of view, as was J. B. Rhine's laboratory founded at Duke University. Hence, CSICOP would concentrate on paranormal investigations, though hopefully from a neutral and impartial framework, and it would examine religious claims only insofar as they were testable. *Free Inquiry* and the Council for Democratic and Secular Humanism were later founded (in 1980) explicitly to deal with religious claims, for the new skepticism needs to be applied across the board.

The first meeting of CSICOP had an enormous public impact. There was extensive press coverage from the *Washington Post* and *New York Times* to *Le Monde* and *Pravda*, with virtually all of the major science magazines welcoming the formation of CSICOP. We had crystallized a perceived need that both the scientific community and many in the general public thought had to be satisfied: a response to the growth of paranormal claims. Within a year our new magazine was launched, at first called *The Zetetic* (under the editorship of Marcello Truzzi), and thence the *Skeptical Inquirer* (under the editorship of Kendrick Frazier, who had been the editor of *Science News*). Much to our pleasure, skeptical groups began forming all over the world, so that today there are over 90 such groups from Germany and England to China, Russia, Spain, and Mexico. Moreover, some 60 magazines and newsletters have appeared. Indeed, we have worked closely with national groups to help get their organizations and magazines started.

All of these developments have contributed to the formation of a worldwide New Skepticism Movement. There is now a vibrant and growing International Network affiliated with CSICOP and the *Skeptical Inquirer*. We are all committed to the scientific program: we are skeptical of paranormal and occult claims, unless they have been corroborated and replicated by independent investigators.[11]

Summing Up

One may ask, After more than two decades of inquiry, what can be learned about this entire phenomenon? In the rest of this article I wish to sum up many of the basic findings and conclusions that the skeptical movement has reached about paranormal belief claims.

These are based on literally hundreds, even thousands, of experiments conducted by those associated with CSICOP and/or extensive meta-analyses of others. In summation:

First, the term *paranormal* itself is highly questionable. We decided to use the term only because proponents (such as J. B. Rhine) had used it. We doubt that it is possible to find a paranormal realm separate from or independent of the natural universe. We are seeking normal and natural explanations for phenomena. The best meaning of the term *paranormal* is that there are sometimes bizarre, unexpected *anomalies* that we encounter (as Charles Fort described them), and we are willing to examine them with an open mind, and do not wish to reject them *a priori* and antecedent to inquiry. Murray Gell-Mann, Nobel Prize-winner and a Fellow of CSICOP, at a conference at the University of Colorado in 1986, observed that in one sense we deny the paranormal entirely, because once we find that phenomena can be explained by reference to prosaic causes, then these explanations are incorporated into the natural scientific world-view, and are not separated from it. I reiterate, we have an open mind and are willing to examine anomalies without prejudgment, providing that the claims made by the proponents are responsible.

Anecdotal reports: We have found that many reports of anomalous events are based on anecdotal accounts. While these reports cannot be dismissed out of hand or without a fair hearing, especially if they are seriously offered, skeptics hold that inquirers go beyond mere anecdotes to a more systematic examination of the phenomena. Many anecdotal narratives are based upon private experiences, subjective and introspective in character, or upon memory of past events, which may be unreliable, or upon second- or third-hand hearsay.

It is important that all such reports be carefully sifted through, if possible, before they are accepted. Anecdotes may have a grain of truth and they may supply new and important data, otherwise overlooked. On the other hand, they may involve serious misperception or faulty memory; they may involve stories embellished upon beyond their original meaning; or incidents blown out of proportion to what actually happened, or the deception of the senses colored by suggestion. Many of these alleged anecdotes, if reported second-hand, take on the character of gossip, folk tales, or urban legends. They may contain kernels of new information, or they may be inflated in significance after the fact. There is a tendency for people who believe in the occult to read in mysterious nuances to otherwise prosaic experiences, or to exaggerate the significance of random events. This commonly occurs, for example, in reports of ghostly apparitions, crisis premonitions of death, visitations by extraterrestrial beings, or the accuracy of psychic prophecies. Skeptics ask, Did the event occur as the person states, and is the interpretation placed on the event the most likely cause?

Unless an anecdotal account can be corroborated independently, investigators urge caution about its authenticity. This not only applies to the truth of the event alleged to have actually occurred, but on the occult explanation that is imposed on it because of ignorance of the real causes.

The skeptic says that the report may or may not be true and that if it did occur there may be alternative causal explanations to be made of it. Are we dealing with a real event, or a misperception, hallucinatory experience, fantasy, and/or a misinterpretation of what happened?

Eyewitness testimony: The appeal to eyewitness testimony is the bedrock of our knowledge about the world and ourselves. The data are drawn from direct first-hand experience. It is important, however, that such testimony not be accepted on face value without careful inspection. This is especially the case when the testimony is about anomalous, unexpected, or bizarre events. If a person reports that it is raining heavily outside and he supports the claim by pointing to the fact that he is soaking wet, and if this report does not conflict with our common knowledge about the world, it need not demand weighty evidence (though he may have been squirted with a hose or had a bucket of water dumped on him). We can corroborate such claims by looking outside and/or receiving reports from other bystanders; and/or consulting the barometer. If, on the contrary, a person reports that it is raining pink fairies, skeptical inquirers request that his extraordinary account be corroborated by independent and impartial observers.

Psychologist Elizabeth Loftus of the University of Washington has performed numerous experiments to demonstrate the often fallible and deceptive character of the senses. She found that many bystanders at a robbery or accident often offer conflicting reports, especially where the incident is emotionally charged. This tendency to misperceive may be compounded when someone claims to have seen a statue of the Virgin Mary weep or a miraculous cure by a faith healer. Not only must the report of an observer be carefully analyzed, but the interpretation that is placed upon it must be evaluated. Thus skeptical inquirers ask that wherever possible there be two or more witnesses to an event, that these witnesses be careful observers, and that what they have said can be independently corroborated. Reports of UFO visitations are common throughout much of the world, and these reports often come in waves, often depending on sensationalistic media exploitation. The investigator asks, What did these people really see; can these interpretations be verified? Skeptical inquirers have sought to provide prosaic explanations for unidentified flying objects, which are often identified as planets, meteors, weather balloons, terrestrial rockets or aircraft, or other phenomena.

Extraordinary claims need extraordinary evidence: This principle has been adduced for anomalous accounts. If it is the case that a paranormal event, if confirmed, would overthrow the known laws of science, then one would need abundant evidence to accept it. The evidence must not be skimpy or haphazard, but so strong that its denial would require more credulity than its acceptance. Skeptical inquirers agree that we should not deny evidence antecedent to inquiry; on the other hand if a claim contradicts well-established principles of science, then it would need to be supported by abundant, not flimsy, evidence. A good case has been made about psychokinesis, that the mind can move matter without an intervening physical object or material force, or that precognitive events can be known before they happen. If we were to accept these extraordinary claims, we would require extraordinary evidence. Helmut Schmidt has claimed experimental evidence that persons in the present can retrogressively affect past events in a random generator. This unusual anomaly would seem to violate the laws of physics, and/or it would require that physics be revised to account for it. We would need several lines of independent replication before we can accept the claim.

Burden-of-proof argument: Some parapsychologists, such as John Beloff, have argued that the strongest evidence for paranormal events is in the historical cases of famous mediums and psychics. Eusapia Palladino was tested by numerous scientific bodies. Many found that she had cheated in some cases; others could find no evidence of cheating—hence they attributed the event to paranormal causes.[12] Similarly, it is claimed that D. D. Home, a well-known medium, allegedly floated 75 feet above a London street and performed other strange feats, and that those feats could not be accounted for in normal terms. Beloff maintains that unless skeptical inquirers can explain how these mediums performed what they did in all cases, then these accounts should be accepted as veridical. The skeptical inquirer responds that the burden of proof rests upon the paranormal claimant. It is he who must be able to account for such cases with sufficient evidence; unless this is done, one should suspend judgment and remain skeptical. This is particularly the case in regard to historical claims, where it is difficult to reconstruct the situation under which the alleged effect occurred. That is why skeptics ask for replication in the present before they can accept the phenomenon.

The burden-of-proof argument has been used in religion. Is a believer entitled to believe whatever he wishes about God, unless the skeptic can disprove His existence or demonstrate that the properties attributed to Him do not exist? The skeptic criticizes the logic of the argument in the following manner: If someone were to claim that mermaids exist, the burden of proof is upon him, not the skeptic to disprove the fact.

Fraud: The resort to fraud is notorious in human affairs, including cases in orthodox science (for example, the Piltdown Man hoax). It is especially widespread in the paranormal area. Many mediums and psychics have been found cheating. Although some of the deception might be unconscious, considerable intentional trickery has been uncovered. It is thus important, says the skeptical inquirer, that every precaution against deception be used. In the design of an experiment, safeguards ought to be built in so that the subjects under study cannot fudge the data, whether inadvertently or consciously. C. E. M. Hansel has pointed out that many of the earlier experiments of J. B. Rhine were suspect, since the conditions of the experiments were loose. In the famous Pearce-Pratt experiment for telepathy, Pratt could easily have peeked at the Zener cards by sneaking out of the library to the sender's office, or by using an accomplice. Many scientists have been especially deceived by children. For example, physicist John Taylor, when observing children through a two-way mirror, found that they bent spoons or forks manually. Susie Cotrell was shown to be using the Shulein forced-card trick to deceive observers. In a clever test of her powers, conducted by Fellows of CSICOP, she was seen on a hidden camera to use sleight of hand in shuffling the cards and to peek at them when no one was observing. It is also important that experimental fraud not intervene. A notable case in J. B. Rhine's parapsychology lab dramatizes the problem. Walter Levy was said to have tampered with the evidence for precognitive tests of chicks by altering the data.

There have been blatant illustrations of cheating in the UFO field: for example, Billy Meier in Switzerland and Ed Walters in Gulf Breeze, Florida. The hoaxing of crop circles as evidence of extraterrestrial visitations in Great Britain has been exposed. Similarly for the unmasking of Philippine psychic surgeons and evangelical faith healers by James Randi and the Committee for the Scientific Examination of Religion.

A key point is that scientists who are accomplished in their own disciplines are not necessarily the most careful observers in other domains, and they can often be deceived by clever conjurers posing as psychics.

Experimenter bias: The role of unconscious bias by an experimenter poses a problem in virtually all fields of science. Those who propose a theory are often not the best or most competent judges of the evidential basis in support of it. Experimenter bias may be conscious or unconscious. It may creep in by inadvertent sensory leakage or in grading techniques. A good case is Michel Gauquelin, who was hailed by many as the founder of a new science of astrobiology. Gauquelin claimed to have found a correlation between planetary configurations and professional achievement. Mars in key sectors (1 and 4) was correlated, he said, with being a famous sports champion. There is considerable evidence that Gauquelin selected his sample based on prior knowledge of whether they were born with Mars in key sectors. Hence there was not so much a Mars effect as Gauquelin's bias. Independent scientific inquiries were unable to replicate the efforts.

Noted parapsychologist Gertrude Schmeidler has said that there is a difference between sheep (believers) and goats (skeptics); and that the former are more likely to achieve results than the latter. Whether sheep can consistently show the existence of ESP is questionable. It is the case, however, that experimenters who are sheep may be more disposed to accept as positive any nuances in the data. On the other hand, the reverse may be the case and experimenters who are goats may dismiss evidence because of their antibias. In a debate with Charles Honorton, Ray Hyman has pointed to the need for tightening the experimental design in the Ganzfeld tests by the proper randomization of trials and careful grading techniques. Others have pointed to the questionable grading techniques in the remote-viewing tests of by Targ and Puthoff at the Stanford Research Institute.

Demand for replication: The key argument of skeptical inquirers not only in the paranormal field, but in orthodox sciences as well, is the need for replicable experiments. Skeptics are not convinced that ESP or PK exist. Until psychical researchers can specify antecedent laboratory conditions under which an effect can be observed by independent observers, they say that they have a right to be cautious. The great controversy in parapsychology is precisely on this point: is there a standard replicable experiment, which can demonstrate the existence of psi to the neutral investigator? Unless that condition is satisfied, skeptics remain dubious about the reality of the phenomena.

Magical thinking: Many skeptical inquirers have been puzzled by the ready tendency of many human beings to resort to magical thinking, i.e., to accept without sufficient evidence contracausal explanations. This includes the capacity for adopting paranormal interpretations and/or reading into nature occult forces. There is a tendency to attribute to some individuals miraculous powers. Historically, this applies to the prophets who claim to have had revelations from on high and were endowed with supernatural abilities. This also applies to gurus, shamans, medicine men, psychics, and faith healers—all who are believed to possess magical powers. The person who resorts to magical thinking is more likely to accept the occult and/or psychic explanation without critical skepticism. The miracle worker is taken as an authority and the facts are stretched to validate the healing claim.

Psychological interpretations of the paranormal: Many skeptical inquirers maintain that the key to understanding paranormal phenomena is in human psychology. This means that the capacity of people to accept paranormal phenomena as true without sufficient evidence has its roots in human nature. This has many dimensions: being amenable to suggestibility, being fantasy prone, given to magical thinking, and the general tendency to allow one's personal propensities, desires, and hopes to color the data. Ray Hyman has demonstrated the power of "cold reading" in regard to palmistry. But this can be generalized to many other paranormal fields.

The popularity of astrological horoscopes provides considerable support for a psychological interpretation. There is little or no evidence to support astrology, which is based on an ancient Ptolemaic cosmology and is now rendered obsolete by astronomy. Moreover, astrology has failed virtually all the tests adduced to prove it.[13] All efforts to find a statistical correlation between the moment and place of birth and the position of the heavenly bodies have had negative results. Yet people claim that astrological sun signs and horoscopes are true. For the skeptic the more likely explanation is that truth is in the eye of the beholder. For the palm reader, astrologer, or psychic is often so general in his reading that his diagnoses and prognostications is stretched by the subject so that they are personally validated. Thus, in my view the key to the paranormal is that it is within the *eye of the beholder*. This is what I have labeled the "stretched-sock syndrome," for socks can be stretched to fit any feet.

The transcendental temptation: Why is this so? Perhaps it has its roots in the long evolutionary history of the species and it may have even a genetic basis. Some, such as E. O. Wilson, have claimed sociobiological roots for religiosity; though many skeptics have criticized this theory as not being sufficiently tested. John Schumaker, an Australian psychologist, believes that some illusions are necessary for sanity; and that "the corruption of reality" is an essential ingredient of mental health.[14] To face death or existential nothingness, he said, is difficult for most people, and so they achieve consolation by reading into nature hidden meanings, including belief in the afterlife or the ability to communicate with dead persons. The same explanation can be applied to many other areas of the paranormal. Gullibility is thus fed by the hunger for transcendence.

Hypnosis: One topic that has aroused considerable skeptical controversy concerns the reliability of hypnosis as a source of knowledge. Is hypnosis a special "trance state" induced in a subject, or is the subject simply acting out the suggestions of the hypnotist? It is clear that hypnosis is a useful technique in many areas of practice. It does have its pitfalls, however, concerning a whole range of paranormal phenomena, allegedly verified by hypnotic regression. This is the case in regard to "past-life regressions" used by some researchers as evidence for reincarnation. Budd Hopkins, David Jacobs, and John Mack have introduced hypnotic regressions as evidence for abductions by alien beings, who are allegedly engaged in sexual-genetic experiments. Skeptics have argued that a more likely explanation for such bizarre tales is that the evidence is contaminated by the hypnotherapist, who, using suggestion, tends to implant the ideas in a person and/or assists in conjuring fantasies. The skeptic maintains that we need not postulate prior lives or extraterrestrial abductions in the paranormal realm; for there are still other possible alternative explanations.[15] For example, some otherwise normal fantasy-prone individuals are likely to weave out tales from their imaginations. Often cryptomnesia is at work and ideas or experiences deeply embedded in the unconscious are embellished upon and taken as real. The skeptic is highly dubious of such uses of hypnosis.

Pseudoscience versus protoscience: It is important that a distinction between pseudoscience and genuine science be drawn. Unfortunately, it is not always possible to find a clear demarcation line; and sometimes what is labeled as "pseudoscience" may really be a new protoscience. Marcello Truzzi has pointed out that there is some danger that skeptical inquirers will reject new ideas—protosciences—because they do not fit into the prevailing paradigm. Some criteria for distinguishing a pseudoscience are available: for example, are its concepts clearly defined and noncontradictory, are its many theories falsifiable, are there any tests that would enable us to ascertain whether the hypotheses and theories are warranted? Phrenology and biorhythms were two alleged sciences which after exhaustive testing were found to warrant the label "pseudoscience." One has to be careful since many new fields of inquiry have often had an uphill battle against the scientific establishment. Similarly for many established disciplines. Critics point out that psychology, sociology, anthropology, and political science are riddled with inadequate experimental designs and questionable studies. The better part of prudence is for skeptics to be skeptical not only of pseudosciences, but of orthodox science as well, and to be willing to revise even the most revered principles if they do not succeed under criticism by the community of inquirers. The key point of skepticism is not doubt, however, but *inquiry*; skepticism is only one element in the process of inquiry. It is not the belief or disbelief that is the main issue, but the facts, theories, and methods of verification.

Ridicule: Many of those whom skeptics have criticized resent what they consider to be unfair ridicule. Martin Gardner has pointed out that "a horse laugh may be worth a thousand syllogisms," and that skeptics may rightfully debunk or lampoon outlandish paranormal claims. In the public domain, particularly in the mass media, paranormal claims are most often inflated all out of proportion to the evidential basis. The claim is sensationalized and the public is led to believe it has been verified or documented by scientists, when this may not be the case. In such situations, a dispassionate appraisal may not get public attention, and an outrageous claim may need to be deflated by skeptics by some kind of humorous debunking. Here skeptics have entered the domain of rhetoric and persuasion. It is clear that ridicule is not a substitute for genuine inquiry and that such a resort can only occur *after* an extensive process of investigation. For skeptical inquirers, their commitment is to objective standards of responsible inquiry. How convince the public that there is insufficient evidence for a claim and/or that they ought to suspend judgment, or that the claim is improbable, is an important question for those committed to advancing the program of science. All skeptics concede that their first obligation is to inquiry, and that any debunking must come as a conclusion to their investigations.

Alternative causal explanations: The ultimate goal of all scientific inquiry is not only to describe what has happened or is happening (descriptive knowledge), but to interpret phenomena by means of causal explanations. Here the best talents and creative ingenuity of inquirers must be brought to bear. It is often the case that an anomaly can best be explained in prosaic terms. Events that seem inexplicable may be due to coincidence; a miraculous cure may be due to the power of suggestion or the placebo effect; a statistical correlation may only be an artifact of the data, etc. The program of science can proceed only when someone is sensitive to "the damn facts." One need not deny that anomalies exist; the challenge is to search for deeper causal correlations in order to account for why the facts are occurring. There is continual scientific success in this latter regard, for that which appeared at one time to be mysterious or inexplicable may be explained by reference to general principles or unique historical circumstances. Thus skeptical inquiry is related to the ultimate goal of all scientific research: to adequately describe and account for data and to explain, where possible, how and why they have occurred.

The unsinkable-rubber-duck syndrome: After more than two and a half decades of investigation by skeptical inquirers, we are continually astonished by the fact that no matter how often we criticize paranormal belief claims, they still persist. Indeed, even if they are thoroughly examined and refuted in one age, they seem to re-emerge within the next and people will continue to believe them in spite of evidence to the contrary. This is what I have called the "unsinkable-rubber-duck syndrome." No doubt many are familiar with a carnival shooting gallery, where customers are induced to shoot down moving metal ducks. Here, even if the ducks are successfully knocked down, they pop right back up again.

Given the tendency for "magical thinking," the "transcendental temptation," and "gullibility," skeptics have their work cut out for them. We cannot silently steal away once we have investigated and debunked an outrageous claim. There will always be a need for skeptical inquiry in society. Not only do the old myths crop up to entice a new generation and need responses, but new, often more fanciful claims may be introduced and become fashionable. Thus, I submit that there is a continuing need for skeptical inquiry, and skeptics will always serve as the gadflies of society. Standing in the wings of the theater of life, unable to accept the prevailing nonsense on stage, the role of skeptics is to keep alive the spirit of free inquiry and to ask probing questions—even if those they criticize are deeply offended, and/or in spite of the calumny that may descend upon the skeptics for their criticisms.

The new skepticism thus has an ongoing positive and constructive task in society; and as long as human credulity persists there is a need for skeptics to raise unsettling questions about it. We should continue to provide responsible explanations for paranormal and occult claims; and whatever our findings, to publish our views and make them known to the general public. We should not despair at the tidal wave of irrational beliefs that sometimes confront us. We are committed to the quest for knowledge and truth. In the last analysis, our main goal is *inquiry*, not skepticism, and in this regard the skeptical movement will always have a vital role to play in human culture.

Further Retrospective Reflections

When we first established CSICOP we did not realize we would elicit such an intense response from the scientific community or the public.

In no small measure, the epidemic of paranormal beliefs is due to the rapid emergence of the mass media on a global scale. These media have virtually replaced the schools, colleges, and universities as the chief conveyors of information. The days of the lone scientist conducting research in the lab or of the isolated scholar writing a paper or book for a limited audience have been bypassed. Today new ideas are popularized—whether half- or fully baked—and they are broadcast far and wide even if they have not been sufficiently tested. Apparently the chief interests of most media conglomerates are entertainment rather than information, profit rather than truth, selling products rather that contributing to the sum of human knowledge. Accordingly, paranormal ideas are pandered to a gullible public and the line between fiction and reality is blurred. Psychic wonders, angelic visitations, Virgin Mary sightings, satanic infestations, weeping icons, miraculous cures, prophetic visions, and other paranormal phenomena are exhibited and marketed along with cereal, chewing gum, cold remedies, and laxatives. The public is often confronted with sensational accounts of hidden realms, and pseudoscience is mistaken for genuine science. Even reputable publishers prefer to publish books touting paranormal claims rather than dispassionate scientific critiques. Why is it that of the thousands of pro-astrology, pro-psychic, or pro-UFO books published, very few are skeptical? "They don't sell," is the response of the hallelujah choir within the publishing industry—a sad commentary on our times.

The skeptics thus have a vital role to play: to educate the public about the nature of science and to attempt to persuade media producers and directors that they have some responsibility to develop an appreciation for scientific rationality. One of the roles of CSICOP is to challenge the views of pseudoscience pouring forth daily from the media. It is clear that we cannot operate within the cloistered confines of the academy, but need to enter into the public arena. In monitoring the media, we surely have not sought to censor producers or publishers; we only wish for some balance on their part in presenting paranormal claims, and for some role for skepticism about these claims. Largely because of the media, large sectors of public opinion simply assume that psychic powers are real (clairvoyance, telepathy, precognition), that it is possible to modify material objects merely by the mind (psychokinesis), that psychics can help detectives solve mysteries, that we can abandon the clinical tests of medical science and heal patients by miraculous means, and that the Earth is visited daily by extraterrestrials who are engaging in sexual-biogenetic experiments with humans. The number of paranormal, occult, and sci-fi television programs is increasing. Our objection is that "docudramas" are not labeled as fictionalized accounts but touted as fact. In regard to the many talk shows that constantly deal with paranormal topics, the skeptical viewpoint is rarely heard; and when it is permitted to be expressed, it is usually sandbagged by the host or other guests.

After two decades of toiling in the paranormal marshes, I am persuaded that what we are dealing with in the public is a *quasi-religious phenomenon*. Belief in the paranormal is the poetic equivalent of religion. We live in a culture where any criticisms of the uncorroborated claims of religions are generally considered to be ill-advised or in bad taste. The New Age spirituality that has developed is drenched in occult and paranormal symbols—from near-death experiences to extraterrestrial abductions, from past-life regressions to miraculous healings. This is consistent with the vague religiosity now regnant in modern culture, and especially American society. The popularity of the paranormal worldview, I submit, is a manifestation of what I call the *transcendental temptation*, the tendency of human beings to wish to penetrate the hidden depths of an alleged transcendental reality that cannot be known by using the methods of scientific inquiry. In my view this is a reversion to primitive forms of magical thinking. That is why it is often so difficult to cope with paranormal beliefs, for we are dealing with faith and conviction, not testable theories or hypotheses. This perhaps explains why there is often so much animosity toward science in large sectors of the population, and why antiscientific irrationalism at times overwhelms the dispassionate standards of scientific inquiry. Too many people find the scientific attitude too demanding and rigorous; they want something easier to ingest.

Modern science and technology have transformed the globe and have vastly improved the standards of living and health of large sectors of the population in those societies where it has been applied. Those of us committed to the scientific outlook do not wish to abandon its programmatic goals; we wish to continue to use the methods of science and technology to understand nature and solve human problems. We are willing to suspend judgment about the claims of new forms of reality until they have been tested; they should at least be falsifiable and they need to run the gauntlet of peer review and replication. In this postmodernist age of nihilistic subjectivity, many intellectuals consider this view to be "outdated," and we are criticized for defending the ideals of the Enlightenment. They reject the view that the methods of science and critical thinking are the most effective procedures for testing truth claims and resolving human problems. We maintain that where the methods of science have been used, they have been eminently successful, and we wish to extend these methods to other areas. The methods of science—

measured on a comparative scale with intuition, faith, emotion, and metaphysics—though not perfect, seem to us the best way to gain reliable knowledge.

The frontiers of science are forever expanding, and this means that we constantly have to be prepared to revise our theories. But the fact that our theories and hypotheses change should not be a cause of despair or uncertainty. The fact that we cannot make absolute or final judgments does not mean that we cannot make any judgments: we insist we still have a body of tested beliefs, and these tell us something about the nature of the expanding evolutionary universe and the place of the human species within it.

Critics maintain that the above account of the universe—based on our reading of the natural, biological, and behavioral sciences—all too often is excessively *naturalistic* or materialistic, and that it leaves little or no room for spiritual, occult, or paranormal realms. I personally accept the naturalistic interpretation of the universe. However, in being committed to the scientific outlook, I do not deny the vital importance of human creativity in life, or the significance of passions, feelings, and other dimensions of human experience, but I would insist that in searching for testable hypotheses these dimensions are not relevant. Some may choose to reject this interpretation. I respond that if we are to abandon the methods of objective inquiry we need to have good reasons and evidence to do so.

The defining characteristic of the new skepticism is that we use objective methods to establish truth claims as nearly as we can and whenever they are applicable. This does not mean that we are opposed to the sense of wonder. The great scientific discoveries of the past four centuries have expanded the boundaries of our understanding. As spacecraft probe our solar system and the galaxies beyond on the macro level, or penetrate the micro level of inanimate and organic matter, we discover hitherto unknown dimensions. Our chief caveat is that intuitive or speculative theories need to be corroborated by valid inference and experimental confirmation.

Not all of those who are committed to skeptical inquiry will accept this broader naturalistic interpretation of the sciences. We are not asking them to do so; yet they may find our unraveling of crop circles, spoon-bendings, spontaneous human combustion, or poltergeists helpful. Our work draws upon the interdisciplinary efforts of many researchers; and rather than depending on the so-called experts in fields such as astrology or UFOlogy, as the case may be, many find the work of the skeptical movement highly instructive in specific areas of interest. In maintaining that the broader interpretation of our world is naturalistic, I have no doubt entered the controversial domain of the philosophy of science, and in this age of intense specialization, many may not choose to take that step.

Future Prospects

I have briefly reviewed how far we have come in these past twenty years. The question is, Where do we go from here? I would suggest that our work has only just begun, and that there is a continuing need in contemporary culture for the skeptical movement. Would that we *could* go out of business! Alas, there are always new claims, many often more bizarre or outrageous than previous ones (like the "alien autopsy" or "milk-drinking statues"), that emerge and cry out for examination.

Our task in the future will be to continue to function as Socratic gadflies. This is vital, and it means that scientific skepticism should be applied to borderland questions. It means that we need to keep alive our probing critical methods—no matter how much they may infuriate those whom we criticize. But we need to continue to develop in the public an understanding and appreciation for scientific inquiry and the scientific outlook. Our role in this sense is primarily *educative*.

In the future, we must seek new ways to bring this critical point of view to the general public. We sometimes feel like the lone voice in the wilderness. We believe we have a valuable contribution to make, but we will in the future need to further convince opinion-makers—political and industrial leaders, the directors of corporations, and the masters of the media—that our battle is theirs and that a free and democratic society can survive and prosper only if it keeps alive the appreciation for skepticism and critical thinking.

---

1. Gardner Murphy and R. O. Balbour, *William James on Psychical Research* (New York: Viking, 1969).

2. Quoted in E. J. Dingwall, "The Need for Responsibility in Parapsychology: My Sixty Years in Psychical Research," in Paul Kurtz, ed., *A Skeptic's Handbook of Parapsychology* (Buffalo, N.Y.: Prometheus Books, 1985), p. 172.

3. Amy Tanner, *Studies in Spiritism* (Buffalo, N.Y.: Prometheus Books, 1994).

4. John Coover, "Metaphysics and the Incredulity of Psychologists: Psychical Research Before 1927," in Carl Murchison, ed., *The Case For and Against Psychical Research* (Worcester, Mass.: Clark University Press; reprinted in Kurtz, ed., *A Skeptic's Handbook of Parapsychology*).

5. George R. Price, "Science and the Supernatural," *Science* 122 (1955), pp. 359–367.

6. C. E. M. Hansel, *ESP: A Scientific Evaluation* (New York: Scribner's, 1966). A revised edition was published as *ESP: A Critical Re-Evaluation* (Buffalo, N.Y.: Prometheus Books, 1980). A second revised edition was published, as *The Search for Psychic Power: ESP and Parapsychology Revisited* (Buffalo, N.Y.: Prometheus Books, 1989).

7. Betty Markwick, "The Soal-Goldney Experiments with Basil Shackleton: New Evidence of Data Manipulation," *Proceedings of the Society for Psychical Research* 56 (1978), pp. 250–277.

8. Paul Kurtz, with Bart J. Bok and Lawrence E. Jerome, "Objections to Astrology," *The Humanist* 35, no. 5 (September/October 1975), pp. 4–6.

9. This was no doubt stimulated by the novel, *The Exorcist*, by William Peter Blatty, and later by a film by that name.

10. "The Scientific Attitude vs. Pseudoscience and Antiscience." *The Humanist* 36, no. 4 (July/August 1976), p. 131.

11. I should add a personal note to the above account: Although I was basically a skeptic, I truly began these inquiries with an open mind. For example, I was not unsympathetic to the conjecture that UFOs may be extraterrestrial in origin. Numerous eyewitness reports seemed to me to point in that direction. It was only after extensive examination of UFO reports under the behest of Philip J. Klass that I became convinced that these reports were either spurious or could be given prosaic explanations.

I had also had a good deal of interest in psychical research, having met philosophers Curt Ducasse and H. H. Price and having studied and discussed their writings in this field with them. Moreover, I always suspected that my second wife Claudine possessed telepathic powers and ESP. She had an uncanny ability to read my mind. She insisted that all she could do was intepret my body language. I was not so sure. She would blurt out ideas or desires which I just had entertained. It was unnerving to me. I tried many thought experiments with her in separate rooms (even card experiments) and I thought that what she did was remarkable. Was she reading my mind or was I causing her to hold certain thoughts or images, or were there other explanations? Thus, I truly began CSICOP with an open mind about psychic phenomena.

Indeed, I decided to teach courses at SUNY at Buffalo on "Philosophy, Parapsychology, and the Paranormal." This went on for 15 years. The purpose was to teach students to think critically and to show them how to design rigorous experimental protocols. But my purpose was also for me to test any number of claims to see if there was anything in them. I tested students for ESP, telepathy, precognition, and clairvoyance, using tens of thousands of trials with Zener cards. Moreover, the students broke up into teams of three to five and they designed over a hundred experiments—testing everything from precognition and telepathy using the Ganzfeld protocol, to horoscopes, psychokinesis, Tarot cards, reports of ghost hauntings, ouija boards, palmistry, and UFO sightings. I should report that the results were invariable negative. I never published the results—since these were a self-learning set of experiments. But parapsychologist Betty Markwick once remarked to me that chance would indicate some should have been positive. Why so, if the phenomena did not exist? Or was "the goat effect" blocking the results? In any case, these experimental findings increased my skepticism even more.

Yet I should confess that at this late date that I still have not resolved the question of whether my wife does possess an unexpected ability to read me. I have lingering doubts as to why. She claims that she lacks any special powers and that after living with me for so many years, she knows me inside and out. She knows my moods and what I want and need. But as far as I can recall she was able to interpret my thoughts almost from the very beginning of our romantic relationship.

Psychologists Ray Hyman and James Alcock, both well-known skeptics, concur in her assessment. (I should add that under fairly controlled conditions—not loose—she does not demonstrate this ability). Parapsychologists maintain that under tightened conditions that psi is elusive.

I must confess that I am uncertain of the adequacy of a skeptical explanation. Is Claudine my white crow? William James thought that Lenora Piper (an alleged medium) was his anomalous white crow, though other critics, such as Martin Gardner, maintain that she was not genuine; and I concur in his assessment.

12. E. Fielding, W. W. Baggally, and H. Carrington, "Report on a Series of Sittings with Eusapia Palladino," *Proceedings of the SPR* 23 (1909), pp. 306–569.

13. Roger B. Culver and Philip A. Ianna, *Astrology: True or False?* (Amherst, N.Y.: Prometheus Books, 1988).

14. John Schumaker, *The Corruption of Reality* (Amherst, N.Y.: Prometheus Books, 1995).

15. Philip J. Klass, *UFO Abductions* (Amherst, N.Y.: Prometheus Books, 1989).

4

The Escape to Oblivion

Heaven's Gate has stunned the world. Why would thirty-nine seemingly gentle and earnest people in Rancho Santa Fe, California, voluntarily commit collective suicide (March 1997)? They left us eerie messages on videotapes, conveying their motives: they wished to leave their "containers" (physical bodies) in order to ascend to a new plane of existence, a Level Above Human.

It was a celestial omen, Comet Hale-Bopp, that provoked their departure. For they thought that it carried with it a UFO spacecraft—an event already proclaimed on the nationally syndicated Art Bell radio show when Whitley Strieber and Courtney Brown maintained that a spaceship "extraterrestrial in origin" and under "intelligent control" was tracking the comet. According to astronomer Alan Hale, co-discoverer of the comet, what they probably saw was a star behind the comet. Interestingly, the twenty-one women and eighteen men, ranging in ages from twenty-one to seventy-two, seemed like a cross section of American citizens—though they demonstrated some degree of technical and engineering skills, and some even described themselves as "computer nerds." They sought to convey their bizarre UFO theology on the Internet. Were these people crazy, a fringe group, overcome by paranoia? Or were there other, deeper causes at work in their behavior?

This article first appeared in *Skeptical Inquirer* 21, no. 4 (July/August 1997), pp. 12–14.

Heaven's Gate was led by Marshall Herff Applewhite and Bonnie Lu Nettles (who died in 1985), who taught their followers how to enter the Kingdom of God. They believed that some 2,000 years ago beings from an Evolutionary Level Above Human sent Jesus to teach people how to reach the true Kingdom of God. But these efforts failed. According to documents left on the Heaven's Gate Web site, "In the early 1970s, two members of the Kingdom of Heaven (or what some might call two aliens from space) incarnated into two unsuspecting humans in Houston [Applewhite and Nettles]. . . ." Over the next twenty-five years Applewhite and Nettles transmitted their message to hundreds of followers. Those who killed themselves at Rancho Sante Fe (including Applewhite)—plus the two former members who subsequently attempted to take their lives on May 6, one of them succeeding—did so to achieve a higher level of existence.

Reading about the strange behavior of this cult of unreason, one is struck by the unquestioning obedience that Applewhite was able to elicit from his faithful flock. There was a rigid authoritarian code of behavior imposed upon everyone, a form of mind control. Strict rules and rituals governed all aspects of their monastic lives. They were to give up all their worldly possessions, their diets were regulated, and sex was strictly forbidden (seven members, including Applewhite, were castrated). The entire effort focused on squelching the personal self. Independent thinking was discouraged.

The followers of Heaven's Gate lived under a siege morality; they were super-secretive, attempting to hide their personal identities. They were like nomads wandering in the wilderness, seeking the truths of a Higher Revelation from extraterrestrial semi-divine beings. What has puzzled so many commentators is the depth of their conviction that space aliens were sending envoys to Earth and abducting humans. They kept vigils at night, peering for streaks of light that might be UFOs, waiting for spacecraft to arrive.

We read on their Web page: "We suspect that many of us arrived in staged spacecraft (UFO) crashes, and many of our discarded bodies (genderless, not belonging to the human species), were retrieved by human authorities (government and military)."

This form of irrational behavior should be no surprise to skeptics. I submit that the mass media deserve a large share of the blame for this UFO mythology. Book publishers and TV and movie producers have fed the public a steady diet of science-fiction fantasy packaged and sold as real. Given massive media misinformation, it is difficult for large sectors of the public to distinguish between science and pseudoscience, particularly since there is a heavy dose of "quasi-documentary" films. Why worry about these programs? Because, I reply, the public, with few exceptions, does not have careful, critical knowledge of paranormal and pseudoscientific claims. What drivel NBC, Fox, and other networks have produced! TV is a powerful medium; and when it enters the home with high drama and the stamp of authenticity, it is difficult for ordinary persons to distinguish purely imaginative fantasies from reality. Many people blame the Internet. I think the media conglomerates, who sell their ideas as products, are to blame, not the Internet. We are surely not calling for censorship, only that some measure of responsibility be exercised by editors and producers. Interestingly, the Heaven's Gaters were avid watchers of TV programs on the paranormal.

Skeptics have been dealing with UFO claims on a scientific basis for more than twenty-five years. We have attempted to provide, wherever we could, scientific evaluations of the claims. We have never denied that it is possible, indeed probable, that other forms of life, even intelligent life, exist in the universe. And we support any effort to verify such an exciting hypothesis. But this is different from the belief that we are now being visited by extraterrestrial beings in spacecraft, that they are abducting people, and that there is a vast government coverup of these alien invasions—a "Luciferian" conspiracy, according to Heaven's Gate.

In my view, what we are dealing with is a religious phenomenon, the tendency of many human beings to leap beyond this world to other dimensions, impervious to the tests of evidence and the standards of logical coherence, the temptation to engage in magical thinking. UFO mythology is similar to the message of the classical religions where God sends his Angels as emissaries who offer salvation to those who accept the faith and obey his Prophets. Today, the chariots of the gods are UFOs. What we are witnessing in the past half century is the spawning of a New Age religion. (Nineteen ninety-seven marked the fiftieth anniversary of Kenneth Arnold's sighting of the first flying saucers over the State of Washington in 1947.)

There are many other signs that UFO mythology has become a space-age religion and that it is not based on scientific evidence so much as emotional commitment. Witness the revival of astrology today; or the growth of Scientology, which proposes space-age reincarnation to their Thetans and attracts famous movie stars such as Tom Cruise and John Travolta; or the Order of the Solar Temple, in which seventy-four people committed suicide in Switzerland, Québec, and France, waiting to be transported to the star Sirius, nine light-years away. Perhaps one of the most graphic illustrations of this phenomenon is what occurred on April 21, 1997, when the cremated remains of twenty-four people, including Gene Roddenberry (father of *Star Trek*), Timothy Leary (former Harvard guru), and Gerard O'Neill (scientific promoter of space colonies), were catapulted into space from the Grand Canary island off of the Moroccan coast aboard an American Pegasus rocket. This celestial burial is symptomatic of the New Age religion, in which our sacred church is outer space. The religious temptation enters when romantic expectations outreach empirical capacities.

Science is based on factual observation and verification. It was perhaps best illustrated by the discovery of Comet Hale-Bopp. That the comet has been captured by the paranormal imagination and transformed into a religious symbol is unfortunate. Alan Hale deplored this extrapolation of his observations. Yet the transcendental temptation can at times be so powerful that it knows no bounds.

Incidentally, the paranormal—which means, literally, that which is alongside of or beside normal scientific explanation—was involved in other aspects of the Heaven's Gate theology. The members expressed beliefs in astrology, tarot cards, psychic channeling, telepathy, resurrection, and reincarnation. That is why it is often difficult to ferret out and examine these claims dispassionately, for New Agers are dealing with faith, credulity, and a deep desire to believe, rather than with falsifiable facts; and they are resistant to any attempt to apply critical thinking to such spiritual questions.

Quotations from the Heaven's Gate videotape are instructive. Those who committed suicide affirmed that: "We are looking forward to this. We are happy and excited." "I think everyone in this class wants something more than this human world has to offer." "I just can't wait to get up there." These testimonials sound like those of born-again fundamentalists who are waiting for the Rapture and whose beliefs are self-validating. These confirmations of faith are not necessarily true; they are accepted because they have a profound impact on the believers' lives. Heaven's Gate gave meaning and purpose to the lives of its followers. As such, it performed an existential, psychological function similar to that of other religious belief systems. Obedience to a charismatic leader offered a kind of sociological unity similar to that provided by traditional belief systems.

One might well ask, what is the difference between the myth of salvation of Heaven's Gate and many orthodox religious belief systems that likewise promise salvation to the countless millions who suppress their sexual passions, submit to ritual and dogma, and abandon their personal autonomy, all in quest of immortality? Their behavior is similar to the more than nine hundred Jewish Zealots who committed suicide at Masada in 73 C.E., or the early Christians who willingly died for the faith, or the young Muslim Palestinians today who strap explosives to their bodies and blow themselves to kingdom come in the hope of attaining heaven. I recently visited Cairo and the Great Pyramid of Gizeh, where a ship of the dead had been uncovered. The Pharaohs had equipped a vessel to take them to the underworld, hoping thereby to achieve immortality after death. This has been transformed into a UFO craft in modern-day lingo.

The bizarre apocalyptic theology of Heaven's Gate is interpreted by its critics as absurd and ridiculous; yet it was taken dead seriously by its devotees, and a significant part of the UFO scenario is now accepted by large sectors of the public.

In one sense the New Age paranormal religions are no more fanciful than the old-time religions. Considered cults in their own day, they were passed down from generation to generation, but perhaps they are no less queer than the new paranormal cults. No doubt many in our culture will not agree with my application of skepticism to traditional religion—CSICOP itself has avoided criticizing the classical systems of religious belief, since its focus is on empirical scientific inquiry, not faith.

I am struck by the fact that the Seventh-Day Adventists, Jehovah's Witnesses, Mormons, and Chassidic Jews were considered radical fringe groups when first proclaimed; today they are part of the conventional religious landscape, and growing by leaps and bounds. Perhaps the major difference between the established religions and the new cults of unreason is that the former religions have deeper roots in human history.

The Aum Shinri Kyo cult in Japan, which in 1995 released poison gas into a crowded subway station, killing twelve people, was made up of highly educated young people, many with advanced degrees. Unable to apply their critical thinking outside of their specialties, they accepted the concocted promises of their guru. Thus an unbridled cult of unreason can attract otherwise rational people.

I have discovered in more than two decades of studying paranormal claims that a system of beliefs does not have to be true in order to be believed, and that the validation of such intensely held beliefs is in the eyes of the believer. There are profound psychological and sociological motives at work here. The desire to escape the trials and tribulations of this life and the desire to transcend death are common features of the salvation myths of many religious creeds. And they appear with special power and eloquence in the case of the misguided acolytes of Heaven's Gate, who, fed by an irresponsible media that dramatizes UFO mythology as true, found solace in a New Age religion of salvation, a religion whose path led them to oblivion.

5

Fears of the Apocalypse

Are we living in the last days of civilization? Will the human species and the planet Earth be engulfed in fire storms, earthquakes, floods, or be destroyed by the impact of an asteroid? As we approached the year 2000 we were surrounded by prophets of doom who predicted that terrible disasters awaited us. Obviously the year 2000 had special significance in these scenarios, for it marks the beginning of a new millennium. The year 2000 and the years soon thereafter seem to be the deadline for many end-time prophets. But we may ask: Did the new millennium start January 1, 2000 or 2001? The calendar we use begins at year 1 instead of 0—for a zero was left out in the transition from B.C. to A.D. Thus, a century does not begin with a double-zero year, but ends with it. If this is the case, the new century and millennium began with an *01-year*, not an 00-year.

But it is not clear that 2001 is the beginning of the new millennium, because the Western world measures it by the birth of Jesus Christ. But many Biblical scholars agree that we know very little if anything about him, though many believe that he was actually born four to six years *before* the year A.D. If this is

Remarks delivered at the Second World Skeptics Congress, held at the University of Heidelberg in July 1998 and published in the *Skeptical Inquirer* 23, no. 1 (January/February 1999), pp. 20–24. I have since updated the article, viewing 2000 after the fact.

the case, the third millennium might already may have begun in 1996, not in 2000!

The millennium is actually a human creation of our culture, an arbitrary date in eternity. Why it should be of special significance is muddled, aside from its religious meaning or cultural bias.

Most non-Christian cultures in the world do not measure the calendar by the date of Christ's birth. The Chinese year in 1998 is 4696, the Hebrew calendar 5760. For the Muslims, the calendar begins in 622 C.E., when Muhammad went from Mecca to Medina, and 1998 is actually the year 1420. It is 6236 according to the ancient Egyptian calendar, 2749 for the Babylonian, 2544 for the Buddhist, 5119 for the Mayan great cycle, and 2753 according to the old Roman calendar.

The Gregorian calendar was first initiated by Pope Gregory XIII in 1582, replacing the Roman Julian calendar of Julius Cæsar, which was ten days different from today's. After the decline of Rome, Britain celebrated New Year's Eve on December 25th—until William the Conqueror changed New Year's to January 1, 1066, the date of his coronation. Britain subsequently changed it to March 25th and later, to accord with other countries. The French desired Easter Sunday to be New Year's Day. For the Chinese, New Year's Day is at the end of February.[1]

Thus, January 1, 2000 or 2001 is really a meaningless non-event—an expression of Western socio-cultural prejudice, of no special significance in the nature of things.

Secular Doomsday Prophecies

Nonetheless, there is a perennial concern for the future. Human beings always wish to peer ahead and know what will ensue tomorrow or next year or in the next century. Many of these interests are based on expectations of a better and more promising world. But there are often predictions of gloom, and great apprehension.

Three kinds of forecasts may be distinguished among the Doomsday prophecies. First, *secular predictions*. The 1990s enjoyed a period of great economic optimism, as stock markets, at least in Europe and America, soared. The bulls dashed forward with rosy forecasts. There was sustained technological scientific expansion. Some people even predicted a long boom in which the economic cycle had been overcome. This was based on new industries: telecommunications and the information revolution, biogenetic research, and space technologies. Under this scenario the bulls predicted that Germany and France would overcome their recession, unemployment would be solved, the Asian and Russian economic slump would become a thing of the past, and gross domestic products would continue to expand as prosperity gains. This scenario was one of unlimited horizons. By contrast, the bears focus on the negative: The year-2000 computer bug would wreak havoc everywhere, they warned, oil shortages would appear, either deflation would overcome us or inflation would re-ignite, and the Dow-Jones stock exchange average would plummet from 11,000 to 3,000 in a short period of time. Here the pessimists prevail. Following the scenario of the Dutch Tulip bubble bust, crowd psychology rules the day, as the public is engulfed first by the fervor of speculative binge and then by pessimistic forecasts of doom. One may ask: whose prophecy of the future will prevail—the optimists, pessimists, or neither?

Another key source of present doomsday scenarios is science fiction, in which the future is unusually bleak: either Big Brother will emerge, or complete anarchy will prevail. Science projects doomsday asteroids or comets striking the earth. *Deep Impact* and *Armageddon*, two Hollywood movies, arouse fear and terror, and *Jurassic Park* brings back the dinosaurs to devour us.

Probably the most frightening secular prognostications are environmental scenarios of runaway population growth and devastating ecological pollution.

Many of these forecasts are not end-of-the-world predictions, but they illustrate the difficulties of making long-range extrapolations. Of course there are real dangers—from environmental damage to nuclear war—and we need to be aware of them and to take rational precautions; for example, global warming and the depletion of the ozone layer. I am surely not denying that there are genuine problems that need to be seriously addressed. But not too long ago we were warned that the world would be overtaken by famine, that hundreds of millions—even billions—of people would starve to death, and that the cities and countrysides would be teeming with swollen bellies. Contrary to expectations, India and other impoverished countries have managed to increase their food production, and while there are famines in Africa, the predicted worldwide famine has not occurred.

Demographers told us two decades ago that population growth would increase exponentially and that there was no way to stop it. By the year 2000, they said, there would be seven billion inhabitants on the earth, and by 2020, 15 billion or more. This does not deny that population growth is a serious problem; but, in many parts of the world, there has been a significant decrease in the rate of population growth; and the extreme projections for 2020 are most likely exaggerated.

Some ecologists maintained in the 1960s that by 1980 the atmosphere would be so polluted that we would need to wear gas masks year-round—not even in Los Angeles has this occurred! They warned that many of our lakes and waterways would be so despoiled that all of their fish and plant life would be destroyed. The Great Lakes, they said, would be totally dead. President Lyndon Johnson in 1968 visited the Buffalo River in western New York and ignited it with a match. Massive efforts to clean it up followed. There has been a noticeable increase in the fish harvest in Lake Erie, and the lake seems to be coming back. Ecologists have warned that we would deplete our natural resources and run out of oil, gas, and other fossil fuels in the near future. In the long run they are probably correct, but new resources have been discovered and new sources of energy developed.

A frenzied phobia of the unknown surrounds the additives and chemical wastes of modern technological society. There is fear of cancer-causing agents; everything from fluoride to sugar has been claimed to be noxious.

We have been told by successive Cassandras that the imminent collapse of major banks would bring down the entire world financial system, that galloping inflation was uncontrollable, and that we were on the verge of a depression that would change the face of society. No doubt we will continue to experience recessions, possibly even depressions, in the future. Marx predicted Armageddon for the capitalist system. Millions of pessimists are still waiting for that to occur. They think every recession will lead to a worldwide economic collapse. Interestingly, George Orwell's 1984 has arrived and passed and our freedoms are still intact, much to everyone's surprise.

Overhanging all of this is the sword of Damocles—nuclear energy. Nuclear fears engulfed large sectors of society. Anything related to radiation was considered diabolical. In many countries the public shrinks in terror at the thought of the opening of new nuclear power plants. The greatest fear of all is the fear of a thermonuclear holocaust. We are admonished on all sides that death stares us in the face and that some miscalculation would inevitably trigger a worldwide nuclear war. The results, we were told, will be a nuclear winter and the near extinction of all life on this planet. This was the Age of Anxiety par excellence.

Pessimists become angry at realists who think that civilization and the human species are likely to muddle through periodic crises and mini-crises but still survive these end-of-the-world forecasts. I am only advising that we place them in a balanced perspective. But to say this infuriates those who are convinced that our whole universe will collapse. In one film Woody Allen worried about what modern astronomers have to say about the cosmos, that there are two ultimate possibilities: either the universe will expand into infinity, cool down, and die, or eventually collapse into itself like an accordion.

For many the Apocalypse seems to be almost a wish fulfillment. The mundane world lacks the drama that a fertile apocalyptic imagination produces.

Religious Doomsday Prophecies

A second area for Doomsday scenarios are *religiously based*. Indeed, we today find hundreds of millions of people who interpret the world primarily through a biblical lens and see their own end-of-the-word scenarios. Much of this is based on the Book of Daniel of the Old Testament and the Book of Revelation of the New Testament. But their vision is far more terrifying than anything that mere secularists can dream up, because it is all part of God's plan of punishment for sinners. And it is always imminent. Moreover, only a small portion of suffering humanity will be saved from it. Several Protestant sects, such as the Jehovah's Witnesses, have held apocalyptic theologies in the past.

Today the message that fundamentalist prophets are preaching is one of a millennial Armageddon. They are truly convinced that we are living in "the last days," and they view earthquake tremors, wars, and rumors of war as signs of the impending apocalyptic disaster. The last great battle of Armageddon is approaching, we are warned. Indeed, *this* generation, many of them insist, is the last generation, and this was all foretold in the Old and New Testaments. Jesus said: "I tell you this: the present generation will live to see it all" (Matt. 24:34–35, New English Bible). And "Verily I say unto you, This generation shall not pass, till all these things be fulfilled" (Matt. 24:34, King James Version). Many of Jesus' disciples believed that his admonitions applied to his own generation in the first century A.D. That prophecy did not come true for the early Christians, and almost 2000 years have since passed. We were told by Pat Robertson, Hal Lindsey, David Koresh, Harold Camping, Edgar C. Whisenant, and other evangelists that the generation referred to is *ours*. Even President Ronald Reagan was quoted as saying in the 1980s: "You know, I turn back to your ancient prophets in the Old Testament and the signs foretelling Armageddon, and I find myself considering if we're the generation that is going to see that come about. I don't know if you noted any of those prophecies lately but, believe me, they certainly describe the times we're going through."

In his book, *The Late Great Planet Earth* (a bestseller in the U.S. in past decades), Hal Lindsey claimed that Armageddon is just around the corner. According to biblical prophecies, seven years of terrible tribulation will soon befall mankind. This period is about to begin because the Jewish people after the long Diaspora have finally returned to their ancient homeland in Palestine, which they left after the destruction of the Temple of Jerusalem in A.D. 70. And it is a genuine reality, we are told, because of the establishment of the State of Israel.

Next, Lindsey says, the Israelis will rebuild the temple in Jerusalem. Then a whole series of cataclysmic events will trigger the final Armageddon. A great war will ensue. Israel will be invaded from all sides: by a confederacy from the North (which was said to be the Russians), by the Arab nations, and by a great power from the East (which was identified as the Chinese). During the period leading up to these events, there will also emerge a European confederation—the old Roman Empire, now the European Common Market—headed by an Antichrist preaching a new religion. These years will witness the greatest devastation that mankind has ever seen. The valleys will flow with blood, cities will be destroyed by torrents of fire and brimstone—this, it is said, represents a thermonuclear war, World War III, the most awesome holocaust of all time. At that moment, Jesus Christ will return to rescue in rapture those true believers who accept the word. Christ will reign for a thousand years and eventually establish his final kingdom throughout all eternity.

In a series of books that suddenly swept to the top of the bestseller list, millions of people disappear from the face of the earth. They have been snatched from homes and offices, automobiles and airplanes—all saved by the rapture, which has taken God-fearing Christians to heaven, while the rest of humanity is left behind to suffer the terrible trials and tribulations inflicted by the Antichrist. This is the plot of the fictionalized apocalyptic series, *Left Behind*, by fundamentalist preacher Tim LaHaye and Jerry B. Jenkins.[2] LaHaye ominously forewarned on his Web site that the year 2000 computer problem could trigger a "financial meltdown" as prelude to the world's destruction.

Fears of the "last days," it has been claimed, appeared at the end of the first millennium. Charles Mackay, in his 1841 work, *Extraordinary Popular Delusions and the Madness of Crowds*, depicted the epidemic terror that seized Christendom in the middle of the tenth century, as people expected the last judgment.[3] Some said that Mackay's account was pure hyperbole. In any case, the first millennium passed without the destruction of the world! Why should it occur in the second?

Many people have believed in the end-of-the-world scenario based on the Bible, and they often thought that it applied to their own age. A graphic illustration is the case of William Miller and his followers in the nineteenth century. Miller, a fundamentalist Protestant preacher from Vermont (and precursor of the Seventh-Day Adventists) studied the Bible carefully. He was convinced that the world would come to an end in his own day, sometime between March 21, 1843, and March 21, 1844. He based his analysis upon a specific biblical passage that draws on the Book of Daniel. "And he said unto me, Unto two thousand and three hundred days; then shall the sanctuary be cleansed" (Dan. 8:14, King James Version). Miller interpreted "days" as "years." Since the prophecy was dated 457 B.C., the end of the world, he said, would occur two thousand and three hundred years later, in 1843. The Millerite groups—which numbered in the thousands—sold their possessions and awaited the final day. But, as we know, nothing happened. When 1843 passed he extended his prediction by another year, but again nothing happened. This forecasting of the end of times has been repeated many times throughout history. The same thing is most likely true, in my judgment, of present-day predictions of Armageddon.

Other religious traditions have prophetic-apocalyptic themes: Buddhism awaits Lord Matrieya, Islam the Madhi; Orthodox Judaism the Messiah; and

Native American Indians wish to return to nature as it was before the European invasion. For those who use the Mayan calendar, the world will end in 2012.

It is clear that a state of belief may help create a self-fulfilling or suicidal prophecy. A widely held belief can have profound political and social ramifications, especially if it is held by people in positions of power. Apocalyptic thinking may lead those are under its sway to do little or nothing to prevent overwhelming disaster, fatalistically awaiting what is inevitable; or they may so act as to allow it to come true, believing that they are fulfilling divine prophecy. The problem with faith in prophecy is that it can take control of the future out of the hands of those best able to shape it. We are supposedly impotent and helpless creatures awaiting our fate, unable or unwilling to exert any influence to rectify or modify the course of events. The fixation on apocalypse grows out of fear of the unknown, and it is fed by hope for redemption. Often when the prophecy is falsified, the convictions of the believing group are intensified and the prophecies extrapolated.[4]

In democratic societies we need an informed public capable of wise decisions and without fantasy. We know of the dangers that distorted, apocalyptic, survivalist, conspiratorial, or pseudoscientific ideologies have had on societies.

New Age Doomsday Prophecies

A third kind of doomsday prophecy is that offered by *New Age cults*. Skeptics have examined a great number of the paranormal claims that are proliferating today from psychics, fortune tellers, seers, and gurus of various kinds. These include the failed predictions of Edgar Cayce, "the Sleeping Prophet," who warned of a massive shifting of the poles in the years 2000–2001. They involve a number of suicide cults, such as the UFO-related "Heaven's Gate" and the French-Swiss-Canadian space-age religion, "The Order of the Solar Temple,." Japan's "Aum Shinrikyo" cult, and the many New Age cults proliferating in Russia today. There are also numerous astrological predictions of disaster due to planetary alignments, such as the so-called "Jupiter Effect." And psychics are having a field day in their Armageddon prophecies. How many times are those who claim to have precognitive or psychic powers correct in their prophecies? The track record, I submit, is extremely weak. We can and do make predictions about the future based on evidence and rational inference, and often these predictions are reliable. But those made on the basis of mystic power, psychic intuition, or astrological forecasts prove to be no more accurate than anyone's wild guesses. Those who make such claims often fit a prophecy or vision to present circumstances after the fact, or they make the prophecy so general that it can be related to virtually any case. This has been done with the predictions of the ever-popular

Nostradamus, the sixteenth-century seer. His quatrains have been read by every generation, including the present one, and his prophecies have been adapted to all sorts of circumstances in every time period. Often what is taken as prophetic is only due to coincidence; events are not preordained and predetermined as the prophetic tradition maintains. The future depends upon our own actions in the given situations. There are no special secret paths to knowledge of the future.

We live in a highly developed scientific and technological society. We face awesome problems. If we are to solve them, we must draw upon the best critical intelligence available. We need to use our rational powers, not abandon them. In free societies anyone is entitled to his convictions. Yet democracy presupposes an educated citizenry. When apocalyptic faith is intermingled with ideology, it can have deleterious social, political, and military consequences. It is at this point that all those committed to skeptical inquiry have an obligation to carefully examine those claims being made about our collective future, whether they are based upon so-called revealed prophecies or not, and to submit them to empirical criticism. There is thus a compelling need for critical examination of the prophecies of doom—whether secular, religious, or New Age—for these have serious implications for the world at large.

---

1. For fuller discussion of this, see Richard Abanes, *End-Time Visions: The Road to Armageddon?* (New York and London: Four Worlds Eight Windows, 1998).

2. The four books, all by Tim LaHaye and Jerry B. Jenkins, are *Left Behind* (1995), *Tribulation Force* (1996), *Nicolae* (1997), and *Soul Harvest* (1998), all published by Tyndale House Publishers.

3. Charles Mackay, *Extraordinary Popular Delusions and the Madness of Crowds* (New York: Crown, 1980).

4. See Leon Festinger, Henry W. Riecken, and Stanley Schachter, *When Prophecy Fails: A Social and Psychological Study of Modern Groups That Predict the Destruction of the World* (New York: Harper and Row, 1956).

6

Scientific Tests of Astrology

Paul Kurtz and Andrew Fraknoi

An estimated 1,200 newspapers in North America carry Astrology columns. While many editors chuckle and tell you that no one takes these columns seriously, the evidence does not bear this out. For example, a June 1984 Gallup poll showed that 55% of American teenagers (ages 13–18) believe that astrology works. Continuous exposure to the ideas of astrology in newspapers contributes to that credulity.

Astrologers assert that astrology has a successful record stretching back 4,000 years and that this record speaks for itself. Yet dozens of scientific tests of astrological columns, charts, and horoscopes clearly contradict this claim.

The present formulation of astrology was largely codified by Ptolemy in the second century C.E. The basic premise is that the position of the heavenly bodies at the time and place of an individual's birth influences or is correlated with his or her personality, physical characteristics, health, profession, and future

First published in *Skeptical Inquirer* 9, no. 3 (Spring 1985), pp. 210–211.

destiny. Classical astrology regarded the earth as the center of the universe, with the planets, stars, sun, and moon orbiting around it The heavenly bodies were originally considered divine and possessing "magical" characteristics. Thus Mars, thought to be the color red, represented the god of war and signified courage and aggression. Venus was soft and white and was the goddess of love and beauty.

What does science have to say about astrology? First modern astronomy has negated its key principle: that the earth is the center of our solar system. We now know that the planets circle the sun, that our solar system is on the outskirts of a galaxy, which itself is only a part of an expanding universe that contains millions of galaxies. Moreover, new planets (Uranus, Neptune, Pluto) have been discovered that were unknown to ancient astrologers. It is interesting that the presumed astrological influences of the planets did not lead astrologers to discover them long before astronomers did.

Second, we now know that a person's personality and physical characteristics are determined by his or her genetic endowment inherited from both parents and by later environmental influences. Several decades of planetary exploration have confirmed that there is no appreciable physical influence on the earth from planetary bodies. Indeed, the obstetrician hovering over the infant during delivery exerts a much greater gravitational pull than the nearest planet.

Third, there have been exhaustive tests of astrological claims to see if they have any validity. Astrologers predict that individuals born under certain signs are more likely to become certain personality types that become politicians or scientists. Thus you would expect the birthdates of these two groups to cluster in those signs. John McGervey, a physicist at Case Western University, looked up the birth dates of 16,634 scientists listed in *American Men of Science* and 6,475 politicians listed in *Who's Who in American Politics* and found the distributions of these signs were as random as for the public at large.

Are some signs relatively more compatible or incompatible with each other, as astrologers maintain? Professor Bernard Silverman, a psychologist at Michigan State, obtained the records of 2,978 couples who married and 478 couples who divorced in Michigan in 1967 and 1968. He found no correlation with astrologers' predictions. Those born under "compatible" signs married—and divorced—just as often as those born under "incompatible" Signs.

In order to look for trends favoring astrological signs ruled by Mars (courage and aggression) as opposed to signs ruled by Venus (love and beauty). James Barth and James Bennett at George Washington University examined the horoscopes of men who re-enlisted in the Marine Corps between 1962 and 1970 No such correlation was found.

What about the often-heard claim of famous astrologers that they have made countless correct predictions over the years? Astronomers Roger Culver and Philip Ianna examined 3,011 specific predictions by well-known astrologers and astrological organizations. The results indicated that only 10% of these predictions were realized. The public reads the predictions in newspapers and magazines; the fact that 90% of these predictions never come true is not publicized.

Newspaper charts and horoscopes deal primarily with the sun signs rather than with other so-called planetary influences. Even astrologers admit that the sun-sign astrology featured in newspaper columns has little reliable basis for prediction of the day's events Incidentally, very few astrology columns agree on what is supposed to occur.

Why then do so many people believe that astrology works? Careful inspection of astrological predictions in a typical newspaper column shows that the statements are so general and vague that they can apply to anyone.

The results of one experiment shows how these statements sometimes seem to work. C. R. Snyder, a psychologist at the University of Kansas, and his colleagues drew up a personality description that incorporated the characteristics they found most people believed they possessed. They showed this description to three groups of people, each of whom was asked to rate, on a scale of 1 to 5, how well they were described by it. The individuals in the first group were told that it was a universal personality sketch, and the average rating was 3.2. Individuals in the second group were asked for the month in which they were born and were then told the statement was a horoscope for their signs. On the average, they rated it 3.76. The individuals in the third group were asked for the day on which he or she was born and were told that the description was his or her *personal* horoscope. This group rated the same description on average of 4.38. Apparently those who want to believe will do so!

Newspapers should let their readers know that astrology columns should he read only for their entertainment value and that they have no reliable basis in scientific fact.

Note—This essay was mailed to 1,500 newspapers in the U.S.A. and Canada in an effort to get them to label their astrology columns as follows: "The following astrological forecasts should be read for entertainment value only. Such predictions have no reliable basis in scientific fact." Currently, the following newspapers are running this or a similar disclaimer: *The Recorder* (Greenfield, Mass.), *The Sun* (Westerly, R.I.), *The Telegraph* (Nashua, N.H.), *Union Leader* (Manchester, N.H.), *Press* (Asbury Park, N.J.), *News* (Buffalo, N.Y.), *Citizen* (Auburn, N.Y.), *Post-Gazette* (Pittsburgh, Penna.), *Gazette* (Indiana, Penna.), *Mirror* (Altoona, Penna.), *Courier Times* (Bucks, County, Penna.), *Review* (weekly) (Philadelphia, Penna.), *News Journal* (Wilmington, Del.), *Times & World News* (Roanoke, Va.), *Herald Courier* (Bristol, Va.), *Observer-Times* (Fayetteville, N.C.), *News Topic* (Lenoir, N.C.), *Ledger Enquirer* (Columbus, Ga.), *Times* (St. Petersburg, Fla.), *News* (Tuscaloosa, Ala.), *Advertiser* (Montogmery, Ala.), *The Register* (Mobile, Ala.), *Oak Ridger* (Oak Ridge, Tenn.), *Commercial Appeal* (Memphis, Tenn.), *NE Miss. Daily Journal* (Tupelo, Miss.), *Daily Jeffersonian* (Cambridge, Oh.), *Record Courier* (Ravenna, Oh.), *News* (Salem, Oh.), *Press-Gazette*

(Hillsboro, Oh.), *Star* (Indianapolis, In.), *Enquirer* (Battle, Creek, Mich.), *Telegram* (Adrian, Mich.), *Daily News* (Hillsdale, Mich.), *Mining Journal* (Marquette, Mich.), *News-Republican* (Boone, Ia.), *News-Advertiser* (Creston, Ia.), *News* (Kenosha, Wisc.), *Journal* (Milwaukee, Wisc.), *Post-Bulletin* (Rochester, Minn.), *Times-Courier* (Charleston, Ill.), *Gazette* (Mattoon, Ill.), *Post-Dispatch* (St., Louis, Mo.), *Star* (Kansas City, Mo.), *Journal World* (Lawrence, Kan.), *Daily World* (Hiawatha, Kan.), *Courier* (Houma, La.), *Advocate* (Baton Rouge, La.), *Democrat* (Sherman, Tex.), *Tribune-Herald* (Waco, Tex.), *Leader* (Orange, Tex.), *News* (Port Arthur, Tex.), *American Statesman* (Austin, Tex.), *Daily News* (Sun City, Ariz.), *Arizona Daily Star* (Tucson, Ariz.), *Citizen* (Tucson, Ariz.), *The Sun* (Las Vegas, Nev.), *Times* (Los Angeles, Cal.), *News* (Hemet, Cal.), *Press Enterprise* (Riverside, Cal.), *Tribune Herald* (Hilo, Hi.), *Advertiser* (Honolulu, Hi.), *Ka Leo O Hawaii* (Honolulu, Hi.).

7

The "Mars Effect"

by Paul Kurtz,
with Jan Willem Nienhuys and Ranjit Sandhu

I
Gauquelin's claim

Classical astrology has little if any empirical support from science. Some advocates of astrology, however, have maintained that there is new evidence for astrological influences in the work of the Gauquelins. French psychologist and writer Michel Gauquelin, in collaboration with his wife, Françoise Schneider-Gauquelin, wrote that although classical astrology was mistaken, there were "astrobiological" or "cosmobiological" correlations between planetary positions and birth times on the one hand and personality traits and professional

This article is from the *Journal of Scientific Exploration* 11, no. 1 (Spring 1997), pp. 19–39. It has been slightly modified and shortened. It is in response to an article by Suitbert Ertel and Kenneth Irving in the same issue.

achievements on the other—between Jupiter and military men, Saturn and scientists, Mars and sports champions, etc. Since Mars had the highest correlation, a vigorous discussion of the "Mars effect" has been going on for several decades, and it has engaged skeptical scientists on both sides of the Atlantic. What are we to make of this so-called effect?

The planet Mars rises and sets just like any other celestial phenomenon. Mr. and Mrs. Gauquelin divide the time between rising and setting into six equal intervals, numbered 1 through 6. Likewise, they divide the time between setting and rising into another six equal intervals, numbered 7 through 12. These sectors coincide with one of a dozen or so popular astrological house systems, namely that of Placidus, though the Placidean numbering is different.

The Gauquelins suggested that sports champions were somewhat more likely to be born when Mars is passing through the first sector (approximately the first two hours after the rise of Mars) and the fourth sector (roughly the two hours after culmination). Interestingly, in the traditional astrology of Ptolemy (*Tetrabiblos*), the two most important points in the house divisions are the Ascendant ("oroscopos") and the Midheaven or *Medium Cœli*—which are the initial boundaries of the Gauquelins' sectors 1 and 4.[1]

It would appear that the chance of being born in either the first or fourth sectors is 2 out of 12, or 16.67%. A small adjustment is necessary, however, to take two factors into account: (1) the astronomic factor, namely the positions of Mars as seen from Earth, or more specifically from the latitude of France, and (2) the demographic factor, namely the daily pattern of births (more in the early morning, fewer in the evening). This adjustment has been estimated at about 0.5%, making the chance expectation 17.17%.[2] Sports champions, said Gauquelin, were born in the first and fourth sectors about 22% (more exactly, 452 in 2,088, or 21.65%) of the time. The deviation was too small to be of any practical use. One must meticulously collect hundreds of cases to observe it at all. Yet if Gauquelin was correct, the deviation was theoretically interesting.

Michel Gauquelin collected champions' names from sports directories, and then tried to locate their actual birth data in the town registries. In support of his claim, he published in 1955 a total of 567 French champions with their names and birth data (plus one erroneous name).[3] In 1960 he reported 915 additional foreign champions, together with 717 "less well known" sports people that served as a control, but without specific names and data.[4]

He added further data to his files from a replication by the Belgian Comité Para (more on this below). With Gauquelin's help, the Comité Para derived a sample of sports champions, which by 1968 produced 330 new names (mostly of French champions).

Gauquelin added another 276 names (among whom were 113 aviators and 76 rugby players) to his total sample, to yield 2,088 "well-known" champions.[5] Meanwhile he collected piecemeal another 278 "lesser" champions before 1976.

We mention this, because in the discussions Michel Gauquelin and others have stated several times that the 2,088 consisted of 1,553 champions collected first, followed by the Comité Para test of 535 champions.[6]

The Test by the Belgian Comité Para

As mentioned above, the Belgian Comité Para, beginning in 1967, attempted to test Gauquelin's thesis.[7] Their 535 champions consisted of 205 already in Gauquelin's 1955 book (it was thus not an entirely fresh sample) and 330 "new" ones. In 1976 the Comité Para published its final report,[8] and found that 22.2% of these sports champions were born with Mars in sectors 1 or 4. (We shall hereafter refer to the percentage born with Mars in sectors 1 and 4 as the Mars percentage.) The Comité Para maintained, however, that Gauquelin's theoretical expectation (of about 17 percent) was not computed correctly. There was thus some dispute between the Comité Para and Gauquelin about whether the test constituted a replication. The Comité Para thought that demographic factors were not properly taken into account: the births of the athletes were not uniformly distributed in the time-period studied (1872–1945), and the daily patterns of births varied during this period. Gauquelin insisted that the Comité Para's test had confirmed his hypothesis. The Comité Para denied it.

Gauquelin had helped to supply the data for the test of the Comité Para. However, the circumstances surrounding the data compilation of the test are most unclear. Ertel claims that the 332 "new" champions of the Para test (a counting error; it should be 330) had already been collected by Gauquelin in 1962, along with 76 Belgian soccer players that had not been used in the Para test.[9] Luc de Marré states that at the meeting between Gauquelin and the Comité Para in 1967 the list of 535 names was already decided upon.[10] This claim is hardly credible; it presupposes that the Comité Para was clairvoyant and knew in advance the precise number of champions about whom they would receive information from town halls. The Comité Para collected 430 French champions from their main source book, but Professor J. Dommanget has provided documents indicating that data of 589 champions from this book were requested.

Concerning the Belgian soccer players, it was decided to select only the 43 who had been chosen to defend the glory of Belgium at least 20 times. It is unknown how that decision was arrived at and if any prior knowledge of the Mars effect among Belgian soccer players played a role in that decision. If Ertel's information about the year 1962 is accurate then Gauquelin knew already the Mars positions of 119 Belgian soccer players when the decision about the cut-off at 20 was taken. We do know that above that cut-off the Mars percentage happens to be 21% and below that line it is only 12%.

We think there is sufficient reason to reject the result of the Para test. There are too many doubts surrounding the process of data gathering.

The "Zelen Test"

The dispute between Gauquelin and the Comité Para concerned the expected "Mars percentage" for the general population. Marvin Zelen, then a professor of statistics at State University of New York, now at Harvard, proposed a test of the baseline percentage. This became known as the "Zelen test," and it was developed in cooperation with astronomer George Abell and Paul Kurtz. Zelen recommended Gauquelin randomly draw 100 or 200 names from his sample of champions,[11] and then compare their Mars sectors with all other births occurring at the same times and places.[12] Zelen designed this test to help determine the baseline Mars percentage, and also to control for various other demographic aspects that had so far not been a matter of dispute.

Michel and Françoise Gauquelin assembled birth data on 16,756 ordinary persons born at about the same times and places as a subsample of 303 champions. They observed that the Zelen method yielded a theoretical prediction of 51.4 births in sectors 1 and 4 among the 303, i.e. 16.83%. More precisely, this result means that the "true" percentage is between 16.3% and 17.4% (95% confidence limits) and that there is no reason to suppose that the astrodemographic correction should vastly exceed 0.5%. There was again some dispute as to the validity of the test, particularly since the Gauquelins did not follow Zelen's original protocol.[13] For example, Gauquelin did *not* draw the names randomly. His total sample of 2,088 champions included 42 Parisian athletes, and he included all 42 in his subsample of 303. He selected the remaining champions from those who had been born in capitals of Departments of France or Provinces of Belgium.

The Gauquelins also chose the matching non-champions in Paris from only one of the 20 arrondissements. Strictly speaking, this was a breach of the protocol, but it is difficult to see what difference it could make for the expected percentage, as the weight of "Paris" in the 16.83% was less than one-seventh. A more important deviation was Gauquelin's decision to examine only capitals of departments and provinces, though this might mean no more than a few tenths of a percent. Nonetheless, the results suggested that demographic factors were not the explanation of the "Mars effect."

The Gauquelins pointed out that among their 303 champions were 66 Mars-champions, i.e., 66 born with Mars in sectors 1 and 4. Given the expectation of 51.4, they wrote that this was "clearly significant at the 0.05 level." Now "significant" in statistics merely means "worth a closer investigation," even though it is often misinterpreted as "incontrovertible proof." Zelen, Abell, and Kurtz's comments on the Zelen test constituted such a closer investigation.

Zelen pointed out that the subsample of 303 was not randomly drawn from the 2,088. More specifically, about half of the "excess" of 15 Mars-champions came from Paris. In other words, the comments of Zelen, Abell, and Kurtz constituted a very mildly formulated suggestion that it was not the astrodemographic factor, but some peculiarity associated with Gauquelin's data handling and collection, that might be the ultimate explanation of the Mars Effect.

Some critics have interpreted these comments as inadmissible sample splitting. However, the core of these comments constituted a legitimate inquiry. If a non-random procedure compromises the representativeness of a sample, then surely it is permissible at least to discuss the effects of such deviations from the protocol.

Much of the ensuing controversies have centered on these remarks about champions from Paris and elsewhere. Dennis Rawlins was much more outspoken in his conviction that the main problem might be Gauqelin's data handling. He predicted that the outcome of the Zelen test would not been seen as the exclusion of an astrodemographic explanation of Gauquelin's findings, but instead would mistakenly be seen as an independent test of the Mars effect. He advised that the Zelen test episode should be treated as a tactical error. With the wisdom of 20/20 hindsight Rawlins no doubt was correct. The Zelen test was proposed and undertaken in the true skeptical spirit of seriously examining the somewhat implausible claim of a giant astrodemographic effect, possibly in the hope of finding a naturalistic explanation of the Mars effect.

The U.S. Test

Since it was Gauquelin himself who had done almost all the data gathering in support of the Mars-effect claim, an independent replication was called for. When Marvin Zelen first suggested the Zelen test, he also said that at least one further replication, on a fresh sample, would be necessary. George Abell put this suggestion into print: "if . . . [Gauquelin's] results hold up, then it is necessary to repeat the experiment with a new sample, say in the United States."[14] So the genesis of this test actually predates the formation of CSICOP, which is why we call it the U.S. test. And even before the publication of the results of the Zelen test, Paul Kurtz, Marvin Zelen, and George Abell met with Michel Gauquelin and together they outlined plans for a test in the U.S.

Zelen, Abell, and Kurtz constituted themselves as an *ad hoc* committee to devise and supervise the test. It was a blind experiment, with the data drawn by students at the State University of New York, Germain Harnden and Frank Dolce. Dennis Rawlins in San Diego calculated the positions of Mars. Although the American group consulted with Gauquelin throughout, he had no direct role in compiling the data. The American group used five sports dictionaries—*The*

Lincoln Library of Sports Champions,[15] *Who's Who in Football,*[16] *Who's Who in Basketball,*[17] *Who's Who in Boxing,*[18] and *Who's Who in Track and Field.*[19]

The U.S. researchers believed that consulting sports directories or Who's Whos of sports champions would be the most reliable guide. These volumes generally publish lists of the highest achievers in sports and the best-known champions. Some do so by listing athletes across many sports, and others only provide a Who's Who for specific sports. Of the millions and millions of individuals engaged in competitive sports in America, these directories only contain a few thousand champions, the *crème de la crème*, as it were. These volumes were compiled by editors and authors who were surely unaware of Gauquelin's hypothesis. Some of them contain citations of several hundred of the leading champions in a specific sport. The *Lincoln Library of Sports Champions* contains 493 entries derived from all of the fields of sports. *Who's Who in Football* contains 1,397 of the most famous names from the very beginning of the sport to 1974.[20] *Who's Who in Basketball* contains 921 names, *Who's Who in Boxing* 499 names, and *Who's Who in Track and Field* 420 names. When we delete the champions born outside of the U.S., the champions for whom insufficient birth data are supplied, the duplicate entries, the coaches, umpires, referees, reporters, managers, promoters, team owners, and so forth, we are left with a grand total of 2,419 eligible champions.

These numbers suggest that the standards used were comparable to Gauquelin's own, which had yielded his 22% hypothesis; for these 2,419 eligible champions are from a country with five times the population of France. Gauquelin's 1,356 French published champions number more than half of this amount, and that is *after* he had selected the "best" and after the loss due to the untraceability of champions' birth data.

Given the then recently enacted Privacy Act in the United States, many registries would not supply birth data without the permission of the athletes. Accordingly, the American group deemed it essential to send for the birth data of *all* the sports champions listed in those directories, without selection, provided they were born in states that agreed to supply data. The American group was able to assemble a sample of 408 sports champions. The results were negative, with 55 (13.5%) of the sports champions born with Mars in the first and fourth sectors. With a null-hypothesis of 16.67% the *p*-value was reported at 0.09. Hence, Zelen, Abell, and Kurtz concluded that an effort at replication of a fresh U.S. sample showed no evidence for the Mars effect.[21]

Those who sent for the data did not have any prior knowledge of the Mars positions. The Mars effect was calculated by Dennis Rawlins in San Diego only *after* the data were received. The U.S. researchers sent for *all* the data and they published *all* of the data received from the states waiving the Privacy Act. They at no time knew the Mars positions before they were included in the sample, nor were any data omitted.

These facts are clearly stated in the report on the U.S. test.[22] Ertel and Irving do not believe it. Ertel had taken the effort to try to badger the former assistants Dolce and Harnden with many questions about the exact procedures 15 years earlier.[23] One of our authors, Ranjit Sandhu, in response to an earlier version of Ertel and Irving's paper, independently reviewed (in late 1995) the original data from the U.S. test. He corroborates that the above test was conducted as the published accounts indicate.

Gauquelin immediately disputed the interpretation of the results of the U.S. test, claiming that too many U.S. champions were not outstanding enough.[24] For example, he argued that the names listed in *Who's Who in Football* were "surely too many to represent the top athletes." He wrote that the selections should have been made from *within* the five directories, and one must winnow names from these lists. By what criteria? Only the "most famous," said Gauquelin, and only those, he insisted, who were "internationally known."

But these champions are famous! Anyone who wishes to examine whether the champions listed in these directories are anything less than eminent is encouraged to visit a library and inspect these books thoroughly. He or she will find that very many of these champions are still being mentioned frequently on the sports pages of U.S. newspapers. Gauquelin tried to select a subsample from the total set of 408 by pointing to other American reference books in which they were mentioned. Eventually he included only 192 in his files, and he discarded 216 names entirely, even though they had been published. His selection, however, was clearly made in full awareness of the positions of Mars at the birth of all 408 champions.

Gauquelin's 1979 Test

Gauquelin had meanwhile published in 1979 another test of 432 French sports champions who had not been included in his original studies, which he claimed further corroborated his thesis.[25] The U.S. group was hesitant to accept his conclusion, because the criteria by which Gauquelin selected notable sports champions seemed to vary from test to test. They wondered whether Gauquelin's own *selective bias* was not the real explanation for the "Mars effect." Kurtz, Zelen, and Abell speculated that Gauquelin knew the Mars sectors of athletes beforehand and introduced the criteria *post hoc* in order to favor those with Mars in key sectors.[26]

Gauquelin's study excluded the names of 423 "lesser" champions. Gauquelin never honored the American team's repeated requests that he provide this list. According to Gauquelin these 423 lesser champions were composed of two groups: "minor" French champions taken from Le Roy's *Dictionnaire encyclopédique des sports*, and Italian cyclists taken from the reference books *Vélo 1968* and *Vélo 1970*.[27] Gauquelin said that these three works together contain 42 champions in Mars sector 1. In Ertel's database of Gauquelin's champions there are 24 Italian cyclists marked "GMINV,"[28] and only one of them is born in Mars sector 1. Thus one would expect 399 French "minor" *Dictionnaire* champions, with 41 of them born in sector 1. Between 1979 and 1986 Gauquelin located additional names.[29] According to Ertel, the original "minor" French champions numbered 432, not 423. So Ertel's database contains 455 champions marked "GMIND," though after correction for duplicates the number should be 453. However, these 453 contain only 32 champions born in Mars sector 1. So something does not tally: either Gauquelin's sector count in 1979 is wrong or Ertel's database is incorrect. The numbers Gauquelin reported give the impression that his "control group" had a Mars percentage of 16.8% (71 out of 423) instead of something like 13%.[30]

Gauquelin continued to collect data after he published this test. In 1982 he gathered, on his own, another 159 U.S. champions. By 1986 he had added another 50 French athletes (both "famous" and "lesser"), whose data he said had been untraceable in earlier studies.

The New French Test

Until then the evidence for Gauquelin's "Mars Effect" was based largely on French sports champions collected by Gauquelin himself. So it was proposed that an independent group of French scientists attempt a replication, using data on French athletes. Gauquelin agreed to this proposal.

The protocol for this test was published in the leading French popular science journal *Science & Vie* in October 1982. Of course these French athletes had been gone over thrice already, resulting in publications by Gauquelin in 1955, 1970 and 1979, and it was to be expected that not many new champions could be found. The value of the new test was entirely in its protocol, which covered all aspects of such a test from the setting of criteria to the final comparison with a control sample, and it aimed at a procedure that excluded even the smallest intrusion of Gauquelin's prior knowledge of Mars positions into the selection and data-gathering process.

This new test was performed under the auspices of the French Committee for the Study of Paranormal Phenomena (Comité Français pour l'Etude des Phénomènes Paranormaux, or CFEPP). Many researchers were involved at various times, and the support of two prestigious national institutes (INED, the National Institute for Demographic Studies, and ING, the National Geographical Institute) was enlisted. The French researchers tried to solicit sports journalists to assist them in the selection of champions. The journalists declined, though several recommended the use of the *Dictionnaire encyclopédique des sports*[31] as the primary reference. Gauquelin urged the addition of another reference, *L'athlège*,[32] which the Committee added. The data were compiled independently of Gauquelin. Altogether 1,439 champions were selected, and these resulted eventually (after corrections by Jan Willem Nienhuys) in 1,120 reliable data received. The construction of the control group seemed to present insuperable logistical difficulties. By the time all the champions' data had been received, the CFEPP was plagued by various problems, and was unable to do any more data gathering, which would have required sending out many thousands of letters and gathering an estimated 24,000 names from Paris alone and many more from elsewhere. So a different method was proposed for the control group, namely the creation of a group of fictitious individuals by scrambling the data. Gauquelin agreed with this procedure (which had already been used by the Comité Para) and he was also given extensive opportunity to comment on both the selection criteria and the data received. The protocol stated that Gauquelin's proposals should be taken into consideration, which the CFEPP did by publishing them and analyzing them carefully. Among the 1,120 champions, 207 (18.48%) were born in the 1st and 4th sector, which does not differ significantly from the values obtained from the control group.[33] Thus the French test did not reveal a Mars effect.

Gauquelin's proposals to the French Committee consisted of modifications of the sample. He suggested that certain athletes be removed from the list because "they were not famous enough" and that others be added. His proposals appeared to the French Committee to be extremely biased. He suggested names to be added that the CFEPP had not been able to find, he pointed at data received that contained errors, and he mentioned individual champions and entire groups that were overlooked or overrated, *but these suggestions skewed the results in the direction Gauquelin wanted.* For example, he conveniently recommended data corrections that increased the Mars percentage, and withheld those corrections that decreased the Mars percentage. Regarding the corrections that would neither increase nor decrease the Mars effect, he mentioned only one-sixth. The CFEPP researchers concluded: "In our considered judgment, the Mars effect study demonstrates *some bias in the selective process on the part of M. Gauquelin.*"[34]

One of our authors, Nienhuys, carefully reviewed the CFEPP's study. He found a few errors and omissions, but these did not change the results of the study. Nienhuys formulates the conclusion to be drawn from the French test as follows: "*the whole point in this laborious test was to find out what remains of the Mars effect when one starts from scratch without the help of Gauquelin. The answer is: nothing.*"[35]

Gauquelin committed suicide on May 20, 1991, in Paris, and Ertel has written that he left instructions that all his data be destroyed, implying that the skeptics had "worn him out."[36] Gauquelin seemed seriously ill in January of that year, and it is said that he privately expressed negative opinions about skeptics.

However, most of the skeptics who worked with Gauquelin were personally cordial, even though they raised legitimate questions whether there was sufficient evidence to corroborate his thesis.

II
The "Eminence Effect"

A new dimension to the controversy is the work of Suitbert Ertel, who claims to find independent corroboration for Gauquelin's thesis. He and Kenneth Irving attempt to dismiss the negative tests disconfirming Gauquelin and to show why the Mars effect is still valid.

They base their method on Gauquelin's *post hoc* analysis of the U.S. test, in which he claimed that "internationally famous sports champions" (of a sample selected by him) showed a higher percentage born in Mars key sectors than the sports champions who were merely famous. The latter group had a Mars percentage far below the expected 17% attributed to "ordinary" people. It is at this point that the entire procedure became rather ludicrous, bordering on the bizarre. The independent tests of Gauquelin's thesis ultimately settled for simple criteria such as being mentioned in an authoritative source and meeting general across-the-board minimum quality requirements. The introduction of extra eminence criteria introduces a great deal of latitude into the analysis of data of people with known Mars positions.

In fact, Gauquelin's criteria of fame shifted from publication to publication. He would change criteria midstream. For example, in some studies only Olympic Gold Medalists would be included as sufficiently famous internationally; for other studies Silver and Bronze Medalists might be included.

Ertel claims to be able to resolve the question of "eminence" on more objective grounds, by proposing that we count the number of citations of an athlete in various directories. Ertel and Irving maintain that a citation count might mean only that an athlete was "referred to at least once." Referred to in what manner? A passing remark to an athlete or to a non-sport-related matter should not properly be counted as a citation or an indicator of eminence. Ertel assembled 18 directories, most of them European, and he claims to find a correlation between them and the Mars effect. The Gauquelin "Mars effect" hypothesis says that highly qualified champions show a high Mars percentage. The Ertel "eminence effect" hypothesis says that any group of athletes will show an increasing relation between "eminence" and Mars percentage. So if the Mars percentage happens to be low in a sample, the "eminence effect" still has a chance, thus allowing the claimant to bet on two horses for the price of one.

The contents of dictionaries are based on athletes' achievements. However, many items in a dictionary are not related to sporting achievement. Often a dictionary will mention many recent "hopefuls" at the expense of champions of the past. The use of many dictionaries carries the risk of introduction of a new bias. If one branch of sport happens to have a high Mars percentage, it is attractive to validate this by using a specialized dictionary for that branch of sport. If an investigator wants to argue that American sports people are less famous than Europeans, all he needs to do is avoid the use of American sources. In any case, there is *a priori* no reason to think that the mere mention in a directory is a better indicator of an athlete's quality than the achievements of the champions themselves. And of course, until a test has unequivocally shown the contrary, there is also no reason to assume that Mars has anything to do with sports.

In his "Commentary" on the CFEPP investigation, Nienhuys presented a method of rating sports people by their achievements.[37] That method is—in its present form—perhaps not so suitable for comparing champions from different countries, but at least it avoids the arbitrariness in the choice of sources. Ertel decided in 1988 not to look at the sporting achievements themselves. Was that because he did not know how, or because the method gave unsatisfactory results?

Using his eminence criterion, Ertel selects "eminent athletes" from the U.S. and CFEPP tests, and claims that this subsample supports the Mars effect. But he argues this point by *discarding* data from the U.S. and CFEPP tests *post hoc*. Ertel's entire procedure seems to us to be impermissible. Further, Ertel's conclusion that the CFEPP test confirms Gauquelin's hypothesis was largely based upon his study of earlier incomplete and only partially corrected data. Strangely, Ertel did *not* include any of the five directories used in the U.S. test in his eminence appraisal, though they are easily available through interlibrary loan. Nor did he consistently use *L'athlège* or *Dictionnaire encyclopédique des sports*, the key French directories used by both Gauquelin and the French Committee. Moreover, Ertel drops and adds dictionaries in subsequent studies. These omissions are puzzling in a test that he claims is objective. Ertel's eminence test thus is a function of the directories that he had in his possession at that time or that he borrowed from Gauquelin, and it is not based on *all* of the directories available—and this might be attributed to Ertel's own bias in selecting directories.

This eminence-effect hypothesis took its inspiration from Gauquelin's efforts to dispute the U.S. test; so it is not strange that Ertel would claim that the U.S. test provided evidence for the eminence effect. But it is invalid to use the same data twice in such a way: once to provide the inspiration for a conjecture, and then to "explain" that same data by the conjecture. Incidentally, the evidence here is very weak: when a one-sided test yields $p = 0.06$, it is clearly nonsignificant.[38]

What does the eminence effect show here? In 1988 Ertel observed that there was apparently a more or less linear relation between the number of times a Gauquelin athlete was mentioned in 18 specific sources and the athlete's chance of having been born in Mars sectors 1 and 4. Yet Koppeschaar (1992) observed that the total aggregate of Gauquelin's French champions did not show much of an eminence effect.[39] This was confirmed by the CFEPP test. Ertel's database in 1988 included 933 of the 1,066 CFEPP champions. Though his results looked interesting, he made many errors in attributing citations to the *Dictionnaire encyclopédique des sports*. We have corrected these. We have also corrected the Mars calculations, using the sectors as computed by the CFEPP. The following table shows the result.

Number of citations:	0	1	2	3	4	5	6	7	4+
Number of athletes (N):	130	385	270	95	30	17	5	1	53
In primary sector (M):	28	62	52	23	6	5	1	0	12
M as percent of N:	21.5	16.1	19.3	24.2					22.6

Citation counts for 933 CFEPP athletes. Percentages of numbers 30 and lower are omitted. The last column is the sum of all columns of 4 or more citations.[40]

As one can see, there is no trend, which is not surprising because the "eminence effect" had already been found to be statistically insignificant if only the French champions were considered.[41] Ertel also reports that the Comité Para sample does *not* exhibit the eminence effect.[42]

Though there is no trend as such, the oft-quoted champions do have a somewhat higher Mars percentage. This calls for a closer investigation. Such a higher percentage is only meaningful if we can be absolutely sure that no data are suppressed. From the example of the 216 U.S. champions that Gauquelin discarded we see that this is doubtful.

Ertel has contributed something of value to this discussion. He visited Gauquelin in Paris in 1986 to obtain the data on Gauquelin's unpublished sports champions. It was known, of course, that Gauquelin had published the names of 2,889 champions, and from Gauquelin's publications it is obvious that he was continually collecting data. In his publications of 1960 and 1979 he mentioned 118 Germans, 599 Italians, and 432 French and Italian sports people that he had used as control groups, altogether 1,149. So there were many more names in his files, and it is not surprising that he had not yet published all of them. But there are two surprises. The first is the large number (347) of additional and unexpected unpublished data (raising the total of all Gauquelin champions to 4,385, of whom 6 had two near-identical records), and the second is the large negative Mars effect in the total of unpublished data. In 1982 Michel and Françoise Gauquelin published their version of an American test. It contained 351 names, including 192 from the previous U.S. test. But they did not retain the 216 other names of the U.S. test in their files[43]—an egregious procedure.

Ertel and Irving, however, corroborate the conclusions of the U.S. and French tests, namely that Gauquelin had allowed his bias to intervene in the selection process. Ertel and Irving state that:

> Gauquelin had occasionally referred to his exempting low-eminence athletes from analysis, which is a legitimate procedure in principle, *if done without awareness of planetary positions.* Ertel suspected, however, that on occasion Gauquelin in fact might have been aware of Mars positions when he decided whether or not an athlete was or was not eminent enough to be added to the final sample. With Gauquelin's permission, Ertel sought out and analyzed this unpublished data, finding that *indeed, Gauquelin tended not to exclude marginally successful athletes from his high-eminence sample when Mars at their births was in either the rising or culminating zones.* In other words, he tended to rank Mars G–sector cases among low-eminence athletes more favorably than non–G sector cases. . . . This indicates that Gauquelin must have been aware, to a certain degree, of Mars-sector positions . . . (emphasis added).[44]

Ertel's discovery of a bias in Gauquelin's data should have been reason to dismiss all of Gauquelin's data. However, Ertel did not do so. He assumed that a bias in judging people's athletic prowess was Gauquelin's only bias, and he developed his new "eminence" definition of the Mars effect. Moreover, from Ertel's collective writings it seems that he is free to define "eminence" in whatever way he likes, and use any method he likes to demonstrate the "increasing" eminence characteristic.[45] Thus the eminence effect hypothesis tests merely Ertel's ingenuity.

Let us explore Ertel's discovery of Gauquelin's bias further. In his comments on the champions collected by the CFEPP, Gauquelin objected to several names because their birth data did not seem "reliable" enough, arguing that certain birth records that were difficult to find might be the wrong records. Gauquelin, of course, did not reject all records that were difficult to find, and we can examine those that he retained. During the Belgian Comité Para's investigation a total of 88 champions turned up whose birth records we may say were truly difficult to find—for example, those born in Paris or in a place other than what the dictionary stated, or those born in a place with a fairly common name (like Saint-Etienne, Fontaine, Montreuil, or Saint-Nazaire), or those in which the actual birth month did not agree with the month found in the dictionary, including all cases where the dictionary gives the wrong year or only the year. Among these 88 the Mars percentage is 30.7%. These numbers refer to the champions taken from the *Dictionnaire des sports.*[46]

The champions in Gauquelin's 1979 publication were partly obtained from Le Roy's *Dictionnaire encyclopédique des sports.* Of these, 134 were not French, and among these 134 there are 37 that were difficult to find. These 37 have a Mars percentage of 35.1%. Gauquelin also extracted 224 famous French champions (born before 1950) from Le Roy's *Dictionnaire*, and these contain 40 difficult-to-find champions, with a Mars percentage of 27.5%. If we combine these three groups, we get 165 people with a Mars percentage of 30.9%. That is very high, even compared to Gauquelin's 22% hypothesis. These champions are as a group not better qualified than the groups from which they are taken.

The 1963 *Dictionnaire des sports* contained many more potential candidates for selection, namely French people born in either France or Algeria. Though Gauquelin later found data for a few of them, he was never able to find information on many others—at least they are not in Ertel's files. The CFEPP investigation yielded 34 of these "untraceable" champions. Among these 34 only 2 are born in Mars sectors 1 or 4.

Also, the CFEPP found 104 champions that were similarly difficult to find, as the month or place of birth was different from what the source indicated. Of these, 15 were born in sectors 1 or 4. However, 21 of these 104 were not in Ertel's files, and of these 21 only 1 was born in Mars sector 1 and none in Mars sector 4. If we combine these two groups we get 48 people that are missing from the files, with a Mars percentage of 6.25%. That is very low, and even more so compared to the 31.5% among those that were found by Gauquelin.

This suggests that Gauquelin was suppressing data he thought "unreliable," and also that the data of the champions born in a favorable Mars position were not rejected as easily as the others. Possibly this happened more often with champions about whom he had information from different sources.

Ertel's finding can be summarized by the observation that the champions who occur in many books, especially books known to Gauquelin, have a somewhat higher Mars percentage than the others. Could this be due to a Gauquelin bias? Ertel says no, because Gauquelin may have been selectively publishing, but he did not discard data. But it is rather clear that Gauquelin was taking unwarranted liberties with the data. The evidence in short is (1) conflicting numbers between his 1979 publication and Ertel's database, (2) the muddled matter of the 76 Belgian soccer players that were never published, (3) the deletion of 216 Americans, and (4) the matter of the difficult-to-find cases. Moreover, (5) in his comments on the CFEPP investigation, Gauquelin was strangely silent about 39 champions that he almost certainly must have tried to find, but that are not included in Ertel's database.[47]

In the light of these five points the 1988 Ertel eminence effect becomes only mildly interesting, rather than an ultimate proof that science as we know it must be revised drastically. It suggests that it was primarily not fame but having available several sources of possibly conflicting information that correlated with Gauquelin's selection bias. The 1995 Ertel eminence effect raises another matter. It still relies heavily on Ertel's assumption of the integrity of Gauquelin's data, which we question.

We indicated that we believe there is sufficient reason to reject the result of the Comité Para test. And as the doubts also extend to the foreign champions collected by Gauquelin, we see no reason to consider the eminence effect as anything but a side effect of Gauquelin's bias. Whether Gauquelin's bias was intentional or not is irrelevant; his data are unreliable, scientifically speaking.

III
Conclusion

What are we to draw from this protracted controversy? Researchers have spent decades patiently sifting through the claims of the so-called evidence adduced to support the Mars effect. There are two possible inferences:

First, that there is a genuine Mars effect. If this were the case, however, it would apply to only about 2,888 sports champions in the Western world, and would exclude many other famous sports champions (published and unpublished and discarded by Gauquelin). If the Mars effect was real, it should be confirmed by independent researchers. The U.S. and French tests have been unable to replicate the "Mars effect."

Second, that the Mars effect is based upon Gauquelin's bias. There are several rather compelling indications that this is the case. His reactions to the U.S. test showed his efforts to redefine eminence, in full knowledge of the results, after the test was over. An examination of his files showed that he was doing the same thing privately with his own data. He also tried to influence the French CFEPP test in various ways by adding, deleting and changing records. We have adduced evidence that both in the 1960s and in the 1970s he discarded data that he thought unreliable. Perhaps some of this evidence could have been discovered 20 years or longer ago, if scientists at that time had focused less on astronomy and more on Gauquelin's procedures in data collection. In other words, the key witness who claimed a remarkable effect turns out to be unreliable, and we must return a verdict of "not proven." The witness is probably the victim of his own illusion.

Some proponents of Mr. Gauquelin's hypothesis have repeatedly accused skeptical researchers of being biased. These charges have been hurled against the Belgian Comité Para, the U.S. group, and the French CFEPP. Yet the many scientists and scholars associated with this work who questioned Gauquelin's theories have exerted every caution to be fair-minded and objective. Regrettably, pro-paranormalists often accuse "establishment scientists" of being dogmatic. But Gauquelin's theories have not been summarily rejected with an appeal to infallible authority. They have been carefully examined, and a great deal of effort has been spent on that.

We conclude that after persistent and painstaking examination, there is no evidence for the Mars effect, and Ertel and Irving's effort to save the floundering fiction have likewise failed. It is time, we submit, to move on to other more productive topics.

1. Dennis Rawlins, "Report on the U.S. Test of the Gauquelins' 'Mars Effect.'" *The Skeptical Inquirer* 4 no. 2 (Winter 1979–1980), pp. 26–31, esp. p. 27.

2. Ibid, p. 30.

3. Michel Gauquelin, *L 'influence des astres: étude critique et expérimentale* (Paris: Dauphin, 1955).

4. Gauquelin, *Les hommes et les astres* (Paris: Denoël, 1960).

5. Gauquelin, *Sports Champions 1–2089* (Paris: LERCCP, 1970).

6. For example, in "The Truth about the Mars Effect on Sports Champions" (Michel and Françoise Gauquelin, *The Humanist* 36, no. 4, July/August 1976, pp. 44–45) the Gauquelins refer to "the committee's results for 535 sports champions . . . our former results for the group of 1,553 other champions." In the next issue of *The Humanist* (George O. Abell, A. A. Abell, and Michel and Françoise Gauquelin, "A Test of the Gauquelin 'Mars Effect,' " *The Humanist* 36, no. 5, September/October 1976, p. 40) this evolved into 1,553 champions from the 1960 publication and a separate sample of 535 making a total of 2,088. Michel and Françoise Gauquelin ("The Zelen Test of the Mars Effect," *The Humanist* 37, no. 6, November/December 1977, pp. 30–35) refer in their report on the Zelen test to "our first group of 1,553" and "the Comité Para's group of 535," and in 1979 they distinguish "the effect observed by the Belgian Comité Para (22.2 percent) and by us (21.4 percent)," i.e. 119 in 535 and 333 in 1,553. (See also Michel Gauquelin, "Letter," *The Skeptical Inquirer* 3, no. 2, Winter 1978–79.)

7. Jim Lippard records in his "Chronicle of Events" in Suitbert Ertel and Kenneth Irving's *The Tenacious Mars Effect* (London: Urania Trust, 1996) that the Comité Para completed its data gathering on October 22, 1968, and he quotes a source: Michel Gauquelin, *Birth-Times: A Scientific Investigation of the Secrets of Astrology* (New York: Hill and Wang, 1983). Jean Dommanget says that the first meeting between Gauquelin and the Comité Para took place in 1967 (unpublished paper read at the European Skeptical Conference of 1994).

8. Comité Para, "Considérations critiques sur une recherche faite par M. M. Gauquelin dans le domaine des influences planétaires," *Nouvelles brèves* no. 43 (September 1976), p. 327–343.

9. Suitbert Ertel, "Raising the Hurdle for the Athletes' Mars Effect: Association Co-Varies with Eminence," *Journal of Scientific Exploration* 2 no. 1 (1988), pp. 53–82.

10. Suitbert Ertel and Kenneth Irving, *The Tenacious Mars Effect* (London: Urania Trust, 1996), pp. pp. SE–18, 19, and 50.

11. Zelen specifically referred to "Gauquelin's sample of 1,553 sports champions." Apparently Zelen had been led to believe that there was a neat batch of pre-Comité Para champions that could be used to generate a null-hypothesis for the new batch of Comité Para-champions.

12. Marvin Zelen, "Astrology and Statistics: A Challenge," *The Humanist* 36 no. 1 (January/February 1976), pp. 32–33.

13. Marvin Zelen, Paul Kurtz, and George Abell, "Is There a Mars Effect?" *The Humanist* 37 no. 6 (November/December 1977), pp. 36–39.

14. George Abell, "One Astronomer's Views," *The Humanist* 36 no. 1 (January/February 1976), pp. 33–36.

15. *The Lincoln Library of Sports Champions* (Columbus, Oh.: Sports Resources Company, 1974).

16. Ronald L. Mendell and Timothy B. Phares, *Who's Who in Football* (New Rochelle, N.Y.: Arlington House, 1974).

17. Ronald L. Mendell, *Who's Who in Basketball* (New Rochelle, N.Y.: Arlington House, 1973).

18. Bob Burrill, *Who's Who in Boxing* (New Rochelle, N.Y.: Arlington House, 1974).

19. Reid M. Hanley, *Who's Who in Track and Field* (New Rochelle, N.Y.: Arlington House, 1973).

20. Incidentally, Ertel constantly lumps together American football and European soccer and confuses these two different sports (see Ertel and Irving, *The Tenacious Mars Effect*, p. SE-56, note 33). Ertel's arbitrary methods for classifying sports reach their bizarre extreme in his suggestion that basketball is more a form of art like ballet (p. SE-54, note 31).

21. Paul Kurtz, Marvin Zelen, and George Abell, "Results of the U.S. Test of the 'Mars Effect' Are Negative," *The Skeptical Inquirer* 4 no. 2 (Winter 1979–1980), pp. 19–26; Rawlins, "Report on the U.S. Test of the Gauquelins' "Mars Effect," pp. 26–31.

22. Kurtz, Zelen, and Abell, ibid., pp. 21–23.

23. This letter is mentioned in an abridged version of J. Lippard's "Chronology of Events" (Ertel and Irving, *The Tenacious Mars Effect*, p. A2–26).

24. Michel and Françoise Gauquelin, "Star U.S. Sportsmen Display the Mars Effect," *The Skeptical Inquirer* 4 no. 2 (Winter 1979–80), pp. 31–43.

25. Michel Gauquelin, *The Mars Effect and the Sports Champions: A New Replication on 432 Famous Europeans with Publication of Their Birth and Mars Data* (Paris: LERRCP, 1979).

26. Paul Kurtz, Marvin Zelen, and George Abell, "The Contradictions in Gauquelin's Research: Rejoinder," *The Skeptical Inquirer* 4 no. 4 (Summer 1980), pp. 62–68.

27. Michel Gauquelin, *The Mars Effect and the Sports Champions* (1979), pp. 21, 28.

28. GMINV seems to mean "Gauquelin Minor *Vélo* champions." Similarly, GMIND seems to mean "Gauquelin Minor *Dictionnaire* champions."

29. Ertel, "Raising the Hurdle for the Athletes' Mars Effect."

30. The 453 "lesser" champions in Ertel's files contain 61 Mars-champions (13.5%), and the "lesser" champions found by the CFEPP had a Mars percentage of 12.2%.

31. Bernard Le Roy, *Dictionnaire encyclopédique des sports, des sportifs et des performances* (Paris: Denoël, 1973).

32. Marcel Rossini, editor-in-chief, *L'athlège 1951: Biographies des plus grands champions français de tous les sports* (Paris: Kléber, 1951).

33. The CFEPP reports that the control group yields 18.2% as "theoretical estimate." This seems to be the result of a slowly convergent algorithm, and Nienhuys found about 17.7%, a value close to what Ertel claims to be correct. This implies a p-value of about 0.42, i.e. a chance of about two in five of accidentally getting a value that deviates at least as much from 17.7% as the CFEPP's result. Even with this modification, however, the results are still not significant.

34. Claude Benski, Dominique Caudron, Yves Galifret, Jean-Paul Krivine, Jean-Claude Pecker, Michel Rouzé, Evry Schatzman, and Jan Willem Nienhuys, *The "Mars Effect": A French Test of Over 1 000 Sports Champions* (Amherst, N.Y.: Prometheus Books, 1996), p. 31.

35. Ibid., p. 145.

36. Ertel writes:

> The root of the Gauquelin tragedy might be found in his struggle of many years, to no effect, for acknowledgement of his discovery in mainstream science. Great efforts at defending his empirical observations against successive attacks from three skeptical organizations had worn him out. In each of them he became entangled with ill-will and strategies so dubious some members of the adversary camps even left their organizations in protest. Michel Gauquelin stayed on the battlefield for nearly three decades, but toward the end of his life he repeatedly complained that the strain of those decades of combat had used up his physical resources.

Gauquelin did not leave behind any document explaining his decision, but there is one deplorable hint. By his last will he demanded that all empirical data amassed through his lifetime, more than 30,000 birth documents on file in perfect order, must be destroyed. His will was put into effect, and it is almost inevitable to understand his act as a charge, not only directed at those who had not played fair with him but directed at all scientists not serving and suffering as much as he did in the pursuit of scientific truth ("In Memory of Michel Gauquelin," *Journal of Scientific Exploration* 7, no. 1, 1993, pp. 5–7).

The information about Gauquelin's "last will" is only a friend-of-a-friend tale: "I was told by one of Gauquelin's friends who said he had contacted relatives who had told him that Michel wanted the data to be burned" (e-mail message of November 14, 1994). The only thing that seems certain is that Gauquelin's files are gone. They might have been destroyed by people who were unaware of their value and who fibbed about it afterwards. Ertel's inflated rhetoric is unconvincing. All genuine research scientists hope that after their deaths their results, or at least their honor, will survive. Ertel ascribes to Gauquelin an uncharacteristic petty meanness. If Gauquelin thought his data of any value, should he not have made them available to any friend or colleague that was interested in them? If Gauquelin had actually left instructions to destroy his entire data file, this could only raise the most serious questions about the integrity of his research.

37. Benski, et al., pp. 137–138.

38. Suitbert Ertel, "Update on the 'Mars Effect,'" *Skeptical Inquirer* 16 no. 2 (Winter 1992), pp. 150–160.

39. C. E. Koppeschaar, "The Mars Effect Unriddled." In: J. W. Nienhuys (ed.) *Science or Pseudo? The Mars Effect and Other Claims. Proceedings of the Third EuroSkeptics Congress, October 4–5, 1991, Amsterdam*, vol. 8 of "Skeptische Notities" (Utrecht: Stichting Skepsis, 1992), pp. 162–184.

40. Ertel's files did not contain 133 of the 1,066. And according to Ertel and Irving, in *The Tenacious Mars Effect*, there are 17 more that are absent. This suggests that Ertel is unable to search his own files properly.

41. Jan Willem Nienhuys, "Dutch Investigations of the Gauquelin Mars Effect," *Journal of Scientific Exploration* 7 (1993), pp. 231–292.

42. Ertel and Irving, p. SE–16.

43. Ertel also discards these 216 names (Ertel and Irving).

44. Ertel and Irving, p. XX.

45. An illustration of the failure of Ertel's eminence criterion is his recently published test of *1083 Members of the French "Académie de Médicine"* (coauthored with Arno Müller; Waldmohr: A. P. Müller Verlag, 1994). This refers to a correlation with eminent physicians and the planet Mars. In this he explicitly contradicts his own eminence criteria on key points; for the Mars effect *decreases* as higher levels of eminence are achieved; he also abandons his own citation-of-biographical-dictionaries method to determine eminence. We quote from this study.

> For Mars the eminence relationship in the present study was less satisfactory. The effect *decreased* at higher eminence levels, but did not increase at low eminence levels. However, it is possible that G% for certain planets (here Mars) *is less related to eminence* for certain professions (here physicians) (p. 28, emphasis added).

> The great majority of members of the Académie de Médicine did not obtain any citation in 586 biographical dictionaries indexed by Arlan Appelletier. Therefore *a count of citations cannot be used as a measure of eminence* (p. 19, emphasis added).

Ertel changes the criterion of "eminence" and uses instead the physicians' ages of admission to the Academy. He ranks the total group of 1,083 according to this age. Then he splits the group into six almost equal portions. The first portion are the 181 youngest academicians. The next portion are the 180 next youngest academicians, and so on. As the total Mars percentage (with the wider Ertel definition) among these academicians is 25.2%, we can compare the expectations on the basis of this percentage with the actual numbers.

Age groups	1	2	3	4	5	6
Group size	181	180	181	180	181	180
Expected Mars number	45.6	45.4	45.6	45.4	45.6	45.4
Actual Mars number	40	50	45	44	47	47

This is after Ertel decided for himself that a division into 6 groups (and not into 3, 4 or 5 groups) would be most appropriate. By showing the results only in graph form Ertel masks the actual numbers.

We submit that the numbers display only one peculiarity: they are unusually close to their expected values. A chi-squared test yields $p > 0.9$, in other words, it rarely happens (1 in 10 times) that actual values are all this close to the expected values. Subdivisions into another number of groups give even flatter pictures. Since the French Academy physicians served as the original inspiration for the planetary hypotheses, the Mars percentage of 25.2% cannot very well serve as support for this hypothesis.

Yet Ertel believes that this table shows that planetary effects increase up to medium eminence and then decrease at high eminence. He calls this "curvilinear." We would say the eminence hypothesis falls dead flat. Incidentally, his co-author Müller does not agree with Ertel's interpretation, and instead finds the results "ambiguous" at best.

Further, in *The Tenacious Mars Effect* (p. SE–43), Ertel's table 10 is a textbook example of invalid statistics. We merely discuss the column referring to "all athletes" combined. The number of these is said to be 1,683. This number is wrong. Apparently Ertel did not notice 13 champions who occur both in the Comité Para sample and in the CFEPP sample. Then Ertel naïvely includes 5 champions from Gauquelin's proposed additions, plus some of Gauquelin's "corrections," raising the Mars score by 4. More than a year before publication of *The Tenacious Mars Effect* Ertel was informed about the nature of these additions and corrections; he even refers to the very e-mail messages that contained this information. Ertel reports that he scrambled the data 200 times, simply by alphabetically shifting the birth years, a rather crude method. Of these 200 scrambles, 14 yielded a *higher* Mars score than the actual value, but one should, of course, look at *equal or higher*. These 14, divided by 200, yield then a "p-value" of 0.07, which is dubious, because to get a theoretical number like a p-value in this way with any precision, one needs about ten times as many scrambles. Then a few lines lower the average Mars percentage of these 200 scrambles is reported, together with a p-value of 0.09. Given the error of including these Gauquelin proposals, the correct value is probably something like 0.13. As this is a one-sided test, there's nothing special about this. Nonetheless, the result is called "near significant" on the strength of "$p = 0.07$." So this one column yields a pitiful spectacle of inefficient data search, naïve assumptions, deliberate preservation of gross distortions, poor understanding of statistics, and pseudo-scientific jargon. In other columns this is compounded by arbitrary choices of sources to be used to assess eminence, and the number of citations that is most suitable to demonstrate the desired effect (surprisingly this number is 1 and not 2 or 3), and the conclusion is that "a Mars effect is clearly conspicuous." We do not concur. There's only a conspicuous Ertel effect.

46. E. Seidler and R. Parienté, *Dictionnaire des sports* (Paris: Seghers, 1963).

47. Benski, et al., pp. 141–142.

8

In Defense of Scientific Medicine

Growth of Alternative Medicine

The public is being inundated by New Age spiritualistic therapies. Pseudoscientific health cures are highly popular in the media and among book and magazine publishers—visit any bookstore today and compare the shelf space devoted to science books with New Age, Occult, or Paranormal books.

As skeptics, we have encouraged research by the scientific community into these paranormal claims and we have published criticism of them. One question that is often asked by the media and the general public is this: Why should anyone bother to criticize clairvoyance, astrology, phrenology, or numerology? What harm do these do? Aren't they fun? In the past we would immediately respond by referring to blatant quackery in the health area—from faith healing by evangelical hucksters to Edgar Cayce's diagnosis of disease and his alleged cures. The uncritical public acceptance of health fads and diets can be dangerous to the public's health, especially if people substitute these nostrums

Paper read at the inaugural meeting of the Council for Scientific Medicine, held on February 26–28, 1999, in Philadelphia. The theme of the conference was "Science Confronts Alternative Medicine." This conference was jointly sponsored by the Council for Scientific Medicine (CSM) and the Committee for the Scientific Investigation of Claims of the Paranormal (CSICOP).

for competent medical treatment. When we began our skeptical agenda, little did we imagine that alternative or complementary medicine would grow as rapidly as it has, especially in the past decade.

The National Institute of Health established an Office of Alternative Medicine in 1992, which is funded with federal dollars; and there are many new alternative-medicine journals. Many of its leading doctor-gurus, such as Deepak Chopra, Andrew Weil, Bernie Siegal, and Larry Dossey, have published best-selling books that dominate the public's perception of medicine. Moreover, as Marcia Angell and Jerome P. Kassirer, editors of the *New England Journal of Medicine*, point out (September 17, 1998) the multibillion-dollar "dietary-supplement industry" is now exempt from Federal Food and Drug Administration (FDA) regulation; and the public is inundated with advertising claims. The Dietary-Supplement Health and Education Act, which was enacted in 1994, allows herbal remedies to be sold without requiring the manufacturer to prove their effectiveness and safety to the FDA. According to a recent story in the *New York Times* (February 1999), a federal judge ordered the FDA to lift its ban on cholestin, a powder made from a Chinese rice fermented with red yeast. The Agency had banned the import of this unapproved drug, which had been marketed as a dietary supplement. The powder contains a natural form of lovastatin, which is a key ingredient in Mevacor, a cholesterol-reducing prescription drug.

Alternative medicine is growing also because many health-maintenance organizations and insurance companies now cover alternative medicine treatments. According to the *Wall Street Journal* (February 18, 1999), practitioners of the ancient art of healing known as Reiki won't need a license to practice their craft; the New York Massage Board voted to allow them to go unlicensed. Reiki masters allegedly heal with "spiritual energy" that flows through their hands without touching their patients. Ellen Kahne of New York City, according to the *Journal*, claims that she was able to stop her cousin's asthma attack, even though hundreds of miles away! In response to the growth of public interest in alternative medicine, many medical schools are now teaching courses in it. We thus are suddenly faced with the extraordinary growth of alternative therapies, often in competition with scientific medicine.

With this problem in mind, many of us associated with the skeptics movement decided to organize a systematic response to alternative medicine. Thus we created in late 1997 an informal *ad hoc* "Council for Scientific Medicine," and we launched a new peer-reviewed journal, the *Scientific Review of Alternative Medicine*. In my view, the American Medical Association should have organized such a group, but ever since the chiropractic profession successfully sued the AMA, that association has been reluctant to get into the fray. They are at times more concerned with their professional prerogatives than their social responsibilities. Because they have not entered into the fray, we have taken the initiative in organizing this effort.

The goal of the Council for Scientific Medicine is to defend the integrity and the importance of scientific medicine. Health has always been of primary concern to human beings—fearful of disease, pain, suffering, and death, they seek relief. Medical cures were based historically on folk medicine, cultural traditions, and religious superstitions. These remedies no doubt had some basis in experience, but cures were not grounded on rigorously tested knowledge and were often unreliable.

A good illustration of a folk cure is as follows:

> My oldest brother had a toothache, and a man told us: You know them places that be on the inside of a mule's leg looks like it been sore or something. He told us to get a pocket knife and trim some of that off and put it in a pipe and let my brother smoke it. And we did that, and it stopped it.[1]

Everyone knows that grandmother's chicken soup is an excellent remedy for a cold, and that it will relieve symptoms in one week. Of course, without grandma's chicken soup it would take seven days. Folk medicine historically consisted basically of the use of vegetable products or herbs, or various forms of diet and exercise, some of these are no doubt effective, many of them based on the placebo effect. China and India and other Asian countries have a long history of traditional medicine. CSICOP had exchanged delegations with China, and we have visited institutes for Traditional Chinese Medicine in Beijing and Shanghai. One illustration of Chinese folk cures dramatically points to the problem. While in Beijing, James Alcock, a member of our first skeptics delegation to China in 1988, developed a bad cough and he went to a Chinese clinic, which offered to provide him with snake bile. The question we asked was, "Does it work or not?" Of course, the only way to tell is by rigorous testing. Alcock decided not to take it and managed to get some antibiotics.

Scientific Medicine Relatively New

In any case, scientific medicine is a relatively recent development in human history, largely beginning in the nineteenth century, when increased knowledge of physiology and human anatomy was refined. There have been a number of brilliant researchers who have contributed to our understanding, such as Claude Bernard, the French scientist, who used experimental methods to clarify the role of the pancreas and of glycogen in the liver. There have been great breakthroughs in microbiology and bacteriology with the introduction of germ and bacteria theories by Louis Pasteur, Robert Koch, and others. The discovery of the importance of antiseptics was demonstrated by Joseph Lister. Theories about the nature and transmission of infectious disease, such as diphtheria, tuberculosis, yellow fever, malaria, typhoid, tetanus, polio, and the development of vaccines all had important roles in immunization. Likewise important were the great advances in epidemiology, public health, and sanitation. In the twentieth century endocrinology advanced—with the discovery of insulin, cortisone, and sex hormones. In the field of nutrition researchers discovered the important role of vitamins. There have been significant new diagnostic tools, such as x-ray imagery, CAT scans, mammography and sonograms. The great strides in surgery have been impressive, including cardiology, neurosurgery, and organ transplantation. The discovery of antibiotics has made enormous contributions to the cure of infectious disease. We should add to this the discoveries of DNA, biogenetic research, gene therapy, and other innovations on the frontiers of research. All of these achievements have led to the reduction of infant mortality and the extension of life spans—over three decades have been added to longevity rates in the twentieth century in affluent countries. As part of this process was the development, beginning in 1904, of rigorous standards of medical education in medical schools. Thus we see the remarkable effectiveness of modern scientific medicine—all for the benefit of humankind.

The question can be raised: How does scientific medicine relate to alternative medicine? Our response is that we should apply the same rigorous peer-review process to the claims of alternative medical proponents. What does this entail? First, that practitioners of alternative medicine have a coherent, clearly defined explanatory theory that is internally consistent and falsifiable. We are concerned that acupuncture, chiropractic, Qigong, and therapeutic touch, for example, lack such identifiable theories. Second, at the very least, therapeutic practices and medications need to be rigorously tested. Here we are not talking about anecdotal information, hearsay, or self-proclaimed validations by their practitioners, but independent corroboration, double-blind, randomized, controlled clinical tests. We need statistical evidence of the reliability of such cures before we can accept them.

There is an ongoing battle between the advocates of scientific medicine and their critics. Many New Age alternative healers deny that science is applicable. They denigrate the medical establishment. They believe that skeptics dogmatically reject unconventional therapies. They think that there are hidden untapped powers of ancient natural remedies and therapies that need to be released.

Skeptics should not seek to defend the medical profession *per se*. Medical doctors are practical craftsmen, drawing on intuition and their own experience, and some perhaps are not sufficiently familiar with the methods of scientific research. The so-called medical establishment has in the past opposed novel theories and important pioneers, such as Pasteur and Simmelweis, who had to battle against received doctrines.

The medical profession has suffered two waves of criticism in the last thirty years. First, in the late 1960s and early 1970s the field of medical ethics developed. This sought to dethrone authoritarian doctors and to defend the rights of patients. The euthanasia movement is a dramatic illustration of this development; so is the demand for informed choice and the right of patients to resist treatment. After some controversy, medical ethics was accepted by those within the medical community, who, along with philosophers, ethicists, theologians, lawyers and the lay public, have developed new ethical guidelines for treatment. Second, alternative medicine now challenges the medical profession. It seems to me that the only adequate response is to be open to new claims of therapy, provided they are responsibly framed and testable. Thus we need to evaluate such claims and to seek to have them corroborated. We hope this will contribute, in a modest way, to the advancement of medical knowledge—and it should apply to orthodox as well as to alternative medicine.

Some Possible Explanations

The paradox that we face today is that this assault on scientific medicine is occurring in spite of the extraordinary advances that are being achieved. Why is this so? There are various explanations that I can only briefly suggest.

First, the traditional family doctor is being replaced by HMOs, clinics, and by teams of specialists. Many of these have lost the intimate personal relationship that medical practitioners of the past have had.

Second, hopeless patients in the terminal stages of cancer or other debilitating diseases often give up on orthodox scientific medicine and seek alternative cures. They are desperate to seek some help.

Third, many people swear by alternative medicine because they believe it is effective. This, I think, can be attributed to many factors: Many illnesses of the body, if left alone, will in time heal themselves. There are vague pains and maladies, that are undiagnosed and which may in time also dissipate. The placebo effect can be powerful in regard to psychosomatic if not organic illnesses. Medical science is not infallible. There are many diseases we do not understand, nor are cures available. Moreover, the state of the art is constantly changing, and earlier methods subsequently may have to be abandoned or revised. Many patients do not understand the tentative fallible character of the process of scientific inquiry. We need to edify them and especially focus on preventative medicine.

Fourth, alternative medicine has become a highly profitable industry. Food additives, dietary supplements, herbs, and vitamins are being marketed to the public, often with few if any qualifications about their effectiveness. The media-oriented companies that dominate our society often focus on sensationalized reports of miracle therapies, and there has not been a national effort to provide adequate balanced information to the public.

Fifth, the growth of alternative medicine is related to other antiscientific attitudes in society. It is allied with a vague kind of regnant spirituality, especially in the writings of Deepak Chopra and Andrew Weil; and this has an affinity with New Age paradigms. It is also reinforced by postmodern attacks on objectivity in science. If knowledge is ultimately validated subjectively, or by its relationship to a culture, then anecdotal reports and folk medicine would be admissible forms of "validation."

Skepticism has its work cut out for it. For human health is too precious to be squandered by premodern nostrums or postmodern fantasies. We need to submit the claims of health cures to careful evaluation. We need an open mind and should not prejudge the issue before inquiry. We also need to stimulate an appreciation in the public about the nature of scientific medicine and the need for caution about untested remedies.

---

1. Quoted by Frank Reuter in "Folk Remedies and Human Belief-Systems: How Body and Mind Work Together to Make Folk Remedies Seem Successful," *Skeptical Inquirer* 11, no. 1 (Fall 1986), p. 44.

9

Can the Sciences be Unified?

In this bold and provocative book, E. O. Wilson sets himself ambitious goals: He seeks to defend the sciences against the forces that would undermine their integrity, to integrate knowledge across the disciplines and branches of knowledge, and to apply this knowledge for human betterment.

His first task is eminently reasonable. Although the sciences have made impressive strides in understanding nature and human nature, the scientific enterprise has suffered considerable forays against it from a wide range of critics. There is today a concerted effort from many sides to deprecate science and to minimize its achievements. Here Wilson is not referring simply to the growth of belief in the paranormal and the pseudosciences or of fundamentalist religion, but the challenge of a bevy of postmodernist deconstructionists, cultural relativists, ecofeminists, Afrocentrists, neo-Marxists, philosophical Feyerabendians and Kuhnians, and Latourian social constructionists. These critiques emanate from the academy—predominantly from the faculties in the humanities, the arts, and the social sciences—where they have had considerable influence. They add up to the pessimistic appraisal that the sciences express no more than "narrative myths" and that their findings are no truer than any other areas of human endeavor. Indeed, we are told that the modern quest for

A review of *Consilience: The Unity of Knowledge.* By Edward O. Wilson. Alfred A. Knopf, New York, 1998. First published in the *Skeptical Inquirer* 22, no. 4 (July/August 1998), pp. 47–49.

objective methods of knowledge is a chimera. Subjectivists and nihilists today denigrate science and blame it for most of the problems that the world faces. In essence, the postmodernist critics of science are attacking the Enlightenment thinkers of the seventeenth and eighteenth centuries and their conviction that it was possible to discover knowledge of the real world and apply it for human improvement. The goal of the Enlightenment, says Wilson, was "to demystify the world and free the mind from the impersonal forces that imprison it" (p. 21). Now that is under attack by extreme postmodernist skeptics.

Wilson forcefully defends the Enlightenment, which, he maintains, needs to be recaptured and realized, and he agrees with Condorcet (the last of the *philosophes* of the eighteenth century and one of his heroes) that scientific knowledge can make the most powerful contributions to human progress. Science is not a "social construction" (a view held by the influential French sociologist Bernard Latour), though it is conditioned no doubt by the societies in which we live; and the methods of science have enabled us to extend our knowledge dramatically. Indeed, since the Enlightenment science has increasingly expanded the frontiers of knowledge and this has led to the industrial and technological revolutions and the subsequent massive changes that have occurred in world civilizations ever since.

Wilson's second task is likewise reasonable, but far more difficult to achieve. He believes that there is a genuine need to unify knowledge. This he calls *consilience*, borrowing the term from the nineteenth-century English philosopher of science William Whewell. It means, literally, a "jumping together" of knowledge by the linking of facts and theories across disciplines in order to create a common groundwork of explanations.

Wilson properly points out the quandary that we face today. Scientists and scholars can make progress only by the most intense concentration in their specialized disciplines and fields of expertise. If they are to be recognized by their peers and to succeed in their professions, they must make original contributions to knowledge; but this usually means a narrowing of focus, as demanded by the division of labor. This does not permit them much time for dallying in other fields—they can always be accused of dilettantism; nor, regrettably, do they have much inclination to popularize their ideas or interpret them for scientists in other fields or for the general public. E. O. Wilson is a notable exception in this regard, for not only has he made original contributions to research in his own field of entomology (the study of insects), but he displays encyclopedic knowledge and consummate literary skills that have earned him two Pulitzer prizes and enable him to write for a wider public outside of his own specialty.

Wilson's important contributions to sociobiology two decades ago raised a howl of protests from environmentalists, who deplored his emphasis on the genetic conditions of behavior, and from some skeptics who thought that the theoretical constructs of sociobiology had not been empirically tested. Today the intellectual tide has shifted from environmentalism to genetic explanations, and more in Wilson's favor.

Consilience involves a good deal of philosophical reflection. Wilson correctly perceives that although specialization has been effective in extending the frontiers of knowledge, there has been an increasing fragmentation of knowledge so that authorities in the various domains of knowledge are often ignorant of what others have discovered; nor is anyone able to piece together this knowledge in any coherent way. Yet, if the scientific enterprise is to be fully understood and developed, we need to point out the complementarity of the separate disciplines and indeed the convergence of explanations of many of them. Regretfully, although most people welcome the scientific breakthroughs and technological achievements of the present day, their own cosmic outlook is more readily drawn from religion, the humanities, politics, or the arts, rather than the sciences. Scientific illiteracy is widespread, even among the educated classes, and especially among politicians and the leaders of industry. Colleges and universities no longer provide undergraduates with an integrated liberal-arts curriculum in which the sciences play an important role, but instead they offer up a smorgasbord of courses and programs from which students cherry pick in terms of their tastes and preferences.

The task of unifying the sciences has largely been abandoned by philosophers today. Although the logical positivists a half century ago (Carnap, Reichenbach, and others) attempted to unify knowledge, they did so on the basis of logical analysis alone, but, says Wilson, our ignorance at that time of how the brain worked limited their efforts. Ludwig von Bertalanffy also attempted to achieve a unity of the sciences, based on systems theory.

Wilson believes that we must attempt consilience anew, given the great progress in recent decades in many of the sciences, and he offers his own generalized account of what this should include. He readily concedes that this is metaphysical. Yet in his defense, his conceptual framework is not merely speculative, but is grounded in empirical generalizations and interpretations based on the sciences; though they clearly need further experimental verification.

Wilson argues that the natural sciences provide a basis for integrating our knowledge in a way that was not possible in the past, and that these explanations draw upon a reductionist model, which is essentially naturalistic and materialistic. We are now able to draw together a web of causal explanations proceeding from physics and chemistry to biology. Thus, quantum mechanics is the basis of atomic physics, and this is the foundation of chemistry, biochemistry, and molecular biology. These explanations proceed step by step; and explanations of higher levels of organization even on the cellular and organismic level depend upon more fundamental explanations on the micro level.

From the standpoint of the human species, Wilson maintains that the most important concept is that the brain is the basis of the mind and that every mental event has a physical grounding. In the past decade, discoveries have enabled us to integrate our knowledge of human behavior, especially the brain sciences (cognitive neuroscience), behavioral genetics, evolutionary biology, and environmental science. Of crucial significance is the role of evolutionary theory in interpreting knowledge: the human brain evolved by means of natural selection and is an instrument of survival. Scientific inquiry has attempted to transform the brain from its original instrumental survival function to one of understanding nature in its own terms. Our understanding is now enhanced, he believes, because principles of universal rational consilience are provided by the natural sciences.

What is apt to be Wilson's most controversial thesis, and is doubtless open to skeptical critiques, is his effort to integrate not only the natural sciences, but the social sciences and the humanities. This he attempts to do by integrating culture within the context of evolution. For the evolution of the human species, the unique factor that has emerged is gene-culture co-evolution; in addition to the genetic-biological determinants of behavior, there are cultural changes that modify the environment and the processes by which the human species evolved. Culture allows humans to rapidly adjust to changes in the environment, and these adaptations are transmitted to successive generations by custom. Wilson attempts to integrate levels of discovery with conceptual frameworks that include the natural sciences, genetics, biology, anthropology, sociology, economics, and the social sciences. He maintains that genes prescribe epigenetic rules, and these channel the acquisition of culture; culture in turn helps determine which genes survive and reproduce in breeding populations. Human nature for Wilson is not within the genes *per se*, "It is not the genes, which prescribe it, or culture, its ultimate product. Rather, human nature . . . is the epigenetic rules, the hereditary regularities of mental development that bias cultural evolution in one direction as opposed to another, and thus connect the genes to culture" (p. 164).

Wilson offers a schematic interpretation of how the humanities—the arts, ethics, and religion (he is a skeptic about the claims of religion)—could in principle come within the domain of natural science explanations. This is the most speculative aspect of his thesis, and we have a long way to go before this is achieved. The influential American philosopher Richard Rorty denies that the unification of knowledge is desirable, but he seems in turn to reduce science to literary metaphor and to have abandoned rigorous methods of scientific inquiry entirely.

Does Wilson's conceptual schema succeed in tying together knowledge on many levels of organization, or are we not still at the level of pluralistic principles of explanations from several sciences—far short of the reductionist goal, yet on the path to integration? We surely should still attempt to work out a comprehensive reductionist model, even if we have not fulfilled the reductionist ideal fully. Clearly, reductionism has been a valuable research tool, perhaps the most valuable heretofore discovered; we should no doubt continue to use it as a methodological device wherever we can. I think that in principle all phenomena are reducible to their physical-chemical constituents. Yet at the same time it is important that we continue to pursue holistic explanations for more complex systems of organizations, particularly in psychology and the social sciences where we need to deal with phenomena encountered in the contexts under analysis. I have elsewhere labeled this approach "coduction." Here we co-duce explanations, drawing on many sciences. For example, it is difficult, without an overall comprehensive set of explanations, to know how an economist can deal with market phenomena by knowing brain chemistry alone, or a sociologist can interpret systems of social value by reducing them to the laws of physics and biology—not that we should not continually try wherever possible for reductionistic explanations; they will no doubt be discovered and be useful. But these may not provide the whole picture of who and what we are or how we behave. Thus we have a more complex account drawn from many levels of inquiry, and this is still a thoroughly naturalistic account.

Given these caveats, we should welcome Wilson's valiant efforts in *Consilience*—for he provides a positive view of the possible reaches of scientific inquiry. There is so much in this insightful book that I have not touched upon. Many of his claims need further critical scrutiny. Some skeptics will no doubt reject many of Wilson's speculations as unwarranted. In my view we should not ignore the efforts of scientists such as Wilson to seek comprehensive explanations of the universe. Many of the obstacles placed in the path of scientific inquiry in the past have been overcome. Almost at the same time that critics have denied the possibility of knowing this, that, or something else, new sciences have been hatched dealing with these areas.

We should encourage generalists such as Wilson who have the demonstrated virtuosity to take one step beyond the confines of specialization, and offer some coherent picture of what the sciences tell us about the universe. I agree with Wilson that we should try to unify our knowledge. Scientific consilience has advantages over literary, æsthetic, philosophical, or theological attempts at unity. At least these theories can be tested, for they presuppose a common intersubjective world.

Wilson's final task in *Consilience* is to apply scientific knowledge to normative questions. He concludes his book with an ethical platform and plea. He is concerned about environmental degradation, the loss of biodiversity, and the long-range consequences of continued ecological damage to the human species and other forms of life on the planet. He maintains that scientific understanding of how we evolve and an awareness of possible future dangers is essential if we are to avoid irreparable damage to our common global habitat. At a time when many scientists are reluctant to engage in any kind of ethical recommendations, Wilson argues effectively, I think, that we ought to use the scientific knowledge that we have in order to develop wiser social policies. Wilson believes that we should not consider science to be entirely value-neutral, but that we should draw upon the best knowledge available in order to formulate our judgments. (I have suggested the term *eupraxsophy* to mean that we can and should use scientific wisdom to develop good practice.) We should not leave such issues to the wielders of economic, political, or clerical power alone, but should attempt to bridge the divide between scientific disciplines, and to provide some normative help in resolving important ethical and social problems. Thus, some generalized coherent view of what we know about nature and the place of the human species within it is not only intellectually interesting, but it has direct relevance to our ethical values.

10

Should Skeptical Inquiry
be Applied to Religion?

Scientific Inquiry

The relationship between science and religion has engendered heated controversy. This debate has its roots in the historic conflict between the advocates of reason and the disciples of faith. On the current scene, there is a vocal hallelujah chorus singing praises to the mutual harmony and support of these two realms, or "magisteria."[1] I have serious misgivings about this alleged rapprochement, but I wish to focus on only one aspect of the controversy, and ask: To what extent should we apply skeptical inquiry to religious claims?

The central questions that have been raised concern the range of skeptical inquiry. Are there areas such as religion in which science cannot enter? In particular, Should the skeptical movement extend its inquiry to religious questions? Some influential skeptics think we should not. In my view, skeptical inquirers definitely need to investigate religious claims.[2]

This is an abridged version of an article that first appeared in the *Skeptical Inquirer* 23, no. 4 (July/August 1999), pp. 24–28.

Science has always had its critics, who have insisted that one or another area of human interest is immune to scientific inquiry. At one time it was proclaimed that astronomers could never know the outermost reaches of the universe (August Comte), the innermost nature of the atom (John Locke), or human consciousness (Henri Bergson). Today science has made advances in all of these areas. Critics have also insisted that we could not apply science to one or another aspect of human experience—political, economic, social, or ethical behavior, the arts, human psychology, sexuality, or feeling. I do not think that we should set *a priori* limits antecedent to inquiry, we should not seek to denigrate the ability of scientific investigators to explain behavior or to extend the frontiers of research into new areas.

Can There Be a Science of Religion?

Some have argued that religious phenomena—matters of faith—are entirely beyond the ken of science; but this surely is false because the scientific investigation of religion has already made great strides and there is a vast literature now available. We may talk about religion in at least two senses: First, religion refers to a form of *human behavior* that can be investigated. Second, it is used to refer to the *transcendental*, i.e., to that which transcends human experience or reason.

Let us turn to the first area. Religious behavior has been investigated by a wide range of disciplines: Anthropologists deal with the comparative study of primitive religions, examining prayer, ritual, the rites of passage, etc. Sociologists have investigated the institutional aspects of religious behavior, such as the role of the priestly class in society. Ever since William James, psychologists of religion have studied the varieties of religious experience, such as mysticism, ecstasy, talking in tongues, exorcism, etc. Similarly, biologists have postulated a role for religious beliefs and practices in the evolutionary process and their possible adaptive/survival value. They have asked, Does religiosity have a genetic or environmental basis? Others have focused on the neurological correlates of religious piety, still others have attempted to test the efficacy of prayer.

One can deal with religion in contemporary or historical contexts. A great deal of attention has been devoted to the historical analysis of religious claims, especially since the great classical religions are based on ancient documents (the Old and New Testaments and the Koran), as are some of the newer religions (such as the nineteenth-century Book of Mormon). These texts allege that certain miraculous and revelatory events have occurred in the past and these warrant religious belief today; and it is often claimed that belief in them is based upon faith.

I would respond that scientific methodology has been used in historical investigations to examine these alleged events. Archaeologists seek independent corroborating evidence; they examine written or oral accounts that were contemporaneous with the events (for example, by comparing the Dead Sea Scrolls with the New Testament). The fields of "biblical criticism" or "koranic criticism" have attempted to use the best scholarly techniques, historical evidence, and textual and linguistic analysis, to ascertain the historical accuracy of these claims.

Paranormal claims are similar to religious claims—both purport to be exceptions to natural laws. Skeptics have asked: Did D. D. Home float out of a window and levitate over a street in London in the late nineteenth century? Did the Fox sisters and Eusapia Palladino possess the ability to communicate with the dead? And they have sought to provide naturalistic interpretations for reports of bizarre events. No doubt it is easier to examine contemporaneous claims where the record is still available rather than ancient ones where the record may be fragmentary. Yet in principle at least, the religious investigator is similar to the paranormal investigator, attempting to ascertain the accuracy of the historical record. We use similar methods of inquiry to examine prosaic historical questions, such as: Did Washington cross the Delaware? Did Thomas Jefferson sire the children of Sally Hemings? The same goes for religious claims: Did the Red Sea part before the fleeing Hebrews? Was there a Great Flood and a Noah's Ark? I don't see how or why we should declare that these historical religious claims are immune to scientific investigation.

Thus I maintain that insofar as religion refers to a form of human behavior, whether in the past or the present, we can, if we can uncover corroborating data or historical records, attempt to authenticate the historical claims and ask whether there were paranormal, occult, or transcendental causes, or whether naturalistic explanations are available. David Hume's arguments against miracles indicate all the reasons why we should be skeptical of ancient claims— because they lack adequate documentation, because the eyewitnesses were biased, and so on. And this should apply, in my view, to reports of revelation as well as miracles. Extraordinary claims that violate naturalistic causal regularities should require strong evidence. I don't see how anyone can protest that his beliefs ought to be immune to the standards of objective historical investigation, simply by claiming that they are held on the basis of faith. The fact that believers may seek to shield their belief by proclaiming that they have faith that it is true does not make it any more true. The strength of a hypothesis or belief should be a function of the empirical evidence extant brought to support it and if the evidence is weak or spotty, then the faith claim should likewise be so regarded.

Religious belief systems are deeply ingrained in human history, culture, and social institutions that predate science, and thus it is often difficult, if not impossible, to insist upon using the standards of objective skeptical inquiry retrospectively. This is especially the case since to *believe* in a religion is more than a question of cognitive assent, for religion has its roots in ethnic or national identity; and to question the empirical or rational grounds for religious belief is to shake at the very foundations of the social order.

How to Deal with the Transcendental?

There is a second sense of religion that is nonbehavioral. Here the key question concerns the very existence of a "transcendental, supernatural, occult, or paranormal realm" over and beyond the natural world. The scientific naturalist argues that we should seek natural causes and explanations for paranormal and religious phenomena, that we should never abandon scientific methodology, and that we should endeavor to test all claims by reference to justifying evidence and reasons. We may ask, What is the truth value of theistic claims? In the great debate between scientific or philosophical skeptics and theists, agnostics/nontheists/atheists maintain that theists have not adequately justified their case and that their claims are unlikely or implausible. I will not here review the extensive classical argument or the kinds or evidence adduced.

I do wish, however, to focus on one point that has recently emerged in the literature. And this concerns a prior question raised by analytic philosophers about the meaning of "God language." Any scientific inquiry presupposes some clarity about the meaning of its basic terms. Is religious language to be taken literally, descriptively, or cognitively; and if so, are we prepared to assert that there is some "transcendental ground, cause, creator, or purpose" to the universe? Most linguistic skeptics have sought to deconstruct religious language and have had difficulty in determining precisely to what the terms "God" or "divinity" or "transcendental being" refer. Similarly for the vague, often incoherent, use of the term "spirituality," so popular today. They appear to be indefinable, even to theologians, and hence before we can say whether He, She, or It exists, we need to know precisely what is being asserted. Most God talk is nonfalsifiable, in that we would not know how to confirm or disconfirm any claim about His presence or existence. God talk is by definition difficult or impossible insofar as it transcends any possible experience or reason and lurks in a mysterious noumenal realm. There are surely many things that we do not know about the universe; but to describe the unknown as "divine" is to take a leap of faith beyond reasonable evidence.

Linguistic skeptics have held that if we are to make sense of religious language, we must recognize that it has other nondescriptive or noncognitive functions. It does not convey us truth about the world (thus competing with science or ordinary experience), but is evocative, expressive, or emotive in character, or is performatory and celebrative in a social context, or is moral in its imperative function, or it has poetic metaphorical meaning. Thus God talk should be construed primarily as a form of personal and social moral poetry. If this is the case, then religion does not give us knowledge or truth; instead it gives us mood and attitude.

I am not here talking about the historical truth of Jesus' alleged resurrection or Joseph Smith's encounter with the angel Moroni or Muhammad's communication with Gabriel—these are concrete historical claims and in principle at least are available to empirical and rational inquiry and have some experiential content (even though the evidence may be fragmentary or incomplete), but of "divinity" viewed outside of history as a transcendental being or spiritual reality. It is the latter that is incomprehensible almost by definition.

Thus religion should not compete with science about the description and explanation of natural processes in the universe. Science deals most effectively with these questions, not religion. To claim to believe in the theory of evolution, and yet insist the "human soul" is an exception to evolutionary principles because it is created by a deity, is to intrude an occult cause illegitimately. Similarly, to seek to transcend the "big bang" physical theory in science by postulating a creator is to leap beyond the verifiable evidence. To say that this is justified by faith is, in my judgment, unwarranted—the most sensible posture to adopt here is that of the agnostic.

In the last analysis, religion and science are different forms of human behavior and have different functions. We may analogically ask, What is the relationship between science and sports, or science and music? These are different forms of experience, and they play different roles in human behavior. Surely neither sports nor music compete in the range of truth claims. In this sense, religion should not be taken as true or false, but as evocative, expressive, uplifting, performatory, good or bad, beautiful or ugly, socially unifying or disruptive. Historically, the claims of religion were taken as true, but this was a prescientific posture drawing upon myth and metaphor, metaphysics and speculation, not testable claims. Thus "religious truth" cannot be appealed to in order to contest the verified findings of the sciences.

I should add that I do not believe that ethics need be based on religious faith either. To maintain that the proper or exclusive role of religion is within the realm of morality (or meaning) is, I think, likewise questionable, particularly when we examine the concrete ethical recommendations made about sexual morality, divorce, abortion, euthanasia, the role of women, capital punishment, etc. This is all the more so, given that religions often disagree violently about any number of moral principles. I believe that there are alternative humanistic and rational grounds for ethical judgment, based in part on scientific knowledge, a topic that I have written about extensively.

Skeptical Inquiry and Religion

The key question that I wish to address here is, Should skeptical inquirers question the regnant sacred cows of religion? There are both theoretical and prudential issues here at stake. I can find no theoretical reason why not, but there may be practical considerations. For one, it requires an extraordinary amount of courage today as in the past (even in America!) to critique religion. One can challenge paranormal hucksters, mediums, psychics, alternative therapists, astrologers, and past-life hypnotherapists with abandon, but to question the revered figures of orthodox religion is another matter, for this may still raise the serious public charge of blasphemy and heresy; and this can be dangerous to one's person and career—as Salman Rushdie's *fatwa* so graphically demonstrates.

History vividly illustrates the hesitancy of skeptics to apply their skepticism to religious questions. In ancient Rome, Sextus Empiricus, author of *Outlines of Pyrrhonism*, defended the suspension of belief in regard to metaphysical, philosophical, and ethical issues. He did not think that reliable knowledge about reality or ethical judgments was possible. He neither affirmed nor denied the existence of the Gods, but adopted a neutral stance. Since there was no reliable knowledge, Pyrrho urged that compliance with the customs and religion of his day was the most prudent course to follow. The great skeptic Hume bade his friend, Adam Smith, to publish his iconoclastic *Dialogues Concerning Natural Religion* after his death (in 1776), but Smith declined to do so, disappointing Hume. Hume's nephew David arranged for posthumous publication. The French author, Pierre Bayle (1647–1706), perhaps expressed the most thoroughgoing skepticism of his time. In his *Dictionnaire historique et critique*, Bayle presented a scathing indictment of the prevailing theories of his day, finding them full of contradictions. He was highly critical of religious absurdities. He maintained that atheists could be more moral than Christians, and that religion did not necessarily provide a basis for ethical conduct. Nonetheless, Bayle professed that he was a Christian and a Calvinist, and this was based upon pure faith, without any evidence to support it—this is known as fideism. Did Bayle genuinely hold these views, or was his fideism a ruse to protect his reputation and his fortune?

This form of fideism, I maintain, on theoretical grounds is illegitimate, even irrational. For if, as skeptical inquirers, we are justified in accepting only those beliefs that are based upon evidence and reason, and if there is no evidence either way or insufficient evidence, should we not suspend judgment, or are we justified in taking a leap of faith? If the latter posture of faith is chosen, one can ask, On what basis? If a person is entitled to choose to believe whatever he or she wishes, *solely* or *largely* because of personal feeling and taste, then "anything goes." But this anarchic epistemological principle can be used to distort honest inquiry. (The implication of this argument is that if we do *not* have a similar feeling, we are entitled *not to believe*.) One may ask, Can one generalize the epistemological rule, and if so, can it apply to paranormal claims? Is someone thus entitled to believe in UFO abductions, angels, or demons on the basis of feeling and fancy? The paranormal skeptic retort is that where there is evidence to decide the question, we are not justified in believing; though in a democracy we are not entitled to expect others to share our skepticism.

But as a matter of fact, most of those who believe in the traditional religions do not base it on pure fideism alone, but on reasons and evidence. Indeed, no less an authority than Pope John Paul II maintained the same in an recent encyclical entitled "Faith and Reason." In this, the Pope condemns both fideism and atheism. He attacks the naïve faith in "UFOs, astrology, and the New Age." He criticizes "exaggerated rationalism" and pragmatism on the one hand and postmodernism on the other; but he also condemns the exclusive reliance on faith. The Pope maintains that reason and scientific inquiry support rather than hinder faith in Christian revelation and Catholic doctrine. Skeptics might agree with the Pope's defense of reason and scientific inquiry, but question whether these do indeed support his own beliefs.

Thus, in my judgment, acquiescence by skeptics to the fideist's rationalization for his beliefs is profoundly mistaken. Similarly, in answer to those theists who maintain that there is adequate evidence and reasons for their belief, skeptical inquirers should not simply ignore their claims, saying that they are beyond scientific confirmation, but should examine them. Since the burden of proof is always upon the claimant, skeptical inquirers may question both the fideist and the partial-evidentialist in religion, if they do not believe that they have provided an adequate justified case.

Conclusion

The upshot of this controversy, in my judgment, is that scientific and skeptical inquirers should deal with religious claims. Not to do so is to flee from an important area of human behavior and interest and is irresponsible. Indeed, one reason why paranormal beliefs are so prominent today is because religious beliefs are not being critically examined in the marketplace of ideas.

But at the same time I disagree with those who counsel caution in applying scientific skepticism to the religious domain. In my view science should not be so narrowly construed that it only applies to experimental laboratory work; it should bring in the tools of logical analysis, historical research, and rational investigation. In this sense, I submit, religious claims are amenable to scientific examination and skeptical inquiry.

It is possible for a scientist to apply skeptical, scientific inquiry to his or her own specialty with considerable expertise; yet he or she may not be qualified to apply the same methods of rational inquiry to other fields, and indeed may harbor religious beliefs that lack evidential support. Although disbelief about religious claims is higher among scientists (an estimated 60 percent) than the general population (perhaps 10 percent), some scientists fail to rigorously examine their own religious beliefs. They may use rigorous standards of inquiry in their particular fields of expertise, yet throw caution to the wind when they leap into questions of religious faith.

One last issue: to claim that skepticism is committed only to "methodological naturalism" and not scientific naturalism (which sums up the evidence for the naturalistic world view and critiques the theistic/spiritualistic leap beyond) is, I think, profoundly mistaken. To adopt this neutral stance in the current cultural milieu is a cop-out; for questionable religious claims are proliferating daily and they are not adequately evaluated by skeptical scientists. In my view, we need more skeptical inquirers who possess the requisite expertise and are able to apply their investigative skills to religious claims. Such skeptical inquiry is sorely needed today. It could play a vital role in the debate between religion and science.

---

1. Stephen Jay Gould. "Non-Overlapping Magisteria," *Skeptical Inquirer* 23, no. 4 (July/August 1999), pp. 55–61. Excerpted from *Rock of Ages: Science and Religion in the Fullness of Life* (New York: Library of Contemporary Thought/Random House, 1999).

2. I do not believe, however, that CSICOP should, except tangentially, deal with religious issues. But my reasons are primarily pragmatic, not theoretical. It is simply a question of the division of labor. We lack the resources and expertise to focus on the entire range of scientific questions about religion: biblical archaeological, biblical and koranic criticism, linguistics, psychology, anthropology, sociology, the genetic or environmental roots of religion, etc. It would take us too far afield. We have focused on fringe science and specialized in the paranormal, and we have made important contributions here. Skeptical inquiry in principle should apply equally to economics, politics, ethics, and indeed to all fields of human interest. Surely we cannot possibly evaluate each and every claim to truth that arises. My reasons are thus practical.

11

Why Do People Believe or Disbelieve?

I wish in this chapter to focus on two basic questions: Why do people believe in religious doctrines, i.e., why do they accept the tenets of a religion and participate in its practices and rituals? Conversely, we may ask, Why do some people *dis*believe in the tenets of religion and/or reject its practices? Religion is one of the most pervasive and enduring characteristics of human culture. Predictions by scientists and rationalists at the end of the eighteenth and nineteenth centuries that religion would eventually disappear surely were premature because by the end of the twentieth century it remained as strong as ever.

Three dramatic religious events illustrate the perennial power of religious faith in human culture. The first is the huge annual assembly of Islamic pilgrims drawn to Mecca every year. Photographs of an estimated three million devotees who were in Mecca in recent pilgrimages show that they have come from all walks of life and from all classes. The second impressive annual event are the millions of Hindus in India who congregate at the Ganges River in accordance with ancient religious rituals. At a recent event, an estimated ten million people appeared at the Kumbha Mela festival in the small city of Hardiwar for prayer

This is a modified version of a paper presented at a New York Academy of Sciences conference on "Science and Religion," December 4–6, 1998, and published in *Free Inquiry* 19, no. 3 (Summer 1999), pp. 23–27.

and purification. And the third is the re-exhibition at a cathedral in Turin of the shroud that Jesus was allegedly wrapped in and buried. A huge throng of visitors have come from all over the world to view the Shroud of Turin.

Skeptical doubts can surely be raised about the claim that a pilgrimage to Mecca will guarantee Muslim believers entrance to heaven and/or that bathing in the Ganges River will bestow special spiritual benefits. These are sheer acts of faith drawing upon ancient traditions that scientific skeptics would maintain have little basis in empirical fact. There is no evidence that the performance of ritualistic acts of spiritual contrition, either by visiting the Kaaba in Mecca and encircling it three times, or by bathing in the water of the Ganges, will achieve a blessed state of Paradise for Muslims or Atman for Hindus. To point out to the devout disciples of these two ancient religions that the recommended rites are contradictory or have no basis in fact generally fall on deaf ears.

Similarly for the Shroud of Turin, which, according to the best available scientific evidence, was a forgery made in Lirey, France, in the fourteenth century.[1] Interestingly, it was condemned as such at that time by the bishop in the area, for it was used to deceive thousands of pilgrims seeking cures for their illnesses. Walter McCrone, the noted microscopist, has shown that the red color on the Shroud was not human blood, but red ochre and vermilion tempera paint. Joe Nickell has even demonstrated that it is possible to produce a similar image on cloth by a rubbing technique, using the vermilion and ochre pigments that were available at that time in France. Moreover, portions of the Shroud were carbon-14 dated by three independent laboratories, all of whom reported that it was not 1,900 years old, but probably fabricated approximately 700 years ago. These reports were published in the scientific literature and received widespread attention in the press; and skeptical scientists applauded the forensic evidence, which clearly stated that the image on the Shroud was not due to a miracle, but could be given a naturalistic causal explanation.

Yet, much to the surprise of skeptics, who thought that they had decisively refuted the proponents of the faith, the Shroud industry has returned with full force and vigor again and is proclaiming that skeptics were in error. Believers maintain that there were alleged flaws in the carbon-14 process—all rationalizations in the view of skeptics—and that the Shroud was the burial garment of Jesus Christ.

The Origins of Religions

Why do people believe in the above religious claims? Is it because they have not been exposed to criticisms? Most of the classical religious beliefs emerged in a prescientific era before the application of the methods of science. Unfortunately, the origins of the venerated ancient religions are often buried by the sands of historical time—though biblical critics have endeavored to reconstruct the foundations of these religions by using the best scholarly and scientific methods of inquiry. It is often difficult to engage in impartial scholarly or scientific inquiry into the origins of religious doctrines, particularly when those critically examining the foundations of the revered truths are often placed in jeopardy by their societies. Biblical criticism in the Western world has only relatively recently been freed from prohibiting censorship and/or the power of institutional sanctions brought to bear on freethinkers. Koranic criticism is virtually absent in Islamic lands, or if it is done it is only with great fear of retribution; for questioning the divine authority of Muhammad is considered by the Koran itself to be a form of blasphemy punishable by a *fatwa*.

The ancient religions of prophecies and revelations—Judaism, Christianity, and Islam—all claim that God intervened at one time in history, spoke to Moses and the prophets, resurrected Jesus, or communicated through Gabriel to Muhammad. Skeptics maintain that the key claims have never been adequately corroborated by reliable independent eyewitnesses. The so-called sacred books no doubt incorporate the best theological and metaphysical yearnings of ancient nomadic and agricultural societies, and they often express eloquent moral insights by the people of that time; yet they hardly can withstand the sustained critical examination by objective inquirers. The narratives of alleged supernatural intervention that appear in the Bible and the Koran were at first transmitted by oral traditions after the alleged facts occurred. They were written down by second- or third-hand sources, many years and even decades later. They most likely weave into their parables dramatic renditions bordering on fiction, and written by passionate propagandists for new faiths. These sacred books promise believers another world beyond this vale of tears. Their messages of salvation were attractive to countless generations of poor and struggling souls endeavoring to overcome the blows of existential reality. Believers ever since have accepted them as gospel truth; after centuries they became deeply ingrained in the entire fabric of society. Indeed, the great monotheistic religions were eventually intertwined with the dominant political, military, and economic institutions and were enforced by both priestly and secular authorities.

The religion of the ancient Jews, allegedly inspired by Moses and the Old Testament prophets, came to express the ideological yearnings of the Hebrew nation. Christianity was eventually declared to be the state religion by Constantine. Islam, from its inception, was reinforced by the sword of Muhammad. All these faiths, though shrouded in mystery, claim divine sanctification. There are certain common features which each of these religions manifests—historic claims of revelation by charismatic prophets promising eternal salvation; sacred books detailing their miraculous prophecies, prescribing rituals, prayers, and rites of passage; a priestly class which seeks to enforce religious law; great temples, cathedrals, and mosques where the Lord is present in the mysteries of the sacraments. These ancient religions have persisted in part because they have ostracized or condemned heretics and disbelievers. They have gained adherents over time by policies of selective breeding: marriage could only be by members of the same clan or tribe or church, disowning those who married outside of the faith. They sought to inculcate and transmit the tenets of the faith to the young, so as to ensure the continuity of the tradition. The entire artistic, moral, philosophical, economic, social, and legal structure of ancient societies were rooted in religious institutions.

Many liberal theists would accept the above critique of the historic religions by the "higher criticism," especially since the German theologian Rudolf Bultmann attempted to demythologize the New Testament. Yet they maintain that the alleged historical events are to be read symbolically or metaphorically and if they are accepted it is because they give meaning and purpose to life.

Interestingly, we now have data from recent religious sects that emerged in the nineteenth century and are not shrouded in historical mystery. And we are close enough to the events to lay bare the factors at work: the historical records of persuasion and conversion on the part of the founders of these new religions, and the willing acceptance of the faith by receptive believers. Thus we may examine the origins of Mormonism, Seventh-Day Adventism, Christian Science, or the Jehovah's Witness movement to discern if there are similar psycho-bio-sociological patterns at work.[2]

Closer still, twentieth-century skeptics have been able to witness first-hand the spinning out of New Age paranormal religions. A good illustration of this is the power of suggestion exercised by psychics and mediums, often through the use of deception or self-deception, and the receptiveness of so many believers, all too willing to accept claims of supernormal powers by abandoning rigorous standards of corroboration. These processes are even found among sophisticated scientists as well as ordinary folks, who are specialists in other fields, but perhaps not in the art of deception. An entire industry claiming to prove another reality transcending this world is flourishing: belief in reincarnation is based on "past-life regressions," and near-death experiences are often appealed to in order to reinforce belief in the separable existence and immortality of the human soul.

The spawning of the space-age religions in the latter half of the twentieth century is especially instructive for the psychobiology of belief. Scientology was invented by Ron Hubbard, who began as a writer of science fiction but then went on to consciously create a new religion. Dianetics and all that it proposes are questionable on empirical grounds; yet countless thousands of people, including famous celebrities, have been persuaded to accept its tenets. UFO mythology is especially fascinating. For Space Age prophets have emerged, rivaling the classical religious prophets, and likewise claiming deliverance to another realm. This is the age of the great human adventure of space exploration, and so people are conscious of other planets in our solar system and other galaxies far beyond. It is also a time in which astronomy has made great strides and telescopes have enabled humans to extend the reach of observations. It is also an age in which science fiction has soared far beyond verifiable hypotheses and in which the speculative creative imagination is unbounded. Beginning with the premise that it is possible, indeed probable, that life, even intelligent life, exists elsewhere in the universe, there is a leap of faith to the conviction that the planet earth has been visited by extraterrestrial aliens, that some earthlings have been abducted, and that intergalactic biogenetic breeding has occurred. Thus the possible has been converted into the actual and fiction transposed into reality. Extraterrestrial visitations from on high have the similar contours of alleged early visitations by divine beings and their revelations on Mount Sinai or the caves of Hijra outside of Mecca, or the road to Damascus, or by the Olympian gods of Greek mythology.

Thus the question is raised anew, How do we explain the willingness of so many people—no doubt a majority of humankind—to outstrip the evidence and to weave out fantasies in which their deepest psychological longings are expressed and their national mythologies fulfilled? How explain the willingness to believe even the most bizarre tales?

I have had close contact over the years with a wide range of latter-day religious gurus and mystics—from Reverend Moon to Ernest Angley and Peter Popoff—and paranormal psychics and seers—from Uri Geller to Jeane Dixon and Ramtha. Skeptics have been challenged to account for the apparent extraordinary feats of their proponents. After detailed investigation their weird claims have been debunked; yet in spite of this otherwise sensible people have persisted in beliefs that are patently false. Indeed, there seems to be a bizarre kind of logic at work: belief systems for which there is entirely scanty evidence or no evidence, or indeed abundant evidence to the contrary are fervently accepted; indeed, people will devote their entire lives to a groundless creed. This has been heralded in the past as *faith* in things unseen or things hoped for. The will to believe in spite of negative evidence has been acclaimed as morally praiseworthy. David Hume thought it a "miracle" that people who believe in miracles are willing to subvert all of the evidence of the senses and the processes of rationality in order to accept their beliefs.

Two Possible Explanations

There are *at least* two possible explanations that I wish to focus on. (There are no doubt others, such as the need for identity, the quest for community, the role of indoctrination, the power of tradition, ethnicity, etc.) In answer to the question, "Why do people believe?," the first explanation is that believers have not been exposed to the factual critiques of their faith. These critiques apply to the cognitive basis of their belief. There are alternative naturalistic explanations of the alleged phenomena, cognitivists maintain, and if criticisms of the claims were made available to them, they would abandon their irrational beliefs. This is no doubt true of some people, who are committed to inquiry, but not of all, for processes of rationalization intervene to rescue the faith.

Accordingly, a second explanation for this is that noncognitive tendencies and impulses are at work, tempting believers to accept the "unbelievable." This disposition to believe in spite of insufficient or contrary evidence has deep roots in our biological and social nature.

In the first instance, cognition performs a powerful role in human life, liberating us from false ideas. In the form of common sense, it is essential, at least up to a point, if we are to live and function in the real world. Ordinary men and women constantly appeal to practical reason to refute unwarranted beliefs. They are forced to maintain some cognitive touch with reality if they are to survive in the natural and social environment. Human beings are capable of some rational thought, and this is the most effective capacity that they have for coping with obstacles that are encountered. Critical thinking is the pre-eminent instrument of human action; it is the most effective means that we have to fulfill our purposes and solve the problems of living. Cognition is the most powerful method for making sense of the world in which we live. From it philosophy and science have emerged, contributing to our understanding of nature and ourselves.

We all know that we need to use practical reason to deal with empirical questions, such as: "Is it raining outside?" Or "How do I cope with my toothache?" And we also apply such methods within the sciences, to deal with issues such as the following: "The dinosaurs were most likely extinguished by an asteroid impact some sixty-five million years ago." Or, "We are unable to cure people by therapeutic touch." Each of these beliefs may be tested by the experimental evidence or by theories accepted as probable or improbable on the basis of these considerations. In addition, an open-minded inquirer may be led to accept or reject any number of propositions, which he or she previously asserted, such as, "There is no evidence that a great flood engulfed the entire globe as related in the Bible."

There is a class of *overbeliefs*, however, for which no amount of evidence seems to suffice, at least for some people. These generally may be classified as "transcendental beliefs." It is here that faith or the will to believe intervenes. By the "transcendental," I mean that which is over and beyond normal observations or rational coherence, and is enhanced by mystery and magic. This surely is what the great mystics have referred to as the "ineffable" depths of Being. Scientific inquiry is naturalistic; that is, it attempts to uncover the natural causes at work. Granted that these are often hidden causes, unseen by unaided observation, such as microbes or atoms; yet such causes can be confirmed by some measure of verification; they fit into a conceptual framework; and their explanatory value can be corroborated by a community of independent inquirers. Transcendental explanations are, by definition, nonnatural; they cannot be confirmed experimentally; they cannot be corroborated objectively.

We may ask, "Why do many people accept unverified occult explanations when they are clothed in religious or paranormal guise?" The answer, I think, in part at least, *is because such accounts arouse awe and entice the passionate imagination.* I have in my earlier writings labeled this "the transcendental temptation,"[3] the temptation to believe in things unseen, because they satisfy needs and desires. The transcendental temptation has various dimensions. It was resorted to by primitive men and women, unable to cope with the intractable in nature, unmitigated disasters, unbearable pain or sorrow. It is drawn upon by humans in order to assuage the dread of death—by postulating another dimension to existence, the hope for an afterlife in which the evils and injustices of this world are overcome. The lure of the transcendental appeals to the frail and forlorn. There may not be any evidence for it; but powerful emotive and intellectual desire to submit to it can provide a source of comfort and consolation. To believe that we will meet in another life those whom we have loved in this life can be immensely satisfying, or at least it can provide some saving grace. It may enable a person to get through the grievous losses that he or she suffers in this life. If I can't be with those I cherish today, I can at least do so in my dreams and fantasies, and if I submit to and propitiate the unseen powers that govern the universe this will miraculously right the wrongs that I have endured in this vale of tears. Thus the lure of the transcendental is tempting because it enables human beings to survive the often cruel trials and tribulations that are our constant companion in this life, and it enables us to endure in anticipation of the next. It is the mystery and magic of religion, its incantations and rituals, that fan the passions of overbelief, and nourish illusion and unreality. There is a real and dangerous world out there that primitive and modern humans need to cope with—wild animals and marauding tribes, droughts and famine, lightning and forest fires, calamities and deprivation, accidents and contingencies. Surely, there is pleasure and satisfaction, achievement and realization in life, but also tragedy and failure, defeat and bitterness. Our world is a complex tapestry of joy and suffering. The transcendental temptation thus can provide a powerful palliative enabling humans to cope with the unbearable, overcome mortality and finitude; and it does so by creating fanciful systems of religious overbelief in which priests and prophets propitiate the unseen sources of power and thus shield us from the vicissitudes of fortune. Humans tend to corrupt their visions of reality, according to John Schumaker, in order to survive in a world that they cannot fully comprehend.[4]

It is only in recent human history that the species has gradually been able to overcome mythological explanations. Philosophy and metaphysics emerged, attempting to account for the world of change and flux in terms of rational explanations; modern science succeeded where pure speculation failed, by using powerful cognitive methods of experimental verification and mathematical inference. What had been shrouded in mystery was now explicable in terms of natural causes. Diseases did not have satanic origins, but natural explanations and cures. The weather could be interpreted, not as a product of divine wrath or favor, but in meteorological terms. Nature could be accounted for by locating the natural causes of phenomena. Astrology's heavenly omens and signs were replaced by the regularities discernible by physics and astronomy. Science abandons occult for material causes. It is the foe of magical thinking, and it is able to proceed by refusing to submit to transcendental deception, at least in dealing with the empirical world. Thus there has been a continuous retreat of magical thinking under the onslaught of cognitive inquiry. The same methods of inquiry used so successfully in the natural sciences were extended to biology and the social sciences. Science thus continues to make progress by using rigorous methods of naturalistic inquiry.

Yet there still remained a residue of unanswered questions, and it is here in the swamp of the unknowable that the transcendental temptation festers. This beguiling temptation reaches beyond the natural world by sheer force of habit and passion, and it resists all efforts to contain it. Rather than suspend judgments about those questions for which no there is evidence either way, it leaps in to fill the void and comfort the aching soul. It is the most frequent salve used to calm existential fear and trembling. Why is this so? Because I think that the *temptation* has its roots in a *tendency*, and this in a *disposition*. In other words, there is most likely within the human species a *genetic* component, which is stronger than temptation and weaker than instinct. The hypothesis that I wish to offer is that the belief in the efficacy of prayer and the submission to divine power persists because it has had some survival value in the infancy of the race; powerful psycho-socio-biological factors are thus at work, predisposing humans to submit to the temptation.

The cognitive explanation for its persistence is that there is cognitive dissonance or misinformation that is the root cause for the fixation on the transcendental and that this can be overcome by rational inquiry. Socrates thought that faith persisted only because of ignorance, and that knowledge would disabuse us of religious myths. This surely continues to play a powerful role in regard to the content of our beliefs. Yet I submit that there is another factor present, which explains the persistence of religiosity, and this is an evolutionary explanation; that is, belief in the transcendental had adaptive value, and those tribes or clans which believed in unseen myths and forces to whom they propitiated by ritual and prayer had a tendency to survive and to pass on this genetic predisposition to their offspring. Thus religiosity is a "heritable" factor within the naked human ape.[5]

What are some of the data in support of a transcendental predisposition? There are the University of Minnesota studies of identical twins,[6] which showed that a significant number of infants who were separated at birth and reared apart under different environmental conditions nonetheless exhibited similar tastes and preferences, and in this case exhibited a tendency to be religious. This predisposition is not necessarily deterministic in a strict sense, and it is absent in a number of cases. The heritable factor is estimated to be fifty percent. E. O. Wilson also maintains that there is some biological basis for religiosity; though one cannot locate this in a specific gene, there are a multiplicity of genetic factors and epigenetic rules.[7] He argues that theological overbeliefs offer consolation in the face of adversity, and that these religious overbeliefs— whether true or false—provide a functional means of adaptation. Those tribes or clans which possessed a safety net of such beliefs-practices may have been better able to cope with the fear of death, and they were also able to pass along to future generations the tendency to be religious. This proclivity may have had some survival value and thus it was transmitted to future generations. E. O. Wilson claims that "there is a hereditary selective advantage to members in a powerful group united by devout belief and purpose.... Much if not all religious behavior could have arisen from evolution by natural selection."[8]

There is a growing body of scientific research which supports this socio-biological explanation: this includes two components: (a) *psycho-biological*, which has some genetic basis, and (b) *sociological*, which has roots in cultural memes and habits. This would involve a coeval gene-meme hypothesis. Evolution is a function of both our *genes* on the one hand and *memes* transmitted by culture and inculcated in the young on the other. Thus, both hereditary and environmental factors have an influence on the behavior of individuals. Though there may be a predisposition toward belief in the transcendental, *how* it is expressed and the content of the beliefs depends on the culture.

Why Do People Disbelieve?

If we are to answer the question, Why do people believe?, we need also to ask, Why do some humans *dis*believe?—for there is a minority of people who remain unbelievers, agnostics, or atheists.[9] There are number of important research projects that I think should be undertaken. To ascertain if there is a genetic tendency—or lack of it—we should study the family trees of both believers and unbelievers. Much the same as we can trace the physical characteristics, such as eye or hair color, short or tall stature, and even genetic diseases in some family stocks, so we should be able to trace the religiosity factor, especially in twins and/or siblings who are reared apart. If we can measure musical talent (MQ) or intelligence (IQ), then perhaps we can also measure the religious quotient (RQ). Similarly, we need to trace the family trees of unbelievers and ask, Is the genetic factor absent and if so to what extent and why?

I have met a great number of unbelievers over the years who tell me that they have been atheists for as long as they could remember, that they never could accept the dominant religious creed, even though many were indoctrinated into it from the earliest. Clearly, we need to go beyond anecdotal autobiographical accounts to systematic studies of how and why people become disbelievers. Many atheists, on the other hand, have related that their unbelief was a result of a slow cognitive process of critical reflection.

Bruce Hunsberger and Bob Altemeyer, in an important study,[10] have attempted to outline the processes of conversion and deconversion in students that they studied in universities in Canada. Edward Babinsky[11] has published autobiographical accounts of why people abandoned their religiosity. We need to study the processes of deconversion for possible genetic explanations: Why do people who were religiously indoctrinated reject their beliefs, how rapidly did they do so, and for what reasons or causes? Conversely, what processes are involved in moving from a state of unbelief to religious conviction? No doubt there are many causal factors at work; we need to sort them out. Hunsberger and Altemeyer have suggested in their study of students that the process of deconversion was predominantly a slow, cognitive process; and that of conversion a rather rapid emotional transformation.

A number of important sociological studies also need to be undertaken. We need to examine the socio-cultural contexts in which religious ideas appear and disappear. We have an excellent data pool today in Russia and Eastern Europe where atheism was the official doctrine of the state. Here enormous efforts were expended for 50 to 75 years to pursue political policies of indoctrination and propaganda, designed to discourage religious belief and encourage atheism. We may ask, What has happened in these countries since the collapse of communism? Is the past political-social influence of atheism enduring, leaving a permanent residue, or is it dissipating?

Similarly, many Western European countries have seen a rather rapid decline in traditional religion in the post-World War II period, especially under the influence of liberalism and humanism. For example, in the Netherlands before the war approximately half of the population identified with Roman Catholicism and half with Protestantism, with a small percentage of Jews and other minorities. This has changed since World War II where there is now a higher percentage of humanists then either Protestants or Catholics. Similar processes have been observed in Norway, England, France, and elsewhere. Why has this happened? Are the polls reliable?

Curiously, only six to eight percent of the American population may be classified as unbelievers.[12] Can we give an account of why this is so and why American society seems to be anomalous, at least in comparison with Western Europe? Interestingly, some 60 percent of American scientists, according to a recent poll, are classified as unbelievers; and 93 percent of so-called elite scientists. Why does this happen? Are there cognitive factors primarily at work? Or are disbelievers anomalous—lacking the genetic disposition. On the contrary, do they represent an advanced form of the evolution of the species?[13]

A Pessimistic Diagnosis

Sociologists Roger Finke and Rodney Stark present some provocative demographic evidence about the growth of churches and sects in the United States that are of special interest to our question.[14] Marshalling an impressive array of census statistics, they argue that, contrary to popular misconception, religiosity was fairly weak in Colonial America. About 17 percent of the colonists belonged to churches. If this proposition is true, then the oft-repeated claim that our forefathers were deeply religious believers is simply untrue. Moreover, the claim that moral purity accompanied religious piety at the founding of this nation is a myth. Nor were so-called traditional family values in dominance. For example, the authors cite data that indicate that one in three births from 1761 1800 occurred within less than nine months of marriage, despite harsh laws against fornication. They also say that the taverns in Boston were more jammed on Saturday night than the churches were on Sunday morning. Moreover, they maintain that, although solid farmers and merchants came to the new world, America was also the dumping ground for people convicted of capital crimes and felonies by English and Irish courts; many "hardened criminals, thieves, blackmailers, pimps, rapists, embezzlers, and thugs" immigrated here. The wild west especially had a surplus of males, many seeking their fortune by any means.

Finke and Stark cite considerable census data to show that there has been a steady growth in church adherence from 1776 until the present and not a decline under the influence of modernist tendencies. Church membership grew, they say, to 34 percent in 1850, 45 percent in 1890, 59 percent in 1952, and 62 percent in 1980 (based largely on a Gallup poll). So we are becoming *more*, not less, religious.

Of special significance is the fact that the so-called mainline churches under the influence of liberalism have steadily lost ground, but fervent fundamentalist and evangelical sects have grown stronger. The authors show this in two historical periods.

In 1776, the dominant Protestant denominations were Congregationalists, Episcopalians, and Presbyterians. By 1850, they each lost heavily in their percentages of the population. Gaining ascendancy were the Methodists, at that time "fire in the belly" evangelicals and Southern Baptists. Roman Catholics continued to gain ground from 1850 on, but this was due at first to heavy ethnic immigration to America from Catholic countries. The Roman Catholic church thus enjoyed a period of steady growth in the late nineteenth and early twentieth centuries.

Since the 1940s the mainline churches continued their decline, including the Lutherans and Methodists, who, according to Finke and Stark, have become far "more reasonable and less fervent" in their religiosity. Indeed, these Protestant bodies have lost anywhere from 40 percent to 70 percent of their memberships. Since Vatican II in the early 1960s, the Roman Catholic church has also suffered massive losses in adherents and membership. Church members have continued to increase, but growth has centered on evangelical and fundamentalist bodies such as the Baptists, Assemblies of God, Church of the Nazarene, Church of God, Seventh-Day Adventists, and the Mormons.

The interesting question for secularists is: Why, at the same time that liberal denominations decline, do conservative evangelical denominations grow? The authors provide a hypothesis that *"religious organizations are always stronger to the degree that they impose significant costs in terms of sacrifices and even stigma upon their members."* They distinguish between *churches* and *sects*. Churches have accommodated to the social context. Sects, on the contrary, are "in a relatively high state of tension with their environment." Once a sect is transformed into a church it becomes more "reasonable" and "respectable," and it may even take biblical criticism and scientific scholarship seriously. But this process of humanization and secularism leads to a decline in membership. It does not lead "to irreligion," they maintain, but to a revival of extremists cults and sects, which are more "otherworldly." The more a religious organization demands sacrifice and commitment from its members, the more likely it is to grow. This involves deep participation and involvement within the congregation of believers. It also involves some social stigma and social deviance.

The secularization of religion, they say, finds its fullest expression in the seminaries, which focus on critical scholarship rather than evangelicalism, and this leads to a weakening faith. It is no secret that the great battle in Baptist and Mormon seminaries and universities today is over the question of academic freedom and scholarship. The fundamentalist churches oppose such liberal tendencies, and it is these churches that are growing in members. As recently as 1990, almost 66 percent of Southern Baptists were in agreement with the view that the Bible is the actual word of God and is to be taken literally, word for word, not metaphorically or symbolically.

The pessimistic conclusions of this study are disturbing to secular humanists. Are the fundamentalist and evangelical churches simply fringe phenomena that will in time decline, under the influence of secularism, modernism, and scientific education? According to Finke and Stark, either this will not happen, or, if it ever does, other extremist sects will emerge to take their place such as the Branch Davidians and radical Muslim fundamentalists. Given this pessimistic approach, can rationalists and humanists develop alternative eupraxsophies and lifestyles independent of religion? Do secular humanists have the commitment, and are they willing to make the sacrifice for the cause of freethought and humanism? If they are not, then, if this study means anything, will they decline in influence and be overwhelmed by new cults of unreason in the future?

A key factor in the growth of religion or atheism undoubtedly is a function of the socio-cultural influences that prevail. Historically, the orthodox religions have sought to punish heresy or blasphemy as high crimes. Infidels have often been excommunicated or burned at the stake. It is only in recent times that democratic societies have recognized, let alone permitted or encouraged religious dissenters to flourish.[15] One might ask, If the condition of tolerance, indeed encouragement, were to prevail, to what extent would religious beliefs wane or be altered? How can this be developed? What are the environmental conditions by which atheism can be induced? What kind of educational curricula would most likely stimulate unbelief?

Can We Develop Moral Substitutes?

A key issue that can be raised concerns the difference between the *content* of the core beliefs and practices of a religion and the *function* of the beliefs and practices. The content may change over time, and there may be an erosion of traditional beliefs and their modification due to cognitive criticisms; but alternative creeds-practices may emerge, satisfying similar psycho-biological-sociological needs and functions. In this regard, I reiterate, we are not dealing with the *kind* of religion that persists or the status of its *truth claims*—which may be irrelevant for many believers—but with the *power* of religious symbols and institutions to provide structure and order, and to give purpose in an otherwise meaningless and perhaps terrifying universe.

If science confirms the hypothesis that there *are* deep socio-biological forces responsible, at least in part, for religiosity in the species, then we need to ask, What can we do about it, if anything? Cognitivists will say that we still should constantly strive to engage in criticism of outrageous doctrines. At the very least this will help to restrain and temper religious fanaticism, protect the rights of unbelievers, and perhaps develop an ethic of tolerance. If religiosity will most likely be with us in one form or another in the foreseeable future, can we develop secular and naturalistic substitutes or moral equivalents for the passionate longing for meaning? Can we serve up sufficient balm to soothe existential *weltschmerz*? Can we develop new symbols to inspire meaning and hope? Can we engender the courage to be and to become? In other words, can naturalistic humanism offer a message as potent as theistic mythology? These are the kinds of questions that we hope science will help us to solve. But they are predicated on our understanding how and why people believe or disbelieve in a religion.

---

1. The Shroud of Turin phenomenon is especially intriguing. I have been intimately involved for over two decades in examining the claims of those who maintain that the Shroud is the authentic burial shroud of Jesus as he lay in his tomb; and I have worked closely with Dr. Joe Nickell and others in establishing a subcommittee of scientists and skeptics to carefully analyze the facts of the case. Moreover, there is a huge Shroud of Turin industry, with organizations, publications, bestselling books, and conferences all devoted to propagating the miraculous character of the Shroud. The fact that a three-dimensional scorched image of a bearded person appears on it, it is said, cannot be explained by any known natural means. Of the 500 or more books published on the Shroud only two or three can be called skeptical of its supernatural origin. See Joe Nickell, *Inquest on the Shroud of Turin*, rev. ed. (Amherst, N.Y.: Prometheus Books, 1998); Walter McCrone, *Judgement Day for the Shroud of Turin* (Amherst, N.Y.: Prometheus Books, 1999).

2. In many new religions the historical records are abundant. In all of these religions, critics have pointed out the role of deception or self-deception, such as Joseph Smith's writing of the Book of Mormon and his accounts of the golden plates delivered by the angel Moroni, which were allegedly lost by Smith. Similarly for the claims of plagiarism made against Mary Ellen White, founder of the Seventh-Day Adventist Church, or the questionable claims of miraculous health cures by Mary Baker Eddy and other Christian Scientist practitioners. Invariably, it is difficult to certify their authenticity once the claims to divine revelation are examined by careful historical investigators.

3. Paul Kurtz, *The Transcendental Temptation: A Critique of Religion and the Paranormal* (Amherst, N.Y.: Prometheus Books, 1986).

4. John F. Schumaker, *The Corruption of Reality: A Unified Theory of Religion, Hypnosis and Psychopathology* (Amherst, N.Y.: Prometheus Books, 1995.)

5. If it is the case that there is a genetic predisposition for religiosity, then we need an operational criterion of it. I would define (theistic) "religiosity" behavioristically: "the expression of piety, the veneration of the mysterious beyond ordinary experience, the cherishing of overbeliefs about the transcendental, symbolic acts of submission to a divine figure(s) in expectation of receiving salvation, the engaging in propitiatory prayer and ritual."

6. N. G. Waller, B. A. Kojetin, Thomas J. Bouchard, Jr., David T. Lykken, Matthew McGue, and Auke Tellegen. "Genetics and Environmental Influences on Religious Interests, Attitudes, and Values: A Study of Twins Reared Apart and Together," *Psychological Science* (1990), pp. 138–142; Thomas J. Bouchard, Jr., David T. Lykken, Matthew McGue, Nancy L. Segal, Auke Tellegen, "Sources of Human Psychological Differences: The Minnesota Study of Twins Reared Apart," *Science* 250, no. 4978 (October 12, 1990), pp. 223–228.

7. E. O. Wilson, *Consilience: The Unity of Knowledge* (New York: Alfred A. Knopf, 1998). See also John C. Avise, *The Genetic Gods: Evolution and Belief in Human Affairs* (Cambridge, Mass.: Harvard University Press, 1998).

8. E. O. Wilson, *Consilience*, p. 258.

9. The readers of *Free Inquiry* and the *Skeptical Inquirer* magazines provide a large pool of unbelievers, a good source for research. A poll of *Free Inquiry* readers indicate 91 percent are either atheists, agnostics, or secular humanists, and of *Skeptical Inquirer*, 77 percent are atheists, agnostics, or secular humanists.

10. Bob Altemeyer and Bruce Hunsberger, *Amazing Conversions: Why Some Turn to Faith and Others Abandon Religion* (Amherst, N.Y.: Prometheus Books, 1997).

11. Edward T. Babinsky, *Leaving the Fold: Testimonies of Former Fundamentalists* (Amherst, N.Y.: Prometheus Books, 1994).

12. "Religious Belief in America: A New Poll," *Free Inquiry* 16, no. 3 (Summer 1996), pp. 34–40.

13. If one were to conclude that there was a heritability factor, and if one believed that atheism should be encouraged in the population, then one might wish to encourage atheists to marry atheists and to bring up the children as atheists, so as to increase the number of atheist offspring. Often a minority religion grows not so much by conversion but by outbreeding other sects. Another suggestion perhaps might be taken (with tongue-in-cheek) is that atheists be cloned so as to increase their number!

14. Roger Finke and Rodney Stark, *The Churching of America, 1776–1990: Winners and Losers in Our Religious Economy* (New Brunswick, N.J.: Rutgers University Press, 1992).

15. See the book by David Berman, *A History of Atheism in Britain: From Hobbes to Russell* (New York: Routledge, 1990).

Part Two

Beyond Religion

12

First Things First

A Definition of Humanism

Can humanism provide a substitute for traditional religious or New Age paradigms? If we are to answer this question, we need to deal with first things first; that is, we need to clarify what we mean by the term "humanism." Perhaps it is disconcerting to begin with this linguistic question. One might ask: Can philosophers ever get beyond definitions? Don't we already understand what we mean by the term "humanism"? Bertrand Russell at one time observed that philosophers are supposed to clarify puzzling questions, but often they begin with a concept or term that is patently clear, at least to common sense, and after logical analysis they lay down such a thick cloud that we end up hardly knowing what is meant at all. I surely do not wish to begin by engaging in definition-mongering.

I do wish to present, however, what I consider to be a minimal core definition of "humanism." I do this in light of a volume that I edited twenty-five

Delivered on Saturday, December 6, 1997, at "A Philosophical Examination of Atheism, Agnosticism and Humanism," the founding meeting of the Society of Humanist Philosophers. Published in the inaugural issue of *Philo*, a new journal sponsored by the Society of Humanist Philosophers, Spring/Summer 1998.

years ago entitled *The Humanist Alternative: Some Definitions of Humanism.*[1]
There I asked thirty well-known humanists to offer their definitions of what
"humanism" meant, and they ended up with a great variety of alternative
definitions.[2] One may ask, Is there a clear definition of humanism that all
humanists will agree upon? It has been notoriously difficult historically to
develop a philosophical platform that will gain widespread assent, even by its
adherents. Often philosophers who join together are allied by what they are
against, rather than by what they are for.[3]

One may ask, Does humanism represent a distinctive philosophical school,
such as empiricism, rationalism, pragmatism, logical positivism, or analytic
philosophy? Is it akin to the traditional metaphysical schools such as Platonism,
Aristotelianism, idealism, or materialism? Does humanism offer an ethical
theory, such as utilitarianism or neo-Kantianism, and does it present a
distinctive normative stance? There are certainly many major schools of
philosophy that have been identified with humanism; and many major thinkers
in the contemporary world, from Marx and Freud to Sartre, and Camus, Dewey,
and Santayana, Carnap and Ayer, Quine, Popper, Flew, and Hook, Habermas
and Ferry, who have considered themselves to be humanists. And many
qualifiers have been added to fine-tune what is meant. Thus we have
naturalistic, scientific, or secular humanism; atheistic or religious humanism;
Christian, Judaic, or Zen humanism; Marxist or democratic humanism;
existentialist or pragmatic humanism. And historical terms have been used to
characterize epochs, such as classical Græco-Roman humanism, Renaissance
humanism, or Enlightenment humanism.

Are we entering a bottomless morass where "humanism" is used so widely
that it means all things to all men and women, such as "justice," "democracy,"
"socialism," and "libertarianism," and can the term be stretched like a pair of
socks to fit any size feet? Few in the past would admit to being antihumanistic;
it's like being antihuman—until recently, that is, when both postmodernists and
fundamentalists have railed against humanism. Today many disciples of animal
rights indict humanism, accusing it of being partial to the human species,
whereas their commitment, they maintain, is to all forms of life on the planet.

Before I attempt to define humanism, let me say that I am not explicating an
essentialist definition; there is no humanist essence writ large in the nature of
things. There are only common usages and a historical transition that terms
undergo as meanings evolve. What is often at issue is not simply what has been
meant in the past, but how we ought to use the term in the future. The term
"humanism" thus has both a descriptive and prescriptive aspect. It is descriptive
in the sense that it enables us to classify a number of thinkers and/or schools
under its rubric, but it is normative in that it may involve a new application of
the concept. There is one caveat: there are many *precursors* of the humanist
outlook historically, in the sense that they express one or more features of

contemporary humanism, without necessarily adopting other aspects. Thus, Socrates, Epicurus, Lucretius, Carneades, Spinoza, Hume, Diderot, Holbach, and Voltaire, for example, may be said to have expressed humanist features, without necessarily being full-blown humanists, and it is the contemporaneous meaning of humanism that I wish to explicate.

Humanist Ethics

What then do I mean by humanism? I submit that first of all it expresses a set of ethical values and virtues. Humanists wish to enhance the intrinsic qualities of joyful and creative experiences, and to realize some measure of happiness in this life. This set of humanist virtues is interpreted in a naturalistic framework. Humanist ethics may thus be contrasted with theistic doctrines that seek to denigrate or demean the capacity of human beings to find real satisfaction in this life (the "vale of tears" argument) and that look outside of human life for salvation. Humanists focus on temporal and secular values. They believe that our primary ethical obligation is to enrich life for ourselves and others. This was the essential doctrine of Renaissance humanism at the beginning of the modern period, when the term first came into vogue, as it was for classical humanistic philosophy, which Renaissance humanists attempted to revive.

Humanist ethical principles are autonomous, in the sense that they do not derive from theological or metaphysical premises, but grow out of our own sentient experiences. Most humanists have maintained that we are capable, to some degree, of rationality; that is, although our values are relative to us, they are capable of some modification by reflective deliberation. Some humanists have de-emphasized the cognitive and underlined the passionate character of our valuings. Nevertheless, although values have an expressive, indeed an emotive, quality, they can be evaluated in the light of reason. In any case, humanists deny that human values or virtues are derived from an external divine source *per se*, but are related to human experiences, desires, passions, interests, and/or needs.

Humanists have maintained that we have some degree of personal autonomy in the contexts of choice. We have some power over our lives and some responsibility for our futures. If no deity will save us, they have affirmed, we must save ourselves. And to so argue does not necessarily contradict weak determinism. Humanism in this sense differs sharply with those nihilistic philosophies of despair, which have abandoned any effort to progressively ameliorate human existence. Several postmodernist philosophers, drawing on Heidegger and Derrida, begin by rejecting human autonomy and freedom and the capacity of humans to use reason, science, and technology to improve the human condition. This they share with theologians, who maintain that human beings are so dependent upon God that they are incapable of resolving life's problems by themselves. The basic contrast in outlook is that humanists have some confidence in our ability to resolve problems or to control our own destinies, or at least they think that this is our only viable option. Thus, we have some power to fulfill our goals and aspirations; whereas theists declare that we are ultimately impotent and must depend on spiritual forces for our eternal salvation.

There are other points of contrast: humanist ethics does not have a doctrine of original sin; nor does it have a naïve view that all human beings are by nature good but corrupted by an evil society. Men and women are neither inherently good nor evil, but they can become either or both, given environmental and social conditions; and this is also dependent to some extent on what they do.

Although humanist ethics begins by concentrating on the individual and the actualization of his or her highest values, it also is concerned with the social good, and it implies that it is essential to develop just societies which will maximize both individual and social happiness under conditions of fairness and equity. Humanists have held that each individual has inherent dignity and worth—or at least ought to be so treated. Generally, contemporary humanists (such as Dewey, Popper, and Hook) have maintained that the best way to realize happiness is by means of free, open, and democratic societies, and they have been foes of repressive, authoritarian, and totalitarian institutions, whether political, ecclesiastical, or economic. That is why humanists have fought for human rights as essential safeguards of democracy.

This was essential in the battle of Marxist humanists against totalitarian dictatorships. In referring to the early Marx, of the *Economic and Philosophical Manuscripts*, they emphasized the importance of human freedom and autonomy; and they were foes of all sorts of "alienation," such as found in consumer market economies, but also including the kind of alienation that emerged in repressive, totalitarian, Leninist-Marxist societies. In defending individual human rights and the dignity and value of every person, they opposed insensitive régimes which were willing to repress individuals in the name of some ideal utopian goals. By introducing an ethics of principle, Marxist humanists showed there should be a limit on the kinds of means used. Thus, humanism calls to account any ideological or theological doctrines which had obliterated the *human* from its equation or sought to sacrifice the individual at the altar of an Absolutist dogma. Humanist reformers during Vatican II attempted to liberalize Catholicism by calling for a "human face"; similarly for humanists in Eastern Europe who sought to reform Marxism. I should point out that many or most humanists have urged that there be some recognition of the principles of equality in democratic societies—equality before the law, equality of opportunity, and the satisfaction of basic needs against aristocratic oligarchies. But they have likewise opposed egalitarian schemes that seek to deny human freedom and dehumanize society in the process.

Now, I began this paper by emphasizing the ethics of humanism as essential to the meaning of humanism. This was the view of Sidney Hook in his article "The Snare of Definitions" in *The Humanist Alternative* cited above.[4]

Hook stated, "I should like to propose that humanism today be regarded primarily as an *ethical* doctrine and movement . . . . I would say that an ethical humanist today is one who relies on the arts of intelligence to defend, enlarge, and enhance the areas of human freedom in the world." Although Hook's definition emphasizes the ethical, I think it is too broad and yet does not go far enough. It may be used by some defenders of human freedom, who may be theists. Some neoconservatives had allied with Hook's agenda in defending democracy and freedom against totalitarianism in the world, yet at the same time they have supported salvational theologies (I have in mind diverse political figures such as William Buckley, Irving Kristol, and Margaret Thatcher). Analogously, some proponents of ethical humanism have gone further than Hook and simply sought to identify humanist ethics with humanitarianism, even if religiously inspired by otherworldly virtues or values. Under this interpretation, those who are interested in mitigating human suffering or contributing to human welfare, peace, or tolerance have been called "humanists." This has been applied to a wide range of figures (such as Martin Luther King Jr., Mahatma Gandhi, and even Mother Teresa). Some have equated humanism with a "concern with humanity as a whole" by either referring to the Marxists' effort to build a utopian world, or to B. F. Skinner who, in *Walden II*, attempted to achieve a more harmonious society. These latter theories would also collide with Hook's defense of freedom as a basic value.

I think that freedom and some humanitarian concern are both essential to the definition of humanism. But equally important is the demythologizing of theistic ethics by focusing on secular rather than spiritual values. So that simply to defend freedom as some humanists and other critics of political totalitarianism have done, does not qualify as a definition of humanism, nor does a concern for human welfare mean that one is *ipso facto* a humanist.

Rejection of Theism

This leads us to the second characteristic of contemporary humanism—its rejection of theism and supernaturalism. This is already implicit in the above account of humanist ethics. Here the key idea for ethics is that God is dead and humans are alive. A form of this was proclaimed by Nietzsche in *Thus Spake Zarathustra* at the beginning of the twentieth century. Nietzsche was a foe of both Christianity and socialism as being slave moralities, yet he surely was not an ethical humanist as we understand it. Merely to reject God does not qualify one as an ethical humanist. (Lenin, Stalin, Heidegger, and Madalyn Murray O'Hair were atheists, but were they humanists?)

Many people today—its critics as well as its supporters—simply identify humanism with atheism; and in any definition of humanism they basically begin with a statement that humanists do not believe in God. The test of any normative definition is that it should be broad enough so as to include every person or thing that is signified by the term, but limiting enough so that it is able to exclude those not qualified. At the very least, nontheism seems to me to be a *necessary* though not a *sufficient* condition of contemporary humanism. By saying this, I mean that it is atheistic and/or agnostic. There are various forms of atheism historically, and a person may become an atheist for a variety of reasons: birth, ethnicity, feeling, passion, custom, authority. Personal, idiosyncratic, and autobiographical accounts of atheism are not necessarily rational. Broadly, I would suggest two kinds of nontheism: (a) the rejection of belief in God(s) without rational foundation, a form of dogmatic atheism, and (b) the reflective examination of the case for theism and its rejection because of a lack of rational grounds or because of positive evidence in favor of an alternative nontheistic point of view.

It is the latter (b) that makes most sense to philosophers. Actually, this approach is very close to the kind of agnosticism that T. H. Huxley introduced and defended in the nineteenth century. Huxley wrote:

> Agnosticism is not a creed, but a method, the essence of which lies in the rigourous application of a single principle.... Positively the principle may be expressed in matters of intellect, follow your reason as far as it can take you without other consideration. And negatively, in matters of the intellect, do not pretend conclusions are certain that are not demonstrated or demonstrable.[5]

In the nineteenth century, agnosticism and rationalism shared a common platform. Both presupposed a constructive methodological principle of skepticism: one should use objective methods for establishing knowledge claims as far as possible, and one should not accept beliefs if they have not been properly justified by reasons and evidence. Beliefs that do not come up to this standard can be doubted. This criterion means that our beliefs should be based on the best available evidence and that the grounds for them should be adequate. In regard to beliefs in God and a spiritual, supernatural, or paranormal universe, the agnostic consistently denies these claims because they do not satisfy the demands of objectivity. This form of agnosticism is different from popular forms of agnosticism, which state that either the existence of God is unknowable, or since you cannot know either way, you may opt to believe on the basis of fideism.

The most reasonable conclusion to be drawn from agnosticism in religion is, in my judgment, skeptical atheism. The skeptical agnostic atheist argues that the primary burden of proof rests with the claimant, and that in examining all of the arguments adduced for God, he concludes that there are insufficient grounds for accepting theism, and so he remains an *a*-theist. I agree with Antony Flew that we may begin with the presumption of atheism or nontheism, but in the sense that the claimant has failed to make his case by providing sufficient grounds for it.

By maintaining that his grounds are not sufficient, I mean the following: (a) The semantic critique: God language is vague, ambiguous, indefinable, and literally meaningless, since there are no descriptive designators; such language is emotive or moral or performatory in function but not descriptively true. (b) The classical arguments for God have been refuted: The ontological, cosmological, and design arguments are inconclusive, and in the latter regard the problem of evil undermines the whole notion of an omnipotent, omniscient, all-perfect God. (c) The historical arguments for revelation: The Bible, the Koran, and other such books, based on alleged revelations, are rejected because they are uncorroborated by adequate independent testimony. (d) The argument from miracles: This argument, as Hume pointed out, is questionable, for it is based on unreliable eyewitnesses who are ignorant of the natural causes of the alleged phenomena.

Naturalism

May I sum up the argument thus far: Humanism in its most parsimonious definition, first, provides a set of humanist values and virtues; and, second, espouses some form of agnostic atheism. There are other aspects to humanism, however, that I think are implicit in the above and need to be spelled out. I think it is useful to qualify the term "humanism" with "secularism," and to recast secular humanism so that there is no longer any confusion with other forms of humanism, as a generic term. I have suggested that *secular* humanism (like *pragmatic* naturalism, *scientific* empiricism, *democratic* socialism, or *critical* realism—other philosophical schools so qualified) enables us to overcome the semantic disputes about humanism, for secular humanism takes us one step beyond humanism *per se*.

Secular humanism, I submit, is an authentic school of philosophy on the contemporary scene. Added to the above two characteristics are a third and fourth. I submit that any definition of secular humanism should begin, third, by explicating its commitment to a method of inquiry as its first epistemological principle. By presenting a set of methodological principles, we can relate secular humanism to both the freethought and rationalist traditions. By that I mean (a) that secular humanists oppose any effort to restrict or limit free inquiry in all fields of human interests, including religion. As we are well aware, any kind of basic critical scrutiny of the sacred cows of society, especially dogmatic creeds about God and the holy faith, were considered blasphemous or heretical, and were punished by society. Similarly for many cherished political, ideological, and social customs, which were held immune to investigation or reform.

(b) The central methodological question for secular humanists is, How are we to justify claims to truth? Here the methods of scientific inquiry have been taken as general models for evaluating truth claims. I am not here talking about science in a narrow sense, for scientific inquiry is held to be continuous with common sense, but rather reason, broadly interpreted to include an appeal to evidence, rational coherence, and experimental confirmation. If one cannot find sufficient justifying reasons and/or evidence for a belief or hypotheses, said the rationalist, then one ought to suspend belief. In recent years this had led to an emphasis on *critical thinking*. This model should not be narrowly construed, but should be applied to ethics, society, and politics; indeed, as far as possible, to all domains of human interest. It is precisely the application of the methods of objective inquiry or critical thinking to the God question that has led secular humanists to agnosticism and atheism and the rejection of supernaturalism. Atheism thus follows from this epistemological principle, for it rejects the arguments for God as nonevidential.

Still a fourth principle of humanism—secular humanism, as I have qualified it—is implicit in what I have been arguing for, namely, its commitment to naturalism. Naturalism can be construed in many senses. (a) It can be interpreted as a methodological rule; that is, we should always seek to find natural causes and regularities to explain phenomena and reject occult or nonnatural explanations. Thus, science is programmatic. New sciences are spawned when researchers find how to apply scientific methods to new domains. By using critical thinking in the extended sense, it also seeks to apply rational appraisals in normative domains. (b) But naturalism can also be properly construed as a theory of reality or a cosmic outlook, especially in response to supernatural, paranormal, or idealistic worldviews. Basically, naturalists are nonreductive materialists. The universe does not seem to present purpose or design, nor is there evidence for an ultimate spiritual universe—again a powerful argument for atheism. For the naturalist, the most reliable accounts of nature are provided by the sciences, and this suggests that nature is basically physical-chemical at root, that natural processes are undergoing evolutionary change, and that different manifestations of phenomena appear on different levels of observation. Most naturalists maintain that we do not have evidence for a separable "mind" or "self," nor for the supposition of theism that the "soul" survives the death of the body. The human species is part of nature, not separable from it; our thoughts, feelings, and desires and the social institutions and cultural artifacts that we have created are as much a part of nature as electrons, flowers, planets, and galaxies.

Eupraxsophy

May I conclude with one further commentary? Since *Philo* is published by the Society of Humanist Philosophers, permit me to make some observations about the meaning of the term "philosophy," especially as it is referred to by humanists. "Philosophy" historically meant "the love of wisdom." This applied primarily to the philosopher's quest for theoretical knowledge and understanding. It was the task of the speculative philosophers historically to try to interpret our knowledge in comprehensive terms and to develop a systematic worldview; this has been transformed today into the philosophy of science, where the best that the philosopher can do is to interpret the findings on the frontiers of science. Critical or analytic philosophy is also interested in clarifying the meaning of concepts and language and the criterion of falsification. Now this Society is interested in dealing with such philosophical questions. But all of this is on the intellectual plane. The Society of Christian Philosophers is likewise interested in philosophical questions. They say that they wish to engage in a rational-philosophical inquiry and argument. But they also wish to engage in apologetics for a belief in God. What unifies them is their commitment to the truths and values of Christianity as a religious faith; and they are prepared to live and perhaps even die for their faith.

Now in what sense may humanists be said to be committed to humanism? If we deny that humanism is a religion, as I would—it is not a matter of piety or devotion to an unseen power—then is our commitment to humanism purely an *intellectual* position, or are we willing to live and perhaps even die for our humanistic principles under certain conditions? Surely, we believe in these principles on the basis of cognitive assent; and we are persuaded by a life-long philosophical odyssey; but has it entered into our blood and guts as it were, and does it inspire or move us passionately? It is surely uncomfortable for philosophers *qua* philosophers to talk in this manner. We are not theologians already committed to belief in God, nor are we dogmatic ideologists dedicated to a political or social cause. We say that as philosophers, we are concerned with the love of wisdom, clarity, and truth. Is humanism like empiricism, materialism, or utilitarianism, simply a school of thought of which we are convinced, and can we leave it aside when we are not in our philosophical mode?

Or is it something more? We say that we are ethically committed to humanism. But, alas, philosophical ethics has often been pursued by philosophers on the meta-level, principally by clarifying the meaning of ethical terms and/or seeking to understand the methods of justifying moral judgments— but without necessarily being *engagé*. Surely, philosophical ethics is also normative, but in what sense? Philosophers today often say that we should use reason to resolve dilemmas, or that we should use neo-Kantian, utilitarian, or situational criteria, and/or apply ethical principles impartially. Important as this is, to leave humanism in such a state is, in a sense, to leave it *in limbo*. What does it say about the meaning of life, or how we ought to live? And in particular, how does it answer the existential desire of ordinary people for meaning? We say that we are atheists, i.e., we reject belief in God as pure folly, but what are we *for*? Can philosophers state what they are for without abandoning the neutrality of cognitive philosophical inquiry?

It is for these reasons that I have proposed a new concept—standing midway between religion on the one side and philosophy and science on the other. It is *eupraxsophy*.[6] Secular humanism, I submit, is a eupraxsophy; that is, it is based upon a cosmic outlook, *sophia*—philosophical, but especially scientific, wisdom based upon an interpretation about what we have learned in the sciences about the universe; but it also has a definite life stance—for it is concerned with *eupraxis*, good conduct or practice. Some have objected to "eupraxsophy" as a neologism. I would defend the introduction of new terms as important, especially where old terms no longer serve. Both "agnosticism" and "pragmatism" were neologisms; so is "eupraxsophy."

A critic might respond: "Aristotle and other philosophers talked about practical wisdom. Isn't that sufficient?" But I reply: "The focus primarily was on *sophia* or wisdom; I wish to focus on *praxis* or conduct; else humanism only offers a parsimonious diet of stale bread and thin soup instead of a robust and lusty alternative to traditional theistic doctrines. It is life-affirming, positive, and constructive. Although based upon reason, philosophy, science, and ethics, it can inspire compassion, dedication, and commitment. Indeed, I submit that unless humanism—secular humanism—can be transformed into a eupraxsophy, it will fail to enlist the minds and hearts of men and women, which it will need to do if it is to gain acceptance. The transcendental temptation and magical thinking are pervasive tendencies in human culture. We ask, Is religion genetic, sociobiological, or cultural in origin? Whatever its source, religious enticements are far deeper than atheists of previous generations have imagined. I believe that as eupraxsophers we *can* and *ought* to engage in persuasive argumentation about the viability of the humanist life stance. Everyone else in society does so—priests, prophets, politicians, and pundits—why not philosophers and eupraxsophers? Humanist philosophers, it seems to me, should thus also address the question of how, and in what sense, humanism can provide an alternative to the religious cults that have so long dominated human imagination and commitment—a cognitive moral and emotional life stance, without piety or worship. Unless we deal with this question, humanism is likely to remain an interesting intellectual movement applicable to a limited number of philosophical inquirers, but of little relevance to life as lived.

1. Paul Kurtz, ed., *The Humanist Alternative: Some Definitions of Humanism* (London: Pemberton Books; Amherst, N.Y.: Prometheus Books, 1973).

2. Those who contributed included Sidney Hook, Joseph L. Blau, H. J. Blackham, John H. Randall Jr., Herbert W. Schneider, Antony Flew, B. F. Skinner, Corliss Lamont, Bernard Phillips, and H. J. Eysenck, among others.

3. As is well known, when Peirce heard what James meant by "pragmatism," which he attributed to him, he declared that he was a "pragmaticist," so as to keep this term safe from kidnappers.

4. Kurtz, *The Humanist Alternative,* pp. 33–34.

5. Thomas H. Huxley, "Agnosticism and Christianity," in *Collected Essays,* vol. 5 (New York: Appleton, 1894).

6. I have changed the spelling of *eupraxsophy* from its earlier version, *eupraxophy*, by interposing an *s* before the suffix.

13

Is Secular Humanism a Religion?

The question "Is secular humanism a religion?" has been debated for years. It continues to be of special significance because religious fundamentalists and many conservatives vociferously insist that "secular humanism is a religion." Thus, they seek to impose creationism in the schools, maintaining that evolution is a "theory" and an expression of the "religion of secular humanism," and they advocate a voucher system, which would provide public funding for private schools, including religious schools. To support their thesis, they maintain that the Supreme Court (whose verdicts on abortion they reject) has declared secular humanism to be a religion. This litany is repeated *ad nauseam*.

The Council for Secular and Democratic Humanism (now the Council for Secular Humanism) was established in 1980 in order to respond to these unfounded charges. At that time we issued a "Secular Humanist Declaration," in which we argued that America is a pluralistic secular republic, and that it is possible to be a good citizen, lead a moral life, and live meaningfully *without* religion. Indeed, millions of men and women in the United States and throughout the world are content to live without benefit of clergy or deity, and they do not characterize their philosophical, scientific, or ethical life stance as "religious."

Originally published as "Introduction: Beyond Religion," in *Free Inquiry* 16, no. 4 (Fall 1996), pp. 4–6.

The misrepresentations of humanism come from several different quarters. It is especially important that we deal with the charges of the right-wing religious critics, particularly since the Christian Coalition has had an enormous influence in the Republican Party. Should it gain power in the future there are bound to be dire political repercussions. Alas, Democrats have often vied with Republicans in professions of religious piety, which in America is often considered to be synonymous with patriotism. The Republican political conventions seem like revivalist prayer meetings, with pronouncements of "God bless America!" in overabundance.

David Noebel, a strong fundamentalist critic of humanism, has presented the case that humanism, including secular humanism, is a religion.[1] He maintains that humanism is a religion because several prominent humanists have held that it is so in the past. It is no secret that humanists differ on this key point, and that many humanists, representing the old-line humanist organizations, believe that humanism is religious. This is based in part on John Dewey's distinction in *A Common Faith* (1934) between the words *religion* (a creed, a set of institutional beliefs and practices) and *religious* (the quality of being committed to a set of ideal ends).[2] No doubt, the fact that humanism in America at its inception in the 1930s and 1940s was closely related to Unitarianism, and that *Humanist Manifesto I,* which was issued in 1933, was endorsed by many liberal Unitarian ministers, is the primary reason for its emphasis on religiosity. This form of religious humanism, of course, rejects the God of traditional theism, and it tries to create a humanistic religion amenable to the scientific outlook. Although such liberal religious humanists do not believe in God, they nonetheless wish to adopt the label of being religious.

Noebel quotes several humanist authors to make the case that humanism is a religion. Indeed, he quotes from my preface to *Humanist Manifesto I and Humanist Manifesto II* (which I drafted in 1973), in which I noted that "humanism is a philosophical, religious, and moral point of view as old as human civilization itself."[3] Now, it is true that I did once hold that humanism could be interpreted as a religious point of view (not a religion). By "religious" I meant a moral commitment to a set of ideals. But I have long since changed my views and have made my new position abundantly clear, arguing for two decades now that it was an error to consider humanism "religious." That is why I adopted the term *secular* humanism, so as to make it clear that this form of humanism was not religious. Surely, people should be allowed to change their minds. St. Paul was at one time a foe of Christianity. Would it be responsible to quote from the days in which he attacked Christianity, knowing that he eventually became a Christian? Noebel knows full well that I have modified my views, for I have published these extensively; yet he chooses to ignore them in his article. Today, a preponderant number of secular humanists reject the view that they are religious.

In any case, I submit that secular humanism is not a religion, nor is it religious. It does not contain a theology, but bases its views of reality on scientific evidence. It does not have a ministry or chaplains. It emphasizes secularity, the autonomous character of humanistic ethics, and the need for human beings to solve their own problems by using the best methods of reason and science.

We may ask, What is religious humanism, which some humanists have espoused? Mason Olds, former editor of *Religious Humanism,* defines religious humanism by reference to the moral ideals and poetic qualities of experience that it expresses. Clearly, there is much that religious humanists share in common with secular humanists. Our chief dissent with religious humanists (like fundamentalists) is the meaning of the adjective "relig*ious*" and the effort of critics to derive a "relig*ion*" from it. If we are to consider humanism "religious" because of its devotion to a set of ideals, then why is not any and everything that a person is devoted to "religious"; and may his or her set of beliefs be labeled as a "religion"? For example, if a person is committed to libertarianism, environmentalism, feminism, or vegetarianism, might we say that he or she is religious and has a religion? If any intensive devotion to a cause is religious, then no one, not even atheists, can deny being called religious. If Miss Reed is pious and devout, prays daily, and attends Mass every Sunday, we may say she is "religious." If Miss Jones rejects belief in God, never goes to Mass, and claims she is an atheist, is she likewise "religious"? If so, then words lose all meaning and Humpty Dumpty has prevailed; for he can make up to be down and down appear up as he so chooses. What a topsy-turvy linguistic thicket.

One may ask, why do religious humanists wish to argue that humanism is religious? Possibly because many religious humanists consider it to be anathema to attack religion in America. Atheists, agnostics, and secular humanists who do so are considered to be acting in bad taste. So many religious humanists seem to be saying, "Look, we are religious like everyone; please don't accuse us of irreligion." Another possible point of difference that has recently emerged among humanists—particularly in the Netherlands—concerns the important role that reason and the methods of science holds for secular humanists in testing truth claims and solving problems. Some religious humanists seem prepared to reject the scientific outlook and are sympathetic to a kind of postmodernist critique of the Enlightenment.

Secular humanists are fed up with the me-too-ism pabulum expressions of religious piety, which are often a mask for hypocrisy, injustice, and intolerance. Secular humanists maintain that the traditional claims of religion based on the Bible (Talmud or Koran) are outdated, more appropriate to nomadic-agricultural societies than to a post-postmodern age. And they believe that we should state this point clearly, even though it may not be popular at the moment. Religious theists are surely not reticent in their attacks on secular humanism and/or atheism; why should we hold back in an effort to be polite? If we don't believe in God and His alleged Commandments as interpreted by latter-day disciples, why not say so loud and clear? Why mute our irreligion or our criticisms of the sacred cows? Why not forthrightly defend the viability of living *without* religion? Clearly, we wish to defend the positive reaches of humanism, but this can only begin with criticisms of otherworldly religious creeds of salvation.

There is today still a third critique of nonreligious secular humanism on the current scene. The distinguished liberal "quasi" theologian and philosopher Professor John Smith maintains in an article and book that humanism is what he calls a "quasi-religion."[4] Even if secular humanists deny that they are religious, he affirms, secular humanism performs functions similar to those of religion. To make his case, Smith quotes extensively from the book that I edited in 1973, *The Humanist Alternative: Some Definitions of Humanism.* This book presents the views of some thirty leading humanists, in which they propose a wide range of definitions about the meaning of humanism. Professor Smith quotes from those articles that seem to support his claims that humanism is a "quasi-religion," but he does not refer to the two dozen or more humanists who do *not* agree with this thesis. The fact that secular humanism expresses a scientific, philosophical, and educational outlook, and that it entails a set of moral ideals and values as an alternative to traditional religion, does not make it "quasi-religious." Many philosophers have espoused ethical and social values (for example, Hobbes and Kant); but this does not mean that they are espousing quasi-religions. Because secular humanists, like theists, are concerned with the meaning of life and seek to provide some moral guidance does not *ipso facto* convert secular humanists into quasi-religionists.

Is this all merely a linguistic quibble about the terms *religion* and *religious?* I think not. For the battle about terms is not *what* they have meant, but what they *ought* to mean. This is not a descriptive question so much as it is a prescriptive and normative one. Quibbling about definitions often masks deeper political, moral, and ideological agendas and interests. This is what happened earlier in this century about the meaning of the term *democracy,* with both believers in democracy as we now define it and their totalitarian opponents attempting to preempt its use. For a variety of ulterior motives, critics and foes, defenders and enemies, have sought to make secular humanism into a religion— though no doubt for different reasons. David Noebel's thesis has powerful ideological implications; for right-wing critics of humanism on the basis of it would seek to limit or ban the role of secular humanism in American public life by claiming that it is a religion and that it thus violates the Establishment Clause.

In order to resolve this issue, I proposed in my book, *Eupraxophy: Living without Religion,*[5] that secular humanists adopt a new term, which I later labeled "eupraxophy." Surprisingly, a great deal of opposition to it came from humanists, who thought that it was a neologism, that they couldn't pronounce it easily, and they didn't see the need for it. In my argument I maintained that humanism is not a religion in the common meaning of that term. The term "religion," I maintained, has been applied to belief in the sacred, in some deity, or transcendental power who is the creative source and ground of the universe and to which human beings owe allegiance, piety, and prayer. The existence of such a being for the secular humanist is highly questionable, for there doesn't appear to be adequate empirical or rational foundations for the claim.

The term *eupraxsophy* suggests that we can develop a set of good moral principles (*eu*) and that we can apply these to the practical life (*praxis*). Moreover, we can develop some wisdom (*sophia*), based on science and philosophy, about the nature of the universe and the place of the human species within it, which is naturalistic. Accordingly, eupraxsophy means "good practical wisdom." Thus secular humanists are not religious; they reject belief in God, yet they are committed to an ethical, scientific, and philosophical outlook. If religious humanists still wish to maintain that they are religious, they surely have every right to do so, but at least secular humanists are *not*.

Is it a mistake for us to continue to insist that *secular* humanists are not religious? What are we to say today, given a new poll, which shows a high level of religiosity existing in the United States, and the fact that perhaps only six to eight percent of the population are religious unbelievers?[6] I realize that some doubts have been raised about the adequacy of the poll, but if its results are somewhat accurate, should we, too, adopt a religious stance strategically, to gain more adherents? Is it unwise to continue to resist the label, and should we, like so many other Americans, accept religion along with motherhood and apple pie? In my view, such professions of piety, even if naturalized and demythologized, are disingenuous and dishonest for they undermine our commitment to truth. On the contrary, we need to defend our right as dissenters to be heard and we should not weaken our right to criticize claims that are unsubstantiated by the evidence—in spite of the risk of offending religionists who often have a holier-than-thou belief in the truth and moral rectitude of their faith.

The puzzle that we face is why the United States during the reign of Pax Americana exudes the old-time religions while large sectors of the world have abandoned them. Many countries in Western Europe have taken a humanistic direction. Religious belief has declined. In England, for example, less than 10 percent of the people attend the various churches, temples, and mosques. Similarly for Norway, the Netherlands, and other countries where humanist belief has increased. Why is America *the* superpower an anomaly in the democratic world?

That is a good question, which I will not address here. Suffice it to say that we should continue to insist that the land of the free and the home of the brave should extend to its citizens who are irreligious the same rights enjoyed by others. We have a right not to be religious, nor to espouse a religion, and to declare forthrightly that we have a viable and meaningful alternative life stance that we are prepared to defend.

1. David A. Noebel, "The Religion of Secular Humanism," *Free Inquiry* 16, no. 4 (Fall 1996), pp. 7–9.

2. John Dewey, *A Common Faith* (New Haven, Conn.: Yale University Press, 1934).

3. Paul Kurtz, *Humanist Manifestos I and II* (Buffalo, N.Y.: Prometheus Books, 1973).

4. John E. Smith, "Humanism as a 'Quasi-Religion,'" *Free Inquiry* 16, no. 4 (Fall 1996), pp. 17–22.

5. Paul Kurtz, *Eupraxophy: Living without Religion* (Amherst, N.Y.: Prometheus Books, 1989).

6. See "Religious Belief in America: A New Poll," *Free Inquiry* 16, no. 3 (Summer 1996), pp. 34–40.

14

Important Lessons on the Collapse of Marxism

Decline of Utopian Thinking

It has been only a short while since communism in the former Soviet Union and Eastern Europe collapsed. Although Marxist regimes still cling to power in China, North Korea, Vietnam, and Cuba, Marxism everywhere appears to be discredited and in disarray.

There are lessons to be learned from the remarkable rise and sudden fall of Marxism-Leninism, and these should be instructive to those of us who look forward to a more humanistic world in the twenty-first century. Of special interest is the fact that Marxists and socialists encouraged atheism, and this provided the freethought movement with important allies in its warfare against repressive religious institutions. Unfortunately, Marxists-Leninists substituted new forms of dogma to replace those they had rejected. It is clear that freethought is still a powerful movement, and we need to demonstrate that it can flourish, independently of left-wing movements. We emphasize that *democratic*

Originally published as "Some Lessons for Humanists," in *Free Inquiry* 14, no. 3 (Summer 1994), pp. 12–13.

secular humanism can be liberal or conservative in its economic and political outlook. The key point is the defense of *freedom* and opposition to authoritarian and totalitarian institutions.

Idealistic utopian thinking is now in disrepute, and with it, the naïve optimism that it is possible to remake human nature and construct a brave new world. Utopians as disparate as Plato, Marx, and B. F. Skinner thought that by bold philosophical and/or scientific planning, one could radically alter the environment and/or humankind itself by such means as eugenic breeding or social engineering and thus improve the human condition. Today we are disillusioned with such utopian promises, and we are especially indignant at the use of the totalitarian state to create the New Human. The collapse of communism has reinforced our belief in the open, democratic society, the importance of human freedom, and the need to defend human rights. Marxist-Leninists were willing to use terror and to sacrifice those who stood in their way. The terrible gulags of Stalinist tyranny and the massacres by Pol Pot and Mao were the bitter result.

We know that the taste for power that revolutions stimulate can lead to great suffering, and that civilized moral conduct can be undermined in the process. We are witness to how state power can be used to unleash savagery and condone barbarism. The movie *Schindler's List* reminds us that not all men and women need succumb to brutal systems, but also that vulgar and evil ideologies can transform civilized people to condone infamous crimes.

When I was growing up, virtually everyone I knew in the intellectual world seemed to believe that capitalism was wicked and that socialism—meaning social justice and some measure of equality—would eventually triumph. Along with the fall of Marxism has come the tarnishing of socialist ideals. It is true that *democratic* socialists were among the first to condemn totalitarian communism, and that they were the strongest critics of Leninism-Stalinism. Moreover, socialist governments in Western Europe have long since abandoned doctrinaire Marxism and have instead sought to reform capitalist systems by making them more humane. Nevertheless, the great faith in "rational planning" that dominated thinking in the pre-World War II era has been discredited. Few today wish to abandon the capitalist market system.

The error of both Marxists and the other socialists was that they minimized the incentive of individual self-interest. Further, they did not appreciate that highly regulated bureaucratic governmental agencies are not as efficient or productive as the private sector. Marxism failed on its own terms because it was unable to deliver the economic goods that it promised; and this, largely, because its ideal picture of human nature was profoundly mistaken.

Humanists are still idealists. But are they utopians? As secular humanists, we are surely skeptical of the reigning religions of the day. Theistic truth claims have no foundations in empirical fact. They are holdovers from primitive prescientific cultures, and they persist in spite of the Age of Enlightenment and the progress of science. These mythic belief systems are no doubt able to maintain their grip because of their ability to indoctrinate the young and, in many societies, because of their access to authoritarian (if not totalitarian) methods of control. They need to be criticized by secular humanists, especially where they engender ethnic hatred.

But a word of caution We surely do not wish to denude the organic moral structures within society that religious institutions, for all of their faults, still provide. We surely do not wish to deny freedom of conscience to those who believe religious dogmas. We simply seek to protect the rights of unbelievers. Our goal is to build secular humanistic institutions as alternatives for those who wish them.

We may ask: *What if*, for some reason, *all* religious bodies were to close their doors? Some stalwart atheists might applaud. But we should recognize that religious institutions among others still play a constructive role in many societies insofar as they inculcate and reinforce moral behavior, propagate an ethic of love, and oppose violations of the common moral decencies. The key dilemma for secularists and humanists is to ask what will replace these moral frameworks. Granted that religious institutions are often hypocritical and many of them insist upon stances that we find repellent, such as their dogged defense of sexual repression and their anti-woman, anti-choice, or anti-euthanasia attitudes. Still, we cannot simply condone the decline of civilized patterns of conduct unless—and this is crucial—there are equivalent systems of constructive moral guidelines to fill the vacuum. That is why atheistic secularism meaning simply the *disbelief* in theistic religion by itself is not sufficient. As I have said, we need to develop the *positive* dimensions of humanism, i.e., the moral framework for civilized behavior.

Thus, an important lesson to be learned from the discrediting of totalitarian utopian thinking in the twentieth century is that we ought to be cautious about the destruction of existing institutions without their adequate replacement by positive alternatives. This in no way denies that we need to think creatively about the future and to come up with possible images of a better tomorrow. These should not be purely utopian, but realistic and capable of attainment. This means, for example, that our belief in rationality, democracy, tolerance, building a world community, and other humanist ideals should not be abandoned. Humanists are often accused of being too idealistic and optimistic: in rejecting the doctrine of original sin we focus instead on the positive possibilities for human growth and development. Human beings are neither intrinsically good nor evil, but capable of either or both kinds of behavior, dependent upon social conditions and individual responsibility. But if this is the case, then moral education should have the highest priority on the humanist agenda, and we should continue to help develop programs to encourage moral values in the schools and other social institutions. We should seek to develop the skills of clear thinking—healthy and constructive skepticism, not nihilistic negativism—but we should also constantly seek to develop an appreciation for the common moral virtues.

Another lesson is that we ought to be cautious about attempting to totally remake human nature. Granted that we wish to use education to fulfill the best in human nature, but since the "transcendental temptation" is such a powerful impulse in the human species, it is essential that we find symbolic equivalents to help satisfy it. I am not in any sense suggesting that a spiritual dimension needs to be added to humanism, but only that humanist ideals need to be *dramatically* rendered so that they have the power to stir the passions and inspire devotion and dedication. Still, we need to find humanist metaphors to give meaning to life and æsthetic equivalents to engage the imagination and renew our fascination with a zest for living. This reinforces my conviction that a humanist eupraxsophy must focus not simply on theory, but on practice, and that moral education focusing on the best that we can achieve is vital for attaining this goal.

Transcending Ethnic Animosities

The tragedy of Yugoslavia brutally illustrates how nationalistic hatreds ethnic, religious, and racial—can consume a population. The twentieth century began with the assassination of the Archduke of Serbia in Sarajevo. This provoked World War I, and led to a bloody confrontation of nations. This century comes to a close with Sarajevo left prostrate because of the internecine religious warfare between Bosnians, Croats, and Serbs. It is repeated by brutal ethnic cleansing in Kosovo. This is especially sad, as these people lived together in relative peace and harmony only a short while ago.

Similar tribal conflicts rocked the African continent—such as the outrages in Rwanda between the Hutu and Tutsi tribes. The depth of their hatred was so intense that there seems to be little compunction about slaughtering hundreds of thousands of innocent men, women, and children simply because they are of a different ethnicity.

The stark lesson to be learned from these reversions to barbarism is the urgent need of humankind to leave behind divisive alliances and animosities of the past and to seek common ground. We welcome the end of apartheid and the emergence of democracy in South Africa (forged after intense negotiations over the years between de Klerk, Mandela, and Buthelezi). Similarly, we applaud the signing of a peace treaty between Israel and the Palestine Liberation Organization as a hopeful first step toward permanent peace in that part of the

Middle East. The road to democracy in South Africa and peace in Palestine will not be easy, and there are likely to be continuing conflicts in the future. But the alternative is the spectacle of Rwanda, Bosnia, or Kosovo.

Humanists surely appreciate ethnic differences, but humankind must transcend the tribal loyalties and dangerous absolutist religious dogmas of the past. We stand for reason, tolerance, mutual respect, shared commonality; and we believe in the urgent imperative to build a genuine world community. These ideals, I submit, are not only realistic, but the only viable options facing humankind today.

15

Rising Above the Ancient Loyalties: Who is a Jew?

In Defense of Assimilation

How is "Jewish identity" to be defined? What does it mean to be Jewish? These have been burning issues for Jews, especially in the twentieth century, when the Nazis attempted to answer these questions and to eradicate both Jews and Judaism. And they are questions faced anew today, given the continuing challenges to the State of Israel. Jews everywhere in North and South America, Eastern and Western Europe, continue to raise these and other troubling questions. Should people of Jewish background strive to persist as a separable and identifiable Jewish minority, or should they seek to assimilate into the mainstream of the culture in which they live?

According to Alan Dershowitz, in his book, *The Vanishing American Jew*,[1] the Jews in America are facing the greatest crisis in their history. For, if present demographic trends continue, they will most likely disappear as an identifiable ethnic group by the year 2076—the 300th anniversary of the American

Originally published as "Who Is a Jew? Rising Above the Ancient Loyalties," in *Free Inquiry* 17, no. 3 (Summer 1997), pp. 54–57.

Declaration of Independence. Or at the very least, he warns, they are apt to be a less vibrant part of American life. This development, he believes, is due to the decline of anti-Semitism in the United States in recent decades (except among fringe groups) and to the widespread acceptance of Jews in public life. Indeed, he affirms that the Jewish minority has prospered and succeeded in America in many fields of endeavor as in no other time or place in history. A central concern in this book is the fact that Jews have become so secularized and secure that a majority have abandoned Judaism and are marrying non-Jews. Dershowitz is concerned that assimilation rates are increasing. Secular Jews have the "lowest birthrate" of any religious or ethnic group in the United States (1.5 to 1.6%—below the 2.19% necessary for replacement).

Alan Dershowitz is perhaps the best-known lawyer in America, especially since serving on the O. J. Simpson defense team. His views are sought out on a variety of topics. When he speaks, many listen. But is his position in opposition to assimilation defensible? Dershowitz says that he is himself a thoroughly secularized Jew and a humanist, and he is agnostic about the existence of God. Yet he believes that it would be a tragedy if the American Jews were to decline or disappear. If present trends continue, the only identifiable group of Jews who are likely to survive, he says, are the most Orthodox Hasidic Jews who have a soaring birthrate (6.4%) and are intolerant of secular values. If so, the remaining Jews will, he believes, become marginalized. He thinks that what is at stake is not simply the religion of Judaism, but its culture, which he says is 3,500 years old, and the considerable creative, intellectual, scientific, artistic, and entrepreneurial talents that he thinks Jewish life has contributed to civilization.

Dershowitz's account of his own religious upbringing is instructive. Born into an Orthodox family in Brooklyn, he studied at a Yeshiva school and kept kosher eating habits until age 25. He later went on to become a Harvard professor and a public spokesperson for all sorts of controversial causes. He still continues to attend synagogue, to observe Jewish holidays, and to appreciate their Jewish "religious" and "spiritual values," though he remains somewhat skeptical about their supernatural claims. The most interesting paradox of his autobiographical account was the fact that, as a father, he became concerned when his son James decided to marry an Irish Catholic girl, Barbara. He feared that his grandchildren would no longer be brought up as Jews. Dershowitz has had to face the fact that the chain linking his grandchildren to historic Jewish culture will be weakened and that their "Jewishness" might disappear. Dershowitz comes to accept the marriage with affection, but not without some guilt. Both James and Barbara are skeptics, and they have exposed their children to their own varied backgrounds in their interfaith*less* marriage, without partiality to one.

Dershowitz's concern about the loss of Jewish identity is shared by many other members of the Jewish community today, particularly Orthodox and

Conservative Jews, who blame secularism for the decline. Dershowitz asks, What can or should be done to stem this tide? He states and rejects three options: First, Jews can return to the strictest Orthodox faith, attempting to blend their "Jewishness" with the demands of modern secular culture. This is not possible for a secular Jew, says Dershowitz, and most Jews in America are secular. Second, they can depart for Israel, where they can assume an Israeli nationality. Most American Jews are loyal to America and would not think of renouncing their American nationality or their devotion to the United States. Or third, they can accept assimilation as an inevitable fact and acquiesce to the disappearance of Judaism and Jewish cultural life. This Dershowitz likewise deplores.

He offers a fourth alternative, the development of a new form of "secular Judaism" that is not supernatural but humanistic, that allows for agnostic dissent, and yet provides for full participation in Jewish culture and Jewish identity.[2] But if this is to be achieved, he believes there must be a redirection in American Jewish life and a new emphasis on Jewish education. He believes that young Jews need to appreciate their "history and heritage" and the values of Jewish culture, which, he says, include an emphasis on learning and questioning, independence of judgment, a humanitarian concern with social justice and ethics, and an appreciation for the arts and sciences. He calls for a "new Jewish state of mind" able to challenge the view that Jews can survive only where they are discriminated against and persecuted. Judaism, he says, can persist "in an open, free, and welcoming society, such as America."

Dershowitz's plea for a secularized Judaism no doubt will find a receptive audience among many American Jews, who have difficulty with traditional theological Judaism. Indeed, some 80% of American Jews who are secular believe that to be a Jew in America means being a member of a "cultural group," and only 35% think that it also means being a member of a "religion." Even for religious Jews, 70% believe that being Jewish means being a member of a cultural group, and only 49% a religious group. But if Judaism is the core of Jewish culture—and therefore "Jewish identity"—can a Judaism stripped entirely of religion retain that identity? Rabbi Alexander Schindler, president of the Reform movement, a supposedly liberal branch, recently defended a decision of his group to exclude a secular humanist Jewish congregation applying for membership, maintaining that "the concept of God" is the very foundation of Judaism. One might ask, Would Judaism without these supernatural foundations still have a viable message for freethinking and skeptical Jews? What would happen if the myth of the "Chosen People" and the belief that Moses received the Ten Commandments from On High were finally abandoned? Dershowitz thinks that secular Jews should read the Jewish historical literature and study the Talmud and Torah. But could a secular approach to the historic Jewish cultural tradition provide enough sustenance for its continuity?

Why not consider a naturalized and humanized Judaism to be only *one* among many pluralistic contributions to human civilization that all educated persons should know about and perhaps appreciate. And why not have this take its place alongside of Egyptian, Greco-Roman, Buddhist, French, Anglo-Saxon, Indian, Chinese, and other cultural traditions? As a member of the human family, should not one learn to appreciate *all* cultural traditions without chauvinistic preference for one's own? Why should the faith of one's forefathers command the devotion of individuals, especially since one's religious and ethnic background is usually an accident of birth or indoctrination, and not one of voluntary choice?

In reading Dershowitz I am struck by how deep-seated his own ethnic and tribal chauvinism is—and by his failure to appreciate the virtues of assimilation, the appeal of interreligious and/or interracial marriages. The United States (and Australia, New Zealand, Canada, and Western Europe to a lesser extent) are becoming truly universal societies, for they have taken steps beyond ancient ethnic, national, and racial chauvinisms. Should we not applaud those couples (including Dershowitz's son and daughter-in-law) who are willing to transcend their ethnic backgrounds and transfer their affection to the broader human community, able to reach out and love "the aliens" in their midst? Rather than bemoan the loss of his grandchildren to Jewish identity, why not applaud the quest for a broader human identity?

Surely Dershowitz is not alone in his partiality to his ethnic background, yet what if his tribal sentiments were generalized? What if Barbara's Irish Catholic parents were to deplore her marriage to James as being outside of their culture and faith? Following Dershowitz's argument, one might assert that Irish Roman Catholic culture has historic roots and values, and an Irish Catholic should resist the loss of grandchildren to this cultural heritage. Similarly for the Southern Baptist, the Muslim, the Hindu Indian, and so on. Isn't this a form of bigotry?

Is it not time to rise to a new plane of moral commitment? Indeed, one can argue that the assimilation of past cultures to a more universal world culture has higher ethical merit. By so arguing, I do not suggest that we suppress the multiplicities of culture or pluralistic life stances—only that we encourage those who wish to transcend the exclusive loyalties of the past and to achieve a more inclusive devotion to the broader moral community of humankind. Jews in America who marry outside of the fold are much like other ethnic minorities who recognize their cosmopolitan backgrounds—many people today affirm that they are part German, or part English, or part Hopi, or part African-American, or part Asian. Dershowitz quotes former White House Chief of Staff John Sununu, who heralds the fact that he is of mixed Lebanese, Greek, and El Salvadoran ancestry: "It is a varied heritage and I am proud of it." Golf champion Tiger Woods, an Asian-African-American, represents the blending of many ethnic and racial backgrounds—what a wonder to behold! Racists may consider this a "mongrelization," but in saying this they only mask their ignorance of their own distant past and the variety of bloodlines that all humans represent.

The fact that most secular Jews, like others in America, have decided to move in this direction is, I submit, an affirmative decision on their part. The search for a "new identity" beyond parochial loyalties should primarily be a question of personal choice, without the constraints of religious traditions or ethnic prejudice. Most of the modern Jews, whom Dershowitz approves of, from Spinoza to Freud and Einstein, were secular Jews who broke from Judaism and were able to contribute to more universalistic values. Dershowitz is convinced that anti-Semitism is *passé* in America, but who can be assured that Jewish achievement will not stoke new fires of resentment? All the more reason why so many secular Jews have concluded that assimilation is a meaningful option for them, as they seek a more integrated life.

A Redefinition of Jewish Identity

This leads to a second question about historic Jewish identity. It is the prevailing assumption that the Jewish people represent a continuous line of descent of 3,500 years, traceable back to the original Jews or Hebrews who lived in Palestine. I would assume that post-Holocaust Jews find abhorrent the claim of the Nazis that there is such a thing as a distinct "Jewish race." Yet, in defense of Jewish identity, oddly enough, there are those Jews, particularly Orthodox, who are defending a similar argument. The belief that Jewish culture represents a sacred chain of descent suggests at least that there is a kind of "ethnic purity."[3] The Jewish people are said to be unique in that they have maintained their group identity for more than two millennia, in spite of the fact that they had no common territorial base, and that they have preserved their ancestral religion, culture, and ethnicity intact. According to the Old Testament story, the Hebrews fled the repressive Pharaoh in Egypt and settled in the Promised Land, Palestine. Occupied by Roman legions, the Temple in Jerusalem was destroyed in 70 C.E., and the Jews dispersed to many lands. Ever since the Diaspora, according to the traditional account, the Jews have attempted to return to their homeland. Interestingly, this view is shared by both secular and Orthodox Jews, and even by the most rabid anti-Semites. A century ago, Theodor Herzl, the father of modern Zionism, thought that the only solution to anti-Semitism was for the Jews to have a state of their own in Palestine—which he said should be secular and not religious.

Orthodox Jews in Israel, in defending the law of return, tie the question of who is a Jew to maternal descent. Orthodox rabbis insist that they alone can determine who is a Jew—excluding Reform and Conservative rabbis. But do the Jews have a continuous religious and/or genetic identity (as even Dershowitz, for example, assumes), or are there discontinuities? And do the modern-day Jews draw upon disparate peoples of the past? Surely neither Christianity nor Islam are identified with a specific racial type, for they have appealed in their long history to a wide range of ethnicities. Secular Jews have argued that the Jews do not represent a separate ethnicity or racial type, but represent a "cultural tradition." Clearly the Jews who lived in India, China, Yemen, Turkey, Africa, and North and South America reflect a variety of cultural values, but also diverse ethnic genotypes, based on intermarriage with the indigenous stock.

In a provocative book, *The Ashkenazic Jews: A Slavo-Turkic People in Search of a Jewish Identity*,[4] Paul Wexler, who teaches linguistics at Tel-Aviv University, maintains that in the first millennia most Jews lived outside of Palestine and throughout the Mediterranean world (for example, one million lived in Alexandria, Egypt, at one time), and they attracted converts of different ethnic backgrounds to the fold. The first Christians were Jews, who converted others to Christianity, which was originally considered a branch of Judaism. Similarly for the non-Christian Jews—Wexler maintains that Judaism at first grew by conversion of non-Jews, mainly pagans, to Judaism. The Sephardic Jews, he maintains, were originally of Arabic and Berber stock. After the expulsion of the Jews from Spain in 1492, they settled in many lands throughout the world.[5]

Wexler focuses his study, however, on the Ashkenazic Jews. The traditional view is that the Jews in Eastern Europe and Poland immigrated there from France and Germany; and that they trace their lineage to the original Palestinian Hebrews. Wexler maintains, on the contrary, that the Ashkenazic Jewish origin was due to the conversion of large numbers of Serbo-Turkic peoples in the Balkans to Judaism, and that they are largely ethnic Slavs. In so arguing, Wexler is recasting the argument proposed by Arthur Koestler in his book *The Thirteenth Tribe*.[6] Koestler held that the Ashkenazi Jews, who make up 80% of the world's Jews today (in spite of the Holocaust), largely resulted from the conversion of the Turkic Khazars in the Caucasus of the eighth century. Koestler's thesis was criticized because of its lack of corroborating evidence. Wexler maintains that the cradle for the Ashkenazi Jews was the Balkans and the mixed Germanic-Slavic areas of Europe in the Middle Ages. His evidence for this is primarily linguistic: he traces Yiddish, the language of the Ashkenazi Jews, to a Slavic (not Germanic) origin. There were undoubtedly later heavy borrowings from German, but Yiddish, he maintains, is originally a Slavic language. Thus, a Judaization process was introduced to a pagan people; they were responsible for transforming and developing medieval and modern Jewish culture. According to Wexler, even modern Hebrew is a development and an accretion, and it is not a return to the original language *per se* (the Palestinian

Jews spoke Aramaic primarily), but is a result of a similar process of Judaization. Wexler grants that the historical record of the Jews between the sixth and eleventh centuries is very fragmentary, but he holds that, coterminous with the conversion of the pagans to Christianity and Islam during this period, there were widespread conversions of pagans to Judaism.

Thus the Ashkenazis are a result of conversions by proselytes and widespread intermarriage and assimilation. He grants that in time the Ashkenazi Jews became a distinct interbreeding ethnic stock and that, like the Muslims and Christians, they eventually attempted to enforce (not always with success) prohibitions against intermarriage or assimilation out of the group. This means that Jews today are the product of a long period of assimilation (both ways) and that this is an ongoing process. Over the millennia the Jews have not only assimilated other peoples into the fold, but tens of millions have left the fold and their gene pools have been dispersed throughout many nations. Anti-Semites no doubt played a role in this process, but it was a two-way street. During certain periods, the Jews were confined to the shtetl and the ghetto, but many Jews also sought to assimilate into the mainstream as a protection against prejudice.

The implications of Wexler's research for the State of Israel are profound. Jewish nationalism and Zionist ideology are wedded to "the sacred chain" thesis. Wexler observes that, given the Israeli-Palestinian conflict today, the belief in an uninterrupted identity of the Jewish people and/or religion from the Palestinian period to the present impedes the systematic study of this historic Judaization process. If he is correct, this thesis need not justify the frenzied effort by Palestinian nationalists to throw the Jews into the sea, no more than that Native Americans need insist that the settlers in America and Canada return to Europe and Africa, or that the Australians give back Australia to the Aborigines. The world is rapidly changing, and immigration and emigration is a pervasive fact of postmodern existence. We should encourage intermarriage, miscegenation, and other such processes, but especially the creation of secular societies, which encourage people of diverse ethnicities to settle and live together and to transcend the ancient loyalties of the past. This, of course, should apply not only to Jewish chauvinists, but to chauvinists of all stripes. Islamic countries in particular need to respect the separation of church and state, develop an appreciation for secularism, and mitigate hostility to non-Muslims in their midst.

From the secular humanist perspective, assimilation is a positive good and is not to be feared. The moral agenda for humanists is to persuade people that we need to go beyond the ancient loyalties of the past and to attain a new ethical level in which all persons become a part of the community of humankind. This may be difficult. But if it is happening in America, why not elsewhere?

1. Alan M. Dershowitz, The Vanishing American Jew: In Search of Jewish Identity for the Next Century (Boston, New York: Little, Brown and Company, 1997).

2. The most forceful proponent of this view is Rabbi Sherwin Wine of Birmingham, Michigan, who has founded a movement known as "Secular Humanist Judaism." It has developed congregations in North America, and also internationally.

3. See Norman Cantor, *The Sacred Chain* (New York: Harper Perennial, 1995).

4. Paul Wexler, *The Ashkenazic Jews: A Slavo-Turkic People in Search of a Jewish Identity* (Columbus, Ohio: Slavica Publishers, 1993).

5. Paul Wexler, *The Non-Jewish Origins of the Sephardic Jews* (Albany, N.Y.: State University of New York Press, 1996).

6. Arthur Koestler, *The Thirteenth Tribe* (London: Random House, 1976).

16

Morality without God

Humanist Ethics

Can one lead a meaningful life, be a loving parent and a responsible citizen without being religious? Many disciples of the Christian Coalition admonish us that anyone who does not believe in the Bible is immoral. Yet tens of millions of Americans are unchurched and millions are secular humanists, agnostics, even atheists, and they behave responsibly.

Indeed, many heroes and heroines of American history have rejected biblical morality and led ethical lives, such as Tom Paine, Robert Ingersoll, Mark Twain, Clarence Darrow, Elizabeth Cady Stanton, Margaret Sanger, Carl Sagan, and Isaac Asimov. Humanistic ethics has deep roots in Western civilization, from classical Greece and Rome, through the Renaissance to the development of modern democratic societies.

The history of philosophy demonstrates the efforts of great thinkers—from Aristotle to Immanuel Kant, John Stuart Mill, John Dewey, and Sidney Hook—to develop a rational basis for ethical conduct. Ethics, they said, can be

Originally published as "The Common Moral Decencies Don't Depend on Faith," in *Free Inquiry* 16, no. 3 (Summer 1996), pp. 5, 7, and the rebuttal in the same issue, on page 6, responding to John M. Frame's rebuttal.

autonomous and needs no theological justification. These philosophers have emphasized the need for self-restraint and temperance in a person's desires.

Plato argued that the chariot of the soul is led by three horses—passion, ambition, and reason—and he thought that the rational person under the control of wisdom could lead a noble life of balance and moderation. The goal is to realize our creative potentialities to the fullest, and this includes our capacity for moral behavior. A good life is achievable by men and women without the need for divinity. It is simply untrue that if one does not believe in God, "anything goes."

So many infamous deeds have been perpetrated in the name of God—the Crusades, the Inquisition, religious-inspired terrorism in Palestine, the carnage among three religious ethnicities in the former Yugoslavia—that it is difficult to blithely maintain that belief in God guarantees morality. It is thus the height of intolerance to insist that only those who accept religious dogma are moral, and that those who do not are wicked.

The truth is that, from the fatherhood of God, religionists have derived contradictory moral commandments. Muslims, for example, maintain that polygamy is divinely inspired; Catholics believe in monogamy and reject divorce; most Protestants and Jews accept divorce under certain conditions. God's name has been invoked for and against slavery, capital punishment, even war. The German and French armies sang praises to the same God as they marched off to slaughter each other in the world wars.

Perhaps one should ask, can a person be truly ethical if he or she has not developed a caring moral conscience? It need not be based upon the fear or love of God, nor on obedience to his commandments, but rather on an internalized sense of right and wrong.

We live in a multicultural world with various religious and secular traditions. Chinese, Japanese, and Indian cultures do not accept Western monotheism, yet persons in those societies can be as virtuous, kind, and charitable as Westerners.

Every civilized community, whether religious or secular, recognizes virtually all of what I call the "common moral decencies": We ought to tell the truth, keep promises, be honest, kind, dependable, and compassionate; we ought to be just and tolerant and, whenever possible, negotiate our differences peacefully.

One needs no theological grounds to justify these elementary principles. They are rooted in human experience. Living and working together, we test them by their consequences; each can be judged by its consistency with other cherished principles. A morally developed person understands that he ought not to lie—not because God or society opposes lying, but because trust is essential in human relations. No human community could endure if lying were generalized.

Genuine moral awareness needs to be nourished in the young; we need to develop character, but also some capacities for ethical reasonings. It is by education that we can develop the best that is within us.

Clearly, there are moral disagreements; and there are new moral principles that have emerged historically. Often the battles for them have been long and arduous, such as the struggle against slavery and for the recognition of women's rights. The need today is to extend our ethical concern to all members of the world community and to find common ground with men and women of differing faiths and ideologies.

Christians, Muslims, and Jews believe in the promise of eternal salvation for those who obey God's commandments. Humanists prefer to focus on this life *here and now,* and they strive to develop the arts of intelligence to solve human problems. They wish to rely on education, reason, science, and democratic methods of persuasion to improve the human condition.

What is the goal of humanist ethics? It is to mitigate suffering and to increase the sum of human happiness, both for the individual and the community at large. Although interested in social justice, humanists nevertheless emphasize the virtues of individuality. They wish to provide the opportunities for individuals to lead the good life on their own terms, though with sensitivity to others' rights. They believe in cultivating the conditions for moral growth. They affirm that life is worthwhile and that it can be a source of bountiful joy. They believe in developing self-reliant persons, who are rational and responsible, who can discover and appreciate truth, beauty, and goodness, and who are able to share these stores of wisdom with others.

Response to Religious Absolutists

Statements by religious fundamentalists that we need political leaders who will uphold God's absolute standards scare the hell out of Americans who believe in liberty. We may ask: Which absolutes? And whose God? And what would happen to our constitutional secular democracy and the First Amendment principle of separation of church and state if these views were to prevail?

What moral standards are without exception? The Bible states, "Thou shalt not kill"; yet believers condone killing in times of war ("Praise the Lord and pass the ammunition") and the death penalty. Likewise, many defend voluntary euthanasia for terminally ill patients out of moral compassion. Yes, in principle we ought not to kill, but this is a *general* rule, not an absolute. And we ought not to steal; yet some justify Robin Hood's actions, particularly when the sheriff of Nottingham is a tyrant.

Many moral dilemmas that we face in life are not between good and evil (a simplistic view of morality), but between two or more conflicting goods, or the lesser of two evils. Here there is no substitute for rational ethical inquiry in evaluating competing goods and rights. This does not imply a breakdown of morality.

Surely religionists and atheists share moral principles and values in common. Their application, however, depends upon intelligent reflective inquiry in concrete cases. Reasonable persons will draw upon objective criteria: the facts of the case, a cost-benefit analysis, weighing the consequences of alternatives, cherished moral principles, etc. It is especially important in our pluralistic democracy, where there are competing conceptions of the good life, that we justify our moral choices on rational grounds.

It is presumptuous of right-wing religionists to proclaim that *their* values are absolute and sanctified by God. Would they accept the pope's proclamation that contraception and divorce are absolutely wrong? Apparently most Roman Catholics do not. Would they accept the Ayatollah's death sentence against Salman Rushdie for blasphemy? If not, on what grounds?

It is downright false to assume that without God "everything is permitted." The lessons of history demonstrate that unbelievers can be good, and believers wicked. All too many absolutists are intolerant and mean-spirited, and have committed all too many infamies. The "road to hell" is paved by fanatics seeking to impose their moral absolutes on others.

Secular humanists have a deep sense of moral obligation to their fellow human beings—without need of clergy or divine sanctions. I would urge evangelists and fundamentalists to exercise tolerance (a key humanist virtue) toward those who do not accept their faith. It is unfair to blame the decline of morality in America on secularism, as they are wont to do. The level of church-going in America is higher than that in other secular Western countries; yet we have the highest rates of violence, crime, and people in prisons. What we need is *not* a return to the old-time religion, but a commitment to reasoned dialogue and the cultivation of ethical wisdom.

17

Humanism and the Idea of Freedom

A dialogue between Baptists and humanists is long overdue. In a multicultural society, such as America, it is important that people from diverse religious and nonreligious traditions engage in discussion to define any differences and more meaningfully to discover any common ground.

As a secular humanist, I am often asked, What does the term "humanism," or indeed "secular humanism" mean? These terms have been attacked by religious fundamentalists on the right for well over a decade. How shall we define "humanism"?

Defining Humanism

The term "humanism" means different things to different people. For some, it has been simply identified with the study of the "humanities." For others, it has been used synonymously with "humanitarianism." Its critics have

This paper was read at the University of Richmond at the first "Baptist/Humanist Dialogue," October 5–6, 1995. It was published in Paul D. Simmons, ed., *Freedom of Conscience: A Baptist/Humanist Dialogue* (Amherst, N.Y.: Prometheus Books, 2000), pp. 34–40. Several Baptist participants were professors at Baptist colleges and seminaries, who felt that their academic freedom had been curtailed. They were disturbed by the demand for conformity in matters of conscience, in interpreting the Bible, and in accepting a submissive role for women.

condemned it as a mere form of "godless atheism." Some have considered humanism to be a new religion, and others a new form of anti-religion. Yet even critics would not consider themselves "anti-human" or "anti-humanistic." Like "peace," "motherhood," or "virtue," it has been all things to all men and women.

Is there any way out of this impasse? Humanism is not "an ideal essence," laid up in some Platonic heaven of abstract meanings. On the contrary, in unraveling its meaning, we see that it has been used primarily to refer to a set of moral principles. And in this linguistic controversy there is a central idea that emerges strongly, namely, the idea of freedom. I submit that throughout its long tradition of the usage the term "humanism" has embodied the sense of freedom. This may surprise many Baptists who share a commitment to freedom of conscience and defended this value in the early days of the American Republic.

Humanism has had a long career in human history. Indeed, it is one of the oldest and deepest intellectual traditions of Western civilization. From the great philosophers, scientists, poets, and artists of the Greek and Roman world, through the Renaissance and the Protestant Reformation, to the development of the New Science in the sixteenth century, the discovery of the New World, and the democratic revolutions of the modern era, the basic humanist value of *liberty* has inspired the noble deeds and passions of countless men and women.

The first principle of humanism, thus, is its commitment to the idea of freedom. But what does that mean? First, freedom of conscience within the inward domain of thought and belief; second, the free expression of ideas; and third, freedom of choice in the moral domain. This latter ideal may trouble many Baptists, but humanists believe that it is implied in the very idea of freedom.

The above ideas have been central to American democracy and were among the Founding Fathers. Thomas Jefferson, the author of the *Declaration of Independence*, affirmed his opposition to any tyranny over the human mind. And James Madison, chief architect of the *Constitution* and the *Bill of Rights*, affirmed that government should make no law abridging freedom of speech or press, or prohibiting the free exercise of religion. American democracy protects all forms of belief. Similarly, many American patriots have defended individual moral freedom, though it must be allied with moral responsibility.

Humanism and libertarianism are thus indelibly intertwined. Humanists in the modern world have been among the chief critics of the authoritarian or totalitarian state and have provided a powerful case in defense of democracy. Indeed, it may surprise many Baptists, but the first intellectual opponents of fascism and communism are humanists who have defended the open society.

What is often overlooked in this debate is that liberty may be endangered by other powerful institutions within society which *de facto* tend to limit the inward domain of conscience, freedom of expression, and moral freedom. I have in mind many established churches, temples, or mosques which may seek to deny the most fundamental of all human rights: primacy of conscience and the right to believe *or*—especially important for humanists—the right *not* to believe. This is especially evident in Muslim countries today, where there is no separation between church and state, and theocracies repress human freedom. In the name of Allah, Salman Rushdie (an avowed secular humanist) was condemned to death by the Iranians as a blasphemer, as was Taslima Nasrin in Bangladesh; no one is permitted to dissent from prevailing Islamic doctrines. Extremist Muslim fundamentalists do not simply excommunicate, they seek to execute! In the history of religious persecution, the Roman Catholic Inquisition no doubt stands out as an infamous illustration of the worst-case scenario: the use of state power to enforce religious orthodoxy. But even where there is a separation of church and state, churches may have powerful influences on adherents, demanding absolute obedience. The threat of excommunication, the censorship of publications, or the limits imposed on professors are unfortunate illustrations of the power of some churches seeking to enforce discipline in a community. Does a church in a free society have a legal right to do that? Does it have a moral right, particularly in a pluralistic democracy? A similar question can be asked of powerful economic forces: the coercive sanctions imposed by a corporation or a company town on its employees, or perhaps a union on its members.

In his famous work, *On Liberty*, John Stuart Mill presents a set of arguments as to why the rights of the minority need to be respected, including the rights of heretics, dissenters or iconoclasts. For Mill, the real question is, How do you deal with the tyranny of the majority? Namely, if a majority of people in the community fervently believe that something is true, do they have a right to exercise coercion, whether subtle or overt, in order to demand conformity to the prevailing orthodoxy? Mill argues that people who deny freedom imply that they are infallible and/or that they have a monopoly on truth or virtue. But who can say with assurance that their beliefs have reached their final formulation, and that they alone have the Absolute Truth? For the humanist, truth is a product of the give-and-take of a free marketplace of ideas, and it depends upon criticism and of response to that criticism if it is to prevail. One should always leave open the possibility that one may be mistaken. Surely the very premise of democracy is that we have something to learn from those who disagree with us. But, said Mill, even if we believe we have the Absolute Truth, not to allow it to be contested by dissenters would mean that it would degenerate into a mere habit of thought. It would lose all conviction and vitality for succeeding generations—unless it were allowed to be challenged. Those who would deny freedom of inquiry perhaps mask a hidden fear that if there were really an open debate, they would lose out in the end. The censor or inquisitor thus seeks to unfairly impose his or her views by insisting on conformity by everyone.

The point is, quasi-public institutions, such as the Church, Corporation, University, or even public opinion, may be as powerful as the government, and individuals should have the right to dissent in the face of such power. Perhaps the strongest argument in favor of freedom of conscience and free expression is that these freedoms will, in the long run, contribute to the public good and to the progressive development of knowledge, for they allow for the emergence of creativity and the uncovering of new dimensions of truth. By closing the parameters of dissent, the quest for knowledge is restricted. Given the great problems that humankind constantly faces, it is essential that new avenues for the discovery of knowledge be encouraged.

The most awesome attack on freedom in recent time was in Marxist-Leninist-Stalinist societies. During the long night of communism, a reign of ideological terror prevailed, and anyone who disagreed with or defied the doctrine of dialectical materialism was severely punished. If Salman Rushdie stands as the symbol today of the idea of freedom in the Islamic world, so Andreí Sakharov, who was a great exponent of secular humanist ideals, symbolizes the yearning for freedom in Soviet society. In American society today many humanists fear that sincere and devout Baptists who believe in inerrancy have become part of an oppressive coalition that will seek to use the state to impose their sectarian doctrines of creed and morality on dissenters.

Freedom

Permit me to apply the idea of freedom very briefly to three areas that need exploration. First, to the question of academic freedom in the university; second, to the scientific investigation of religion; and third, to the area of women's rights.

The university is a unique institution in society, for it has a double function. On the one hand, it is interested in transmitting to students the best knowledge available within civilization and in cultivating an appreciation for the quest for knowledge. This is known as *Lernfreiheit*; that is, it is the right of students to learn and to be able to engage in free inquiry. Students at a university are thus placed in contact with the best minds and the best literature in many domains of human experience and knowledge. They have a right to cultural freedom without censorship or prohibition.

The university, however, is especially valuable because it is the primary institution committed not only to teaching but to research. Here we need to distinguish the college from the multiversity, though I would argue that similar considerations should apply to colleges and seminaries—if they are to achieve intellectual excellence. What is pre-eminent is that institutions devoted to learning are not only repositories of wisdom and truth in many fields of human endeavor, but that they provide fertile soil where professors and researchers can come together and explore cooperatively the quest for knowledge. This is why *Lehrfreiheit*; that is, the right of teachers and professors to do research, presupposes, as its basic principle, academic freedom. Thus institutions of higher learning seek to appoint to their faculties the best qualified minds who are competent in their fields and recognized by peers. And they must give to their faculties the freedom to pursue research, to reach conclusions which, on the basis of their considered judgments, seem to be true, and this entails the right to speak out and publish the results. Any effort by the corporate body to censor or to prohibit is to deny *Lehrfreiheit*, and this is a betrayal of the very idea of learning itself. Academic freedom has a long and distinguished career, and the great universities—from Oxford, Cambridge, the Sorbonne to Harvard, Stanford, and state universities—respect this right. This not only applies to secular, but increasingly to religious institutions as well.

Authoritarian institutions fear new ideas; they persecute intellectuals; and they seek to deny tenure to their professors. Is there a necessary contradiction between an ecclesiastical institution and a university such that an ecclesiastical institution need not permit *Lehrfreiheit*? If this is the case, then a viable university no longer can be said to exist, and the university has become a place for indoctrination; it is not receptive to the quest for truth, nor does it respect the right of dissent. Humanists, of course, will not compromise on this point. To declare than an institution is devoted to higher learning in some sense must entail academic freedom untrammeled by the threats of a Grand Inquisitor.

This leads to the question, What should be the extent or limits placed on freedom of inquiry in regard to religious doctrines? It is again the conviction of the humanist that every domain of human interest, whether economics or politics, the social sciences, natural, or biological sciences, history, literature, philosophy, the arts, or religion, should be amenable to critical investigation. This means that there should be no blocks placed on free inquiry. It means that the Koran, the Bible, or the Book of Mormon should be read like other books, by using the best tools of scientific, linguistic, and scholarly research; and that any claims made in these books can be examined critically and evaluated cognitively.

Now there are those who are opposed to this, and who believe that this kind of free inquiry would endanger faith, upset dogma, or imperil the body of church doctrines. That may or may not be the case. Surely, if one has little hope that an analysis of belief will survive critical scrutiny, or if one believes that questioning beliefs would lead to their destruction, then so much the worse for the beliefs. If we are truly convinced that our beliefs are true, we ought to permit them to be challenged. And that is why in the area of biblical or Koranic or Mormon criticism, the most advanced tools of scientific, historical, and scholarly analysis should be employed.

The third area for discussion is the question of human rights, and in particular, to what extent should they be extended to women? Are not women equal in dignity and value? Do not the interests and needs of women deserve equal consideration with those of men? Or should the role of women in the various institutions of society be relegated to a submissive position, and should women obey men? It is clear that patriarchal attitudes have long dominated our social institutions. The battle of the suffragist movement for the vote gave women political equality. Similarly for the great battles in the economy and in institutions of higher learning today where there is a need to allow women to achieve positions of responsibility. The real question is, Do not the *same* considerations apply to religious institutions? There are some religions today that believe that women should serve in the pulpit to the same extent as men; that the viewpoints of women are entitled to be heard, that their freedoms should be protected and encouraged. Other religions deny this. Is God the Father a male and is sexist language tolerable in a religious context? Humanists agree with the feminist indictment; and indeed many of the outstanding leaders of the feminist movement worldwide have been humanists, such as Betty Friedan, Gloria Steinem, and Simone de Beauvoir. Hence, the cause of women for liberation is continuous with the cause of freedom and this means that biblical language and practice needs to be revised in the light of these considerations.

Rational Inquiry

The concluding point that I wish to raise briefly is the commitment of humanists to rational inquiry. Humanists believe that it is essential that we encourage the tools of critical thinking in society. Belief should not simply be a question of faith or dogma, emotion or intuition, custom or authority, but should be guided by informed judgment, an appeal to evidence and logic, and tested in practice. Humanists maintain that there are areas of reliable knowledge that we share, and that truth is not established by authoritarian declaration but by objective justification. This is particularly the case in institutions committed to inquiry, for they are based on the idea that debate, discussion, dialogue are the very essence of freedom.

Thus the idea of freedom as a humanist value is concomitant with the idea of reason; and humanism may also be defined by its commitment to methods of rational inquiry. It is our conviction that we ought to engage in a dialogue with those with whom we disagree, and that we ought not to seek to impose our views on others by power of force, but we ought to listen in a fair and impartial way to claims made in the free marketplace of ideas, and we ought to try to work out as best we can what seems most likely true on the basis of cooperative, rational inquiry. This is why a dialogue between Baptists and humanists is so important.

Part Three

Neo-Humanist Politics

18

The Need for a New Secular Coalition

It is time for secular humanism to take a new direction: we need to develop a new political agenda. I suggest that we call this *neohumanism* so as to distinguish it from other forms of humanism that are not concerned with social or political issues.

For a long time I have argued that humanists should concentrate primarily on ethical, philosophical, and scientific issues. What we needed was a basic cultural reformation of society. Our main focus was to be (1) on defending naturalism against the reigning supernatural systems of belief; (2) emphasizing the importance of scientific inquiry rather than revelation, mysticism, faith, intuition, or authority; and (3) providing viable humanistic ethical alternatives to theologically grounded moralities.

In the past, I have deplored the efforts of previous generations of humanists to politicize humanism by converting it into a party platform and/or by endorsing candidates for office. We reasoned that one could be a secular humanist and at the same time be a liberal, libertarian, conservative, or radical. Indeed, humanists may differ in their opinions about political and economic policies or political candidates. After all, Christians and Jews can vote

Adapted from "Humanist Politics: The Need for a New Coalition," *Free Inquiry* 18, no. 4 (Fall 1998), pp. 5, 60; and "A New Secular Coalition," *Free Inquiry* 20, no. 1 (Winter 1999/2000), p. 6.

Democratic or Republican, the Green Party or the Conservative Party, socialist or libertarian. Why not the same for secular humanists?

All of the above doubts about involvement in politics I think are still valid; yet at the same time it is a mistake for humanists to withdraw entirely from the political arena or to refuse to take a stand, especially when vital social and ethical principles are at stake and if there are political obstacles to cultural reformation. Humanists should not be politically neutered; they ought to be *engagé* in the key political controversies of the day.

It is clear that religious factions are involved in a big way in politics. They seek to persuade public opinion and influence candidates. The Christian Coalition clearly wishes to convince everybody to accept a biblically oriented agenda. It is against abortion, euthanasia, women's rights, equality for gays, affirmative action for minorities, and it is for capital punishment, a strong military-defense budget, lower taxes, and reduced welfare aid. Similarly, the Vatican intervenes in the American political process by opposing abortion, birth control, euthanasia, and other issues concerning church doctrine; it is forever urging government financial aid for parochial schools.

It is likewise clear that neo-humanists have certain hot-button issues. It is time that we speak out loud and clear as secular humanists. Indeed, there is, I submit, a compelling need today to develop *a new Secular Coalition.*

This Coalition I hope will be able to enlist a wide range of supporters, from neo-humanists, secular humanists, atheists, and agnostics, to liberal religious allies and religious humanists. I hope that this Secular Coalition will focus on a number of core issues: a defense of the strict separation of church and state; a commitment to secular democracy and the secular state; and a public campaign to uphold the rights of *both* unbelievers and believers. Given the growth of religious chauvinism today, I believe it vital that there be a strong advocacy of secularism, not only in the United States, where the First Amendment prevails, but throughout the world. Such a coalition would be able to support candidates and parties who wish to defend the secular state.

Today other new challenges have emerged. I submit that we should be concerned with ensuring free inquiry in the marketplace of ideas. Hence, we should support all efforts to open the communications media to the expression of a wide range of opinions. Unfortunately, powerful conglomerates increasingly dominate or control the news business, often leaving little room for the dissemination of dissenting viewpoints, and they have virtually blotted out the skeptical, rationalist, and humanist viewpoint, emphasizing instead a spiritual-paranormal bias.

We should also be concerned, as humanists, with the growing disparities in wealth and income between individuals within societies and with the widening gap between rich and poor nations on the global scale. Humanists have in the past criticized narrow egalitarian policies, especially where they seek simply to distribute equal shares of the same pie; a viable alternative is to expand the pie, thus increasing the total amount of goods and services that are available. Today as national economies become global and jobs are exported to cheaper labor markets overseas, the disparities widen even further.

Since humanists are deeply concerned with our planetary habitat, preservation of the ecology and population control should be high on our list of priorities. We have an obligation, not only to the totality of humankind on the planet, but to future generations yet unborn. This means that humanists can play a vital role in helping to define a *global ethic* and advancing the cause of a genuine planetary community, thus transcending ancient differences that are no longer relevant in the postindustrial information age. This planetary community would seek to transcend the ethnic rivalries and religious chauvinisms of the past; and it would seek to find common ground between different cultural traditions.

I submit it is time that neo-humanists organize a new secular humanist coalition—planetary in scope—comprising all those who agree with the humanist outlook, humanist ethics, and our basic commitment to the democratic secular state.

19

The McCarthyites of Virtue

So much has been written and said about the Clinton-Lewinsky morality play—what can I add that is new? Perhaps that the situation vividly illustrates the deep *Kulturkampf* between two contending conceptions of morality engulfing America.

The Clash of Two Moralities

Humanism expresses the core ethical values of large sectors of life in American and Western civilization. Coming to fruition in the modern world, humanistic morality prizes individual freedom and autonomy. It believes that individuals should be allowed to express their unique talents, needs, and desires without undue repression by the state or society. The goal is the enhancement of the good life: happiness and well-being for the widest number of individuals.

A key humanist ethical principle is "the right of privacy," which states that society should respect the right of an individual to control his or her own personal life. That includes a person's body, possessions, beliefs, values, preferences, and actions—so long as they do not intrude upon or deny the rights of other individuals.

Originally published in *Free Inquiry* 19, no. 1 (Winter 1998–1999), pp. 5, 61; the response to the critics was originally published in *Free Inquiry* 19, no. 2 (Spring 1999), pp. 61–61.

The principle has been applied to the right of confidentiality, private sexual preferences (between consenting adults), the right to birth control, abortion, euthanasia, and informed consent concerning a person's medical treatment. This entails the principle of tolerance: one need not necessarily approve of the diversity of life styles; one simply permits them to coexist.

This does not deny that there is a public sphere; nor that society does not have the right to regulate conduct or to enact laws consonant with the public good. But there is the recognition that there should be limits to undue intrusion into the private sphere—and this applies to beggars and kings, ordinary citizens and presidents.

Humanist morality holds that individuals have responsibilities to others; it emphasizes the virtues of empathy, compassion, and altruism, and it encourages rational dialogue and the negotiation of differences. It is also concerned with social justice. The good society is one that maximizes the opportunities for individuals to make their own choices. It seeks to change conduct by education and persuasion rather than legislation and compulsion.

The above is consonant with the democratic ethic that has evolved over three centuries. Humanist morality in this sense permeates modern culture. Interestingly, these ethical principles have been shared by liberals, conservatives, and libertarians, all of whom cherish the preciousness and dignity of the individual and the right to self-determination.

A second conception of morality that contends today is premodern. It has its roots in historical religious traditions. This morality is biblical (or koranic); it is guided by a set of absolute moral commandments. Thou shalt not commit what is considered to be sinful: adultery, abortion, euthanasia, homosexuality, etc. Some advocates of this morality would call upon the state to legislate moral conduct. They would censor pornographic literature or the arts. They would invade the bedroom and define the physician-patient relationship. They think that some kinds of behavior are so depraved and wicked that the behavior ought to be prohibited by society. Interestingly, social conservatives and left-wing communitarians have often shared a similar agenda about private morality, wishing to codify and confine it. This is given a special meaning today by the emergence of the Christian Coalition in the United States and of fundamentalist religions in other parts of the world. They are intent on overthrowing humanist morality and imposing a puritanical inquisition.

The Starr Chamber: Prosecutorial Inquisition

No doubt the underlying ethical issue in the Clinton-Lewinsky impeachment drama was the clash of these two conceptions of morality. The new Puritans insist that the president should have no private life; since the White House belongs to us, he is not permitted to do anything immoral in his goldfish bowl. He must be a Paragon of Virtue. Clinton, for them, has committed two unpardonable sins: adultery and lying.

Leading the pack of wolves of the new inquisition, of course, was Judge Kenneth Starr, whose prosecutorial zeal allowed the pornographic report of his investigation to be released to the public. The McCarthyites of Virtue express the conservative religious traditions of American society, including a wide range of different denominations. William Bennett functions as the imperious U.S. *gauleiter* of Vatican morality. Trent Lott and Newt Gingrich are defenders of the official Baptist biblical line: If the Bible condemns homosexuality, it must be wrong. William Kristol and David Frum in the Murdoch-sponsored new conservative ideological journal, *Weekly Standard*, defend a form of Judaistic Old Testament morality. The anti-privacy judge Robert Bork believes that we live in moral chaos (see his *Slouching Towards Gomorrah*) and that we need to return to an age of censorship and prohibitive legislation. Senator Orrin Hatch adds the Mormon defense of absolutist morality. There are others in the coalition: Reverend Richard John Neuhaus, a "holier than thou" former Lutheran prelate, now a Roman Catholic priest and editor of the journal, *First Things*, argues that the empty public square should be filled with the sacred. James Dobson seeks to instill traditional biblical conceptions of the family in the entire society. (The Old Testament is patriarchal and anti-woman. In the New Testament Jesus is anti-family, for he never married and he bade his disciples to leave their families.) Last but not least is John Whitehead, head of the Rutherford Institute. Whitehead funded Paula Jones's lawsuit against President Clinton. What is intriguing for secular humanists is the fact that two decades ago Whitehead led a legal crusade against secular humanism, arguing that secular humanism was a religion and that it had to be extirpated from the schools and all aspects of social life.

Regretfully, the anti-privacy McCarthyites of Virtue had many allies in the media, which spewed forth anti-Clinton verbiage day in and day out. The most egregious examples are Rush Limbaugh and Laura Schlesinger, who host today's two most popular syndicated radio shows. Any standards of fairness have been abandoned. A similar spectacle can be seen on 24-hour television and cable networks, where the large hallelujah chorus bleats forth daily, with very few dissenting voices.

It is clear that a significant sector of the American public was fed up with the charade. It is also apparent that many of those who wish to impeach the president also wished to fundamentally remake all of our institutions: their long-range goal is to solidify their control of Congress, the presidency, and the courts. In my view, they still pose a real threat to the very fabric of our democratic society. Hence, I reiterate my call for a new secular political coalition, involving liberals and libertarians, social democrats and conservatives—all those who believe at the very least in the separation of church and state and the right of privacy.

What we need to make clear in this *Kulturkampf* is that humanist morality has genuine historic roots within our culture, and that humanism is related to the secularization of values going back to the Renaissance. Central to American democracy is the First Amendment, and the respect for the rights of individuals. To seek to impair these cherished principles would constitute a radical assault on our democracy. Hence a danger signal has to be raised high if we are to defend and preserve our liberties against future McCarthyites of Virtue.

Postscript
In response to critics of the above:

I am opposed to perjury. I do not condone lying under oath. I also think that we need to respect the rule of law. But the U.S. Constitution states that the president shall be elected by the people. For an opposition party to seek to overturn the results of the presidential election would undermine the entire legal framework of our democracy and violate the rule of law in a drastic way. There would need to be overriding egregious public acts by the president to require his removal from office.

I think that the right of privacy, even for presidents, needs to be defended. The intrusive role of the Independent Counsel (who used wiretaps and entrapment, etc.) into the private life of the president (engaged in a consensual affair with Ms. Lewinsky) is an inadmissible assault upon individual liberty. The fact that President Clinton sought to conceal it, in my judgment, does not justify his removal from office. If applicable retrospectively, it would mean presidents John Kennedy, Grover Cleveland, Warren Harding, and others would have been impeached.

I am glad that the Senate did not take this drastic remedy. As Chairman Henry Hyde pointed out when he first began his investigation, the president's removal from office can only be justified if there is bipartisan support for it.

I regret the polarization of the country that has occurred. I think that the doctrine of moral absolutism, without the proportionality of application or the failure to recognize the circumstances to which moral principles relate, is the posture that got our country into this mess in the first place. I hope that some means of civility so essential for democracy can be restored to public life.

20

Where are the Secularists?

An all-pervasive religiosity has descended on the United States. Many secularists, humanists, and freethinkers feel besieged, isolated, and alone. Many disturbing changes have occurred in the United States. Indeed, there is now a concerted effort underway to repeal the secular society. The Moral Majority at first was widely opposed, later it was replaced by the Christian Coalition. What was considered to be a right-wing, fringe phenomenon has become part of the mainstream. It dominates the Republican Party. Even the Democrats have adopted large parts of the conservative social-religious agenda as their own. The former "naked public square" that conservatives complained about is rapidly being filled with professions of religious piety.

Apparently, belonging to a religion, whatever it is, is considered a mark of moral character and patriotism. Those who do not profess a religion are considered pariahs. No politician will admit to being an unbeliever. Similarly for leaders in business, industry, the media, and academia. The official religion is "Caprew" (Catholic, Protestant, or Jewish), though this is now being supplemented by "Himubu" (Hindu, Muslim, or Buddhist) and New Age mishmash. It makes no difference which sect a person belongs to so long as one believes in a vague, amorphous, spiritual universe. Even John Travolta and Tom

---

Originally published in *Free Inquiry* 18, no. 1 (Winter 1998–1999), pp. 16–17.

Cruise, proponents of the church of Scientology, have a place in the new American spirituality because at least they belong to a church, however nutty its doctrines.

The paradigm shift toward religiosity now occurring in America is both subtle and widespread. On the extreme end we witnessed the appearance of the Promise Keepers, which attracted tens of thousands of men in city after city, and Louis Farrakhan's Million-Man and the Million-Woman marches. On the other end of the spectrum, mainline churches have declined in membership by 25% in the past 25 years, at the same time that Pentecostal churches and fundamentalist denominations have increased in adherents.

One factor in the growth of this religiosity is the growing power of the mass media. The Telecommunications Act of 1996 exacerbated the trends toward media concentration. We have become a "mediocracy," an entertainment society focused primarily on selling products, entertainment rather than education, feeling rather than thought, fiction rather than truth. This has led to daily doses of spiritual-paranormal programming.

The Telecommunications Act has had another ominous fallout. It has led to the growth of religious radio stations. There are now 1,648 such stations, *an increase of 500 in the past five years!* Religious programming is now the third-largest radio format in the country. There is not one station in America devoted exclusively to atheism or skepticism; indeed, there few programs that express the secular humanist viewpoint.

Perhaps a far more serious phenomenon in the long run is that intellectual criticism of religion in America, particularly by liberal secularists and rationalists, has become muted. It is considered bad taste to attack religion. The last oppressed minority that needs the courage to come out of the closet are the secular atheists!

Historically, small intellectual magazines have been on the cutting edge of thought, providing alternative viewpoints so essential to a free market of ideas. Alas, today there are few if any magazines devoted to secular rationalism. The left-wing *Nation* and libertarian *Reason* attack religion from time to time, but they are notable exceptions, and their interests primarily are political. On the other side is a vast array of conservative religiously oriented journals—*First Things, Public Interest, National Review, Weekly Standard, Commentary*—all part of the renascent hallelujah choir. Among so-called liberal journals, the *New Republic* is enigmatic, the liberal Jewish-American magazine *Tikkun* is clearly religious, and *Utne Reader, Mother Jones*, and the *Village Voice*, and others are all committed to the new spirituality.

One last bastion of secularism is colleges and universities. The battle between faith and free inquiry was won two generations ago, or so we thought. Committed to modern science and high standards of scholarship, these institutions have respected academic freedom, skepticism, and free inquiry. But we should not take it for granted that the colleges and universities will continue to be hospitable to secularism, and that religion in the larger culture will not undermine their autonomy.

Unfortunately, there are now shrill voices demanding their desecularization. One reads constantly in the *Chronicle of Higher Education* how the Southern Baptist Theological Seminary and other Baptist institutions and the Mormon Brigham Young University oppose dissent and deny academic freedom to their faculties. And a movement is now afoot elsewhere to erode secularism. For example, George Marsden, a Protestant theologian at Notre Dame University, has argued that the postmodern thesis that objectivity is an illusion and that there are multicultural forms of truth should also apply to Christians, whose truth claims need to be heard on the campuses. Alan Wolf, a sociologist at Boston University, in the *Chronicle of Higher Education* (September 19, 1997) says that, although he is a "secular academic," he believes that the "rediscovery of religion" is an important new direction for the universities of the future to take—a step backwards, I might add.

As a sign of the times, many neo-conservative academics have now entered the fray against Darwinism. It is no longer the literal fundamentalist Institute for Creation Science that rejects Darwin and defends creationism. The dean of the neo-conservatives, Irving Kristol (professor emeritus at New York University), opts for the design argument to explain human origins. Michael Behe's *Darwin's Black Box: The Biochemical Challenge to Evolution* and Phillip Johnson's *Darwin on Trial: Arguments against Evolutionary Theory and in Favor of Design* continue the assault. Robert Bork, formerly at Yale, in his book *Slouching Towards Gomorrah: Modern Liberalism and American Decline* argues that, given the undermining of Darwinism, "religion will no longer have to fight scientific atheism with unsupported faith. The presumption has shifted, and naturalistic atheism and secular humanism are on the defensive." Even the influential neo-conservative magazine *Commentary* has joined in the attack with a lead article by mathematician David Berlinski on "The Deniable Darwin" (June 1997). I reiterate, perhaps nothing should be taken for granted: the battles of the past for a secular society must be waged again in the future.

We need to ask, where are the secularists? Where are the secular faculty, writers, intellectuals, and activists who will join in the fray? Is it not time that we work together in establishing a new coalition—defending reason, science, skepticism, freethought, and the secular society?

21

Darwin Re-Crucified

A disturbing new dimension has emerged in the creation/evolution controversy. The crusade against Darwinism is no longer the sole preserve of fundamentalist Christians, for many influential religious conservatives have now joined in the fray. One hundred sixteen years after Darwin's death, efforts to crucify him continue unabated. The main complaint of religious conservatives is that the theory of evolution is allied with naturalism, and this is inconsistent with their theistic faith.

Until recently the creationists' campaign had been marginalized in America. It had been predominantly identified with Christian fundamentalists who interpret the Bible literally: the earth, they claim, was created 10,000 years ago *ex nihilo!* Recently I visited the Creationist Museum near San Diego along with students and professors of the Center for Inquiry Institute, which was holding seminars in San Diego on Creation/Evolution and the History and Philosophy of Skepticism. Included in the delegation were Professor Jere Lipps, distinguished paleontologist from Berkeley, and Eugenie Scott, Executive Director of the National Center for Science Education. Scott has waged a heroic campaign against the creationists' demand that "creation science" be taught in the public schools side by side with evolution.

Originally published as "Darwin Re-Crucified: Why Are So Many Afraid of Naturalism?" in *Free Inquiry* 18, no. 2 (Spring 1998), pp. 15–17.

We were appalled by what we viewed. Many of the exhibitions displayed biblical quotations masking as "creation science" interspersed with numerous attacks on John Dewey, Isaac Asimov, Carl Sagan, and other secular humanists. The exhibit of Noah's Ark was hilarious: how Noah could handle the manure factor on board was never adequately explained, nor how Noah could squeeze two dinosaurs on board, or transport kangaroos from Australia, or how the flood could recede so rapidly to allow the millions of species aboard to descend onto dry land!

There are now new efforts by religious conservatives to crucify Darwin. Although these conservative critics reject the literal interpretation of the Bible, they believe that we need to supplement evolutionary theory with some form of "intelligent design." They reject the young-earth theory, given the strong evidence from geology that the earth is at least 4.5 billion years old. Thus, they are willing to accept some form of evolution; but they insist that creation is a factor, either at the beginning of the universe and/or at several important junctures, when God intervened in the process. Polls indicate that these views are now held by a majority of Americans, who apparently are willing to accept both evolution and creation.

The political pressures on scientists and teachers to acquiesce to religious criticisms are thus very great. Unfortunately, the National Association of Biology Teachers (meeting in 1997) modified an earlier statement defending evolution in order to accommodate theism. The original statement read as follows:

> The diversity of life on earth is the outcome of evolution: an unsupervised, impersonal, unpredictable, natural process of temporal descent with genetic modification that is affected by natural selection, chance, historical contingencies and changing environments.

At the behest of two theologians, Alvin Plantinga and Houston Smith, and after considerable debate, they deleted the words *unsupervised* and *impersonal* to leave room for divine intervention. Many proponents of evolution agreed to the change because they did not wish to offend religious sensibilities; they wished to make it possible to do evolution science without raising the war cry that it was atheistic. Whether this strategy was wise remains to be seen.

Symptomatic of the intensified attacks on Darwinism was a two-hour "Firing Line" debate on Public Broadcasting System television that aired in December 1997. The question of the debate was: "Resolved: The evolutionists should acknowledge creation." The affirmative was defended by William F. Buckley, Jr., noted Roman Catholic conservative; Phillip Johnson, Professor of Law at Berkeley; Michael Behe, Associate Professor of Biochemistry at Lehigh University; and David Berlinski. Arguing for the negative were Barry Lynn,

Executive Director of Americans United for Separation of Church and State; Eugenie Scott, who has a Ph.D. in anthropology; Kenneth R. Miller, Professor of Biology at Brown; and Michael Ruse, Professor of Philosophy and Zoology at Guelph University. The burning issue was whether Darwin's theory of evolution implied naturalism and atheism, and whether it needs to be supplemented by some form of creationism.

Buckley did not deny evolution; he only wished to argue that evolutionists "should acknowledge creation as an explanation for cosmic and biological happenings." Pope John Paul II recently reiterated the Roman Catholic Church's support of evolution. The pope qualified this, however. At a meeting of the Pontifical Academy of Sciences (October 22, 1997), he said that, although the Church recognizes the physical continuity between humans and nature, the spiritual soul is "immediately created by God" and the "transition into the spiritual" cannot be observed or measured by science.

Those who defended the affirmative side of the debate sought to do so by finding gaps in Darwinian explanations. Phillip Johnson, author of a series of books attacking Darwin, pointed out that there are arguments among scientists about the various kinds of mechanisms at work in the evolutionary process—for example between Richard Dawkins, Daniel Dennett, Steven Pinker, and Stephen Jay Gould about the importance of natural selection versus punctuated equilibrium. What especially exercised Johnson is the fact that many people use Darwin as an argument for naturalism and atheistic materialism.

Michael Behe said that he supported evolution as a fact, yet he wished to leave room for intelligent-design theory. Such design is manifested, he said, in the creation of the universe, in the fact that life is "finely tuned," and especially in the irreducible complexity of cells. His argument was that Darwinian natural selection fails to account for the evolution of complex biochemical machinery found in every living cell.

The negative team in the debate sought to demonstrate that evolution theory is so well supported by converging lines of evidence from a wide range of sciences that it would be difficult to deny. In response to Phillip Johnson, Eugenie Scott argued that descent with modification and the emergence and extinction of species found in the fossil record can be explained by natural selection, differential reproduction, genetic mutation, adaptation, and other natural processes, without postulating intelligent design. She maintained that it is possible for evolutionary scientists to describe *how* nature evolves without answering the question of *why* it evolved and whether or not there is a creator.

Kenneth Miller responded to Michael Behe by showing that evolution does operate on the molecular level, that the so-called irreducibly complex cellular systems can be explained by it, and that intelligent design is an unnecessary postulation. Paradoxically, Miller maintained that, although he excludes intelligent design from biology, he personally shared Buckley's religious commitment, and that he was not an atheist.

Barry Lynn, head of Americans United for Separation of Church and State and an ardent evolutionist, likewise maintained that he was a Christian, though he rejected both creationism and the argument from design within evolutionary theory. Regrettably, none of the participants in the debate would openly come out for naturalism.

Defending Naturalism

Indeed, there are few in America today who will defend naturalism *per se*; although they may hold it privately, they are reluctant to admit to it publicly.

We may ask, What do we mean by *naturalism*? There are at least three senses. First, naturalism is committed to a methodological principle within the context of scientific inquiry; i.e., all hypotheses and events are to be explained and tested by reference to natural causes and events. To introduce a supernatural or transcendental cause within science is to depart from naturalistic explanations. On this ground, to invoke an intelligent designer or creator is inadmissible. Natural science was able to develop freely in the sixteenth century only when it abandoned occult explanations. Similarly, the Darwinian revolution of the nineteenth century was so impressive because it sought naturalistic explanations for biological phenomena.

There is a second meaning of naturalism, which is as a generalized description of the universe. According to the naturalists, nature is best accounted for by reference to material principles, i.e., by mass and energy and physical-chemical properties as encountered in diverse contexts of inquiry. This is a nonreductive naturalism, for although nature is physical-chemical at root, we need to deal with natural processes on various levels of observation and complexity: electrons and molecules, cells and organisms, flowers and trees, psychological cognition and perception, social institutions, and culture. We cannot at this time reduce the concepts and explanations of psychology, economic politics, sociology, or anthropology to physics and chemistry, but need to leave room for naturalistic explanations on various levels of complexity.

But to so argue does not entail "spirit" or "purpose" in nature, and least of all a divine being for which there is insufficient evidence. The big-bang theory in physics and astronomy is a useful hypothesis introduced to explain a receding universe; it does not imply a creator or designer. To do so is to leap outside of the naturalistic universe. Thus, naturalists are skeptics, atheists, or agnostics about the God question; they reject the existence of the "soul" or belief that it survives the death of the body.

The philosophy of materialism had been developed historically prior to the emergence of modern science. It was attacked by some philosophers because it seemed based on purely abstract metaphysical speculation. Today, it is possible to defend the above form of naturalism, i.e., nonreductive materialism, on empirical scientific grounds. Naturalism thus provides a cosmic interpretation of nature. The universe is basically physical-chemical or material in structure, it is evolving in time; human life is continuous with other natural processes and can be explained in terms of them. To defend naturalism today is to say something significant, for it is an alternative to supernaturalism, which is, in the last analysis, based on a literature of faith and piety, supported by powerful religious institutions, and is unsupported by scientific evidence. It is time, in my view, that scientists defend naturalism forthrightly as the most appropriate generalization of what we have discovered about nature, without retreating into neutral agnosticism or blind faith.

Third, naturalism has an ethical dimension; for it relates human values and principles to the desires, interests, and needs of human beings. The critics of naturalistic ethics attempt to derive ethical values and principles from theological premises. Naturalistic ethics, by contrast, rejects the idea that you have to believe in God in order to be moral. If there is no evidence for a divine plan in the universe at large, then humans are responsible for their own destinies individually and socially. We have the opportunity to give life new meaning without mythological illusions, and to achieve a better life here and now. Naturalistic humanists believe that, although our ethical values are relative to human experience, some degree of objectivity is possible in ethics without depending on purely subjectivistic caprice. They maintain that it is possible to reconstruct our ethical values in the light of rational scientific inquiry.

The new critics of Darwinism properly perceive that, if the implications of Darwinism are fully accepted, this would indeed mean a basic change in our outlook of who we are, what we are, and also how we ought to live. Darwin's "most dangerous idea" is that natural selection and other causal factors provide a more adequate explanation for the descent of humans than the postulation of divine fiat or design. The efforts to re-crucify Darwin now underway, in my judgment, are motivated by fear. I submit that it is important that scientists and skeptics defend naturalism, not only as a method of inquiry, but as a scientific account of the cosmos and our place within it, and the basis for a new humanistic ethics appropriate to the world community. To realize this and accept it with courage could be the harbinger of a new, creative, moral future for humankind.

22

Confronting "the Corporate Mystique"

It is clear that one can be a secular humanist and not accept the neo-humanist social-political agenda that I wish to propose. It is apparent that from belief in God, one can be a monarchist, slaveholder, authoritarian, totalitarian, libertarian, conservative, liberal, or social democrat. Theists have espoused all of the above positions and more historically.

Similarly, there is no necessary connection between being an agnostic or atheist and supporting a specific political party. The same thing is not necessarily true, however, of modern *secular humanism*; for although secular humanists are skeptical about theism, humanism involves a distinct set of ethical principles that put it into opposition to certain political ideologies. Humanists have held that each individual has inherent dignity and value—or at least ought to be so treated. Humanist ethics concentrates on the individual, and the actualization of his or her highest values, but it is also concerned with the social good, and this implies that it is essential to develop just societies which will maximize both individual happiness and social well-being under conditions of fairness and equity. As a consequence, contemporary humanists generally have maintained that the best way to realize happiness is by means of free, open, and democratic societies (I have in mind here John Dewey, Karl Popper, Sidney Hook, Bertrand Russell, etc.); and they have been foes of repressive institutions,

Originally published in *Free Inquiry* 19, no. 3 (Summer 1999), pp. 5, 54–56.

whether political, ecclesiastical, or economic. Humanists thus have fought for human rights as essential safeguards of democracy. They have defended freedom on many fronts—free thought and free inquiry and some degree of moral and sexual freedom. And they have defended also the democratic principle of equality; for example, equality before the law, equal opportunity, etc. Some humanists have argued that humanism also entails some measure of economic freedom—though the degree of regulation of free markets is open to serious debate.

The humanist battle historically was against the Church and its repressive institutions, and also against authoritarian governments and totalitarian states. Today, I submit, a new battle for freedom is emerging, i.e., the battle to be liberated from "the corporate mystique" that now dominates the United States and other economies of the free world.[1] I realize that to say this is akin to a sacrilege, for the corporate mystique is almost never questioned. Indeed, the "corporate mystique" assumes the characteristics of a sacred religion. Powerful corporations now dominate our culture, they are largely unchallenged and are given free rein to do what they want. Any effort to restrain corporate power is today virtually nonexistent. At the beginning of the twentieth century there was a popular outcry against the excessive power of trusts and monopolies, and the Sherman Anti-Trust Act was enacted. This effort has largely been muted in the United States, where merger-mania reigns supreme. Interestingly, mergers and acquisitions have flourished under both Democratic and Republican administrations. The Microsoft and Intel cases are exceptions, for very few corporate conglomerates in recent years have been challenged by the government. Corporate merger-mania now is also rampant in Europe and other parts of the world, though not on the same scale as in the United States.

We are all familiar with the Marxist challenge that confronted capitalism for almost a century. Nationalization of major industries in so-called socialist countries was offered as a panacea. This has been discredited. Communism could not deliver the goods or feed its people. Moreover, it denied them democracy and cultural freedom. As a result, the free-market ideology now reigns supreme. The libertarian view is that free markets should be left unregulated; for these are the best engines for economic growth. The free-market libertarian believes that this will in the long run maximize the happiness of society. Even China has been able to grow by unleashing the power of the free market. Milton Friedman argued "that the only social responsibility of business is to increase profits."[2] We may ask, Does business have any responsibilities for the commonweal beyond that?

During the 1990s America enjoyed unparalleled prosperity. Forty percent of American households were invested in equities, either directly or through retirement plans and mutual funds, and they applauded the great corporations that succeed. These companies are judged by their bottom lines, earnings, dividends, and potential growth. The president of General Motors, Charles Wilson, many years ago said that "What was good for General Motors was good for America and vice versa." Most Americans are impressed by what corporations like IBM, AT&T, Exxon, GE, Coca-Cola, Microsoft, and WalMart are able to deliver. America has become the world's only superpower. Its standard of living is rising; cheaper prices and better services are available—and this is a result, we are told, of the corporate culture in which we live. The budget has been balanced, and there is even a surplus. Hallelujah to the free market! the choruses chant.

Now, perhaps it is a sacrilege to find chinks in the armor of the corporate mystique; but I think that a more balanced appraisal would be helpful. The current economic boom (how long will it last?) is due to many factors, including scientific research and technological innovation. Industry is able to invest in new companies and bring new products to the marketplace; but institutions of higher education, in training the scientific-technological elite and encouraging basic research, have played a key role here. Moreover, the labor movement and the democratization of our institution have also contributed to our prosperity.

Yet if we take a closer look at American prosperity, disturbing trends appear.

First, many members of our society have not shared in the affluence. Indeed, the disparity in income between rich and poor is greater than it has ever been. The top one percent of the population owns $4 trillion in assets. The bottom 80 percent only six percent of total assets. Bill Gates's vast fortune is equal to the net worth of 40 percent of Americans.

Second, as corporations become more global in reach, they find it cheaper to produce goods abroad—in Asia and Latin America. Thus, jobs are exported and American wage rates must compete with those of underdeveloped countries. The working person faces the threat of job insecurity due to downsizing and outsourcing. Temporary and contingent workers replace permanent personnel, with the decline of benefits, seniority, and security—there are still no health or retirement provisions for 40 million citizens.

Third, merger mania continues. In 1998 the total number of merger deals announced rose 76 percent to $1.6 trillion, the highest on record ($2.41 trillion worldwide). These include the Exxon/Mobil merger, Citicorp/Travelers, AT&T/TCI, and this trend continues unabated. Some believe that every industry will end up with two or three oligopolies dominating the market. Many people uncritically applaud these tendencies. The sheer growth in size in corporations is astounding. Several global corporations are more powerful than most of the countries in which they do business. One has to ask the question: What will this enormous concentration of economic power do to democracy?

Fourth, the corporate mystique is such that many people believe that all areas of social life should be privatized. We have seen this happen in the pharmaceuticals industry, hospitals and healthcare, and it is beginning in schools and prisons. Are we willing to allow all of our institutions to be judged by considerations of profit alone? Business is more efficient than government, it is said. But there are, I submit, other values in society besides profit that need to be encouraged.

The American Constitution is based upon a system of checks and balances among the three branches of government. This system has prevented the emergence of one branch of government with overweening power. I submit that we need some checks and balances on the emergence of excessive corporate power. This had been held in check in the past by the existence of countervailing centers of power—which are being seriously weakened today:

(1) The labor movement in the 1930s played a key role. But the influence of labor has been reduced from 34 percent of the workforce in 1954 to 15 percent today. (It is 80 percent in Sweden, 35 percent in Germany.) With corporations becoming international, how can labor play a role when it is at the mercy of threats of international conglomerates to export jobs to Thailand or Mexico, India or China?

(2) Since the Reagan revolution, the countervailing role of the government has been diminished. The Reaganites considered government to be a major problem, and they ignored the increased power of corporations at the same time that they sought to emasculate the power of labor unions. Clinton had moved his administration to the center of the political spectrum. Embroiled in a constant combat against efforts to throw him out of office, his domestic policies were impotent; he was unable to achieve many of his programs. The anti-trust division has been weak. Moreover, corporations have spent $2 billion (in 1996) in financing campaigns, which tend to subvert the political process and prevent anti-trust action from being effectively applied.

(3) Countervailing forces, we are told, are often other corporations, which can compete in financial markets. Often this is based on new technologies which emerge to challenge older companies. There is some truth to this, but I have two caveats. First, in some industries there are only three, two, or even one player— witness Boeing in the U.S., which competes primarily with Airbus on the international scale, or cable companies which dominate regional markets and raise prices with impunity. Second, increasingly these corporations have worked out partnership arrangements (as in the airline and telecommunication industries), which weaken competition and leads to the development of *de facto* monopolies.

(4) We need a new countervailing force, namely voluntary nonprofit movements to influence public opinion, such as the American Civil Liberties

Union, the Sierra Club, the National Organization of Women, the universities, and new political alliances such as the neo-humanist coalition. Many people agree. The free market has increased the wealth of nations enormously. It has led to more efficient industries, lower prices, and increased consumer goods. Economies of scale that reduce prices are important. Similarly, it has contributed to the economic development and prosperity of the Third World by investing in new industries.

But I ask, At what price? Enormous centers of power, such as Exxon/Mobil on a global scale, have emerged with no regulation or restraint, except from the bottom line and the demands for earnings increase by Wall Street investors. I ask, Will this mean a corruption of the political system, even the castration of democracy? If one believes in individual liberty and a free society—as liberals, conservatives, libertarians, and social democrats do—and if one opposes totalitarian control, then one must worry about what the enormous concentration of wealth and power do to our democratic institutions. Perhaps it is time for neo-humanists to raise questions about the corporate mystique. In the past the predominant motto was *pro ecclesia et patria*, for church and state. The motto today, at least in the U.S., is *pro ecclesia et commercia*, for church and corporation. Interestingly, Europe is now controlled by socialist or social-democratic parties in all but two of the fifteen countries. These governments are willing to regulate these corporations for the common good; although they believe in free markets, they also believe that there are other social purposes that society needs to fulfill.

I think that there are remedies within the free-market democratic system to restrain and limit corporate control. Such remedies would not be antagonistic to our economic system, but may help to strengthen it by leading to a genuine capitalism with a human face. I can only touch briefly on some of these: (1) We can continue to extend employee ownership of the stock in the corporations in which they work. (2) Moreover, employee representatives could sit on the boards of directors of corporations—as they do in Germany and other European countries. (3) Shareholders' rights should be encouraged and protected, and the elections of officers and the voting on important policy issues should be submitted to shareholders' approval. (In order to be most effective, perhaps this should apply only to those stockholders who have owned their shares for a year or more.) Another problem here is that so many shares are held by powerful mutual funds. (4) Before a company can arbitrarily move out of a city or state, adequate notice and consultation with representatives in the area should be mandated; perhaps even their approval and/or exit fees should be required. (e) On the international level additional rules and regulations should be enacted and enforced by the World Court and other international agencies. (f) Of vital importance would be the prohibition of corporate lobbies contributing to campaigns—this may do more than anything else to limit undue corporate influence on the democratic process. No doubt there are many other remedies beyond the above that can be suggested.

Now I readily grant that many humanists—who will accept other aspects of the humanist agenda—will demur at what I have said. At the very least, I submit, we need an open discussion in America about the enormous concentration of corporate power, and possible ways of dealing with it. Unfortunately, because of corporate control of the media this is now difficult to do. There are too few voices of dissent. Only Ralph Nader in the 1996 election campaign sought to raise this issue, and George Gerbner of the University of Pennsylvania and the Cultural Environment Movement have focused on corporate domination of the media. Pat Buchanan from the other end of the political spectrum has expressed populist misgivings about the impact on American industry and workers of the North American Free Trade Agreement and other regional and global trade treaties. Eisenhower warned years ago of the military-industrial complex; this has today become the "corporate-conglomerate complex."

In any case, I reiterate that we need to begin a national debate on the role of the corporation in democratic societies. We need, I submit, a new grass-roots citizens' movement to deal with "the corporate mystique."

---

1. For a responsible discussion of this, see the book by Charles Derber, *Corporation Nation: How Corporations Are Taking Over Our Lives and What We Can Do about It* (New York: St. Martin's Press, 1998), pp. x, 374.

2. *The New York Times Magazine*, September 13, 1970.

23

The Global Mediocracy

The emergence of a global mediocracy today poses a special threat to the scientific-rationalist outlook that has had such a powerful effect on civilization since the Enlightenment. This development is accelerated by two factors: First, the emergence of the information age: new technologies have made it possible to leapfrog national frontiers and to transmit by means of satellites and computers information worldwide. Second, these technologies are owned and controlled by huge media conglomerates—the new global mediocracy is not based on monopolistic ownership but on oligopolistic control. These conglomerates produce and sell programs worldwide. They usually appeal to the lowest common denominator and blot out dissenting points of view. In the process the scientific/rationalist point of view is invariably neglected, even rejected. The concentration of wealth and power in fewer and fewer hands within the media industry has an insidious effect upon public beliefs, attitudes, and values. The global mediocracy is an integral part of the transnational corporations that now virtually dominate the world.

First published in *Free Inquiry* 18, no. 3 (Summer 1998), pp. 5, 57–59.

The Key Criterion: The Bottom Line

The large media companies are not primarily interested in scientific information or education *per se*; nor do they even think that they have an obligation to provide the public with the truth, though most do not consciously wish to distort it. Their main interest is in the bottom line, namely, maximizing profits for their financial investors. This means that their chief concern is with selling newspapers and magazines, promoting books, having high box-office sales for motion pictures, and high ratings for television and radio programs. Advertisers demand more viewers for their dollars, and market-share is the key criterion of success. We face a crisis in the age of media—because there is a conflict between entertainment and information, fiction and knowledge, and the mediocracy that we are now confronted with has transformed America into an entertainment society.

The entertainment industry today is designed for television and films that focus on images, color, and sound; they highlight sensationalism and shock, rather than cognitive or reflective thought. This now permeates all other modes of expression, including the mass tabloid newspapers, the major magazines and journals (such as *Time* and *Newsweek*), and indeed the evening news on national television networks. There is a fudging of the lines between news departments and entertainment programming, and it is the entertainment value that usually determines the content of the programs. The huge corporate conglomerates are not interested in ideas being presented in a didactic or rational way, but in packaging them so that they are saleable.

For example, a large media publisher will bring out a book; this is sold to a Hollywood studio which produces a film; it is then programmed for television or sold as serial rights to magazines; there are many re-runs; this is tied in with the music and recording industry; products such as clothes and personal items are created and sold. The Disneyfication of America has taken hold worldwide. Fantasyland appeals to all age groups and is marketed to them in various forms.

The most profitable products of the media conglomerates are those that dramatize violence, sports, sex, comedians, musical crooners, and sensationalized gossip. There is a tidal wave of misinformation and gossip that pours forth daily and seeks to entice the public to buy a book, see a film, watch a television program, and read a magazine—and generate more advertising income.

A strong staple in the American mass media is what I have called "the spiritualist-paranormal worldview." Many of the best-selling books spawned by the mainstream promote a vague spiritualism. In addition to this are the New Age paranormal religions. There is today a great fascination with angels, encouraged by Hollywood and prime-time television and also best-selling books about angels. Incredibly, 80% of Americans claim to believe in angels. Large numbers believe in Satanism and exorcism or in the reality of miracles. Today, there is widespread interest in the efficacy of prayer, including healing from a distance. The UFO-Roswell craze in 1998 and Heaven's Gate suicides are symptomatic of the new space-age religions now flourishing. The return of the Shroud of Turin of late is disturbing. Carbon-14 dating a decade ago clearly showed that the Shroud was some 700 years old, not 2,000 as its disciples maintain. Yet the Shroud industry has become big business, with hardly a skeptical viewpoint heard.

The Growth of the Media Giants

In the past decade mergers and acquisitions have led to a handful of dominant major media companies. These include two giants: Time/Warner, which had $24.62 billion in sales in 1997; and Walt Disney, which had $22.47 billion in sales. A German firm, Bertelsmann AG, which had $14 billion in sales, is now third worldwide. These media giants, of course, know no national boundaries. They own film studios, television networks, cable companies, book and magazine publishers, and newspaper chains. Moreover, they co-own many properties and have interlocking interests.

American capital has invested worldwide. But now the tables are turned and foreign conglomerates are buying American media companies. For example, Bertelsmann is now the major publisher in the United States. It owns Bantam, Doubleday, Dell, Knopf, and Random House (the largest U.S. publishing company). It publishes approximately one-third of all of the trade books sold in the United States. Another powerful company is the News Corporation, which is controlled by Rupert Murdoch. Murdoch owns Harper Collins, a large Anglo-American publisher. He recently purchased William Morrow and Avon, both owned by Hearst, which makes him the third-largest publisher in the U.S. He also owns newspapers worldwide, and satellite and television companies in Britain, Asia, and the United States.

Interconnecting ownerships of many different properties across the board is the result. Thus, Viacom owns Paramount Studios and Simon and Schuster (part of which has just been sold to Pearson, PLC, the largest British media conglomerate), MTV, and Blockbuster Video. Time/Warner owns Warner Books, Little Brown, *Time* magazine, HBO, and cable networks. Time/Warner merged with the largest Internet company, America on Line (AOL). Disney owns ABC and theme parks.

There are no independent television networks left. NBC, CBS, and ABC used to be independent television and radio companies expressing a liberal and pro-scientific viewpoint. Criticized by the right wing as "too liberal" only five years ago, NBC-TV is owned by General Electric, CBS-TV was owned by Westinghouse and has merged with Viacom, ABC is owned by Disney, and

Fox-TV by Murdoch. The same thing is true of independent radio stations, most of which have been gobbled up by chains. Today five companies have bought up hundreds of radio stations and now dominate radio broadcasting. Concentration continues to grow at a dizzying pace.

The voice of the single individual scientist or scholar or the small magazine or organization is dwarfed by these Goliaths.

Thirty years ago there were thousands of independent stores and thousands of publishers. Today, most of the independent stores have closed. There are two major bookstore chains and two major wholesalers that distribute books throughout America. Seven companies dominate 75% of all publishing; 38% of the best-sellers that appear on the *New York Times* best-seller list are published by two of these companies. Most of the small publishers have gone out of business or have been acquired by larger conglomerates. Most of the towns or cities in the United States have only one newspaper left, and most of these are owned by national chains.

This is a worldwide phenomenon. In many European countries the same process is at work, though perhaps not on the same scale. Fortunately, in many European countries there is still public television and radio. In the United States we have National Public Radio and the Public Broadcasting Service for television. Unfortunately, the funds provided these organizations by Congress are threatened with being cut; there is thus considerable trepidation and these public outlets are often cautious about providing dissenting viewpoints about the sacred cows.

Rising to the Challenge

What is to be done? I have argued that we need in the United States to organize and oppose the cultural debasement of ideas and values, and the constant diet of religion, violence, sex, and sensationalism. There are all too few voices in America who have identified this problem—Ralph Nader, who ran for president and received only 600,000 votes in the 1996 election; Noam Chomsky of the Massachusetts Institute of Technology; and George Gerbner at the University of Pennsylvania are some—but these complaints are rarely aired by the mass media. Those who are concerned about democracy in Western societies, I submit, need to mount a citizens' campaign against the power of the global mediocrity. In the U.S.A. we have the Sherman Antitrust Act, which is designed to limit monopolies if not oligopolies, but this is all too rarely applied. The criterion for limiting oligarchical control of the media should not simply be price competition, *but whether such media conglomerates restrict or encourage competition in ideas.* If we are to maintain the vitality of democracy then we should demand that legislatures and congresses break up or limit the power of media conglomerates. We need to convince the public that democracy requires diversity—independent magazines, book publishers, and alternative voices on radio and television.

I believe that the media must be open to diversity, and there are certain practical remedies that I would recommend, such as the repeal of the Telecommunications Act of 1996. This Act allowed major media companies to expand their radio and television market share, with disastrous consequences. There is, I submit, a need to limit ownership in a market by media companies. I also think that the Fairness Doctrine, which was repealed during the Reagan administration, needs to be restored, for it would require stations to give an opportunity for diverse opinions to be heard in a community. I also think that Anti-Trust laws should be enforced, especially when oligopolies intrude on the realm of ideas. There is also some need to create a second nonprofit TV and radio corporation with complete integrity and independence. This might be financed by either a tax on commercial broadcasters and/or the creation of an Endowment Fund.

From the secular humanist standpoint, we need to confront the widespread antiscientific and pro-religious propaganda now dominating the media. We believe in a free interchange of ideas; we do not want the government to regulate what and how we know. On the other hand, in the name of a free market, oligopolies now increasingly dominate public opinion. The scientific and rationalist community needs to organize a public lobby in opposition. We should insist that there be *some* criticism of religious, spiritual, and paranormal claims, and that the scientific-rationalist viewpoint have access to television.

This is a worldwide battle in which the secular humanist and skeptical movement is already heavily involved. But we also need to work out a common global strategy. We should insist, in every country where the media uncritically presents a paranormal-spiritual viewpoint, that the scientific-rationalist critique also be heard. We need to convince authors and editors, producers and the general public about the need to cultivate an appreciation for critical thinking, rationalism, and the scientific outlook. Above all we need to embark upon a *cultural reformation* of contemporary society. That is a long and arduous process, but it is one which, I submit, is essential not only for the future of skeptical inquiry and secular humanism, but for democracy itself.

24

The Population Time Bomb

Neo-humanism cuts across the ideological fault lines of the past and reaches out toward a new humanist consensus about issues that are of vital concern in the global civilization that is emerging.

With this in mind I submit that the population problem should be high on this agenda of neo-humanist political concerns; that is, we should support all international efforts designed to further family planning on the global scale, thus reducing population growth and ecological devastation and improving living standards. This means that we should support both private voluntary efforts by nonprofit foundations and organizations and public funding by various governments of the world. The United States had taken a leadership role in family planning and population assistance in earlier decades. Unfortunately, the Christian Coalition, in alliance with the Vatican, has in recent years sought to stall such efforts in the U.S. Congress—largely because of theological opposition to both abortion and contraception. Humanists need to persuade their fellow citizens—religious and nonreligious alike—that there is a compelling need to provide contraceptive information to the developing world. Religious Americans, including Roman Catholics and Protestant fundamentalists as distinct from their leaders, are willing to use contraceptives at the same rate as other

Originally published in *Free Inquiry* 19, no. 2 (Spring 1999), pp. 5, 57–59.

Americans. Why not make these services available to men and especially women in the developing world who desperately need them?

As a background to this urgent problem, I wish to focus on the severe social consequences of the failure to apply family planning methods in countries such as India. I do this because I attended in 1999 the Fourteenth International Humanist and Ethical Union (IHEU) World Congress in Bombay (now called Mumbai). Some 600 delegates from all over India and the world participated in this Congress, which was dedicated to the theme, "Humanism for Human Development and Happiness." The meeting, hosted by the Radical Humanist Association of India, was held at the M. N. Roy Centre for Human Development. M. N. Roy was the founder of the Radical Humanist Association (in the 1940s), a secular organization dedicated to the progressive improvement of the human condition by democratic means and cultivating the use of reason and science. This is in sharp contrast to the reigning religious-spiritual outlook that still pervades Indian culture.

The central question of the Congress was: What can we do to improve the standard of living and cultural environment of the Indian masses? It is clear that the need to stabilize population growth should be high on the agenda. Many affluent countries have managed to stem the rate of population increase. Although there has been some decrease in the birthrate in Asia, Africa, and Latin America, these efforts have frequently been too little and too late. India vividly illustrates the social disaster that runaway population has caused.

It had been two decades since I last visited India, yet I was not prepared for the extent of poverty and squalor and the great number of beggars that we encountered on virtually every street corner and back alley—this has increased enormously since my last visit—and it deeply shocked delegates from the Western world. India now has over one billion people, and demographers predict that its population will eventually outstrip China's. Twenty years ago the Indian government was committed to making birth-control information available—including contraceptives, vasectomies, sterilizations, and abortions—but these programs were driven by purely demographic objectives, treated women as statistics, and were deeply unpopular. It is significant that in one state in India, Kerala, where for decades individual well-being has been the driving force behind social programs, family sizes have fallen; so population growth has slowed and life expectancy is as high as in the United States. But Kerala is the exception. In most of India today these programs are languishing and the misery index seems to be rising as a result. Many Indians believe that children are "gifts of the gods," or they wish to have large families—especially many sons—to support them in their old age. Our daily taxi-cab driver, a friendly Muslim, related to us that he had six children, and that they lived in a room 10' × 10', yet he wished to have still more children! Unfortunately, many families still do not have adequate contraceptive information or the means to practice birth control.

Obviously, some people might like to have smaller families, but they do not know that it is possible, particularly if they are illiterate.

Many other reasons prompt Indians to strive for large families. A major one is high infant mortality. This is a factor in most poor countries, or at any rate among the very poor in most third world countries. Often women don't want to talk about contraception; they want help to stop their children from dying. There is a need to provide for one's old age in a country without a public welfare system. Then there is also the weight of religion and cultural practice, which limit the power of women. Females are abused from the very start—female fetuses are often aborted, and some, if they are born, are killed by their parents. Generally, women would like smaller families, but they don't have the clout with their husbands. There is also a perception in many developing countries that the North focuses on population in the South and uses it as a neo-colonialist stick to beat it. It is because of such criticisms that, since the 1994 International Conference on Population and Development in Cairo, the focus has moved from contraception or family planning to reproductive health and child care. After all, how could a humanist justify giving a woman contraceptives but leaving her to die in childbirth or her baby to die soon after?

In any case, there is strong resistance to population policies, particularly by both Muslim and Hindu fundamentalists. An estimated 300 million Indians are now below the poverty level. Unless there is a deceleration of these growth patterns, many predict a social explosion in coming years. The infrastructures of cities such as Mumbai are stretched to the limit. Mumbai is India's leading commercial city, yet its water, sewer, and sanitation systems and roads are decaying. The plight of other cities and villages in the interior is far worse. According to Amartya Sen, India's Nobel Prize-winning economist, the literacy rate in India is 52% of adults, and malnourishment strikes 64% of its children. A recent study showed that more than half of the children under 12 in seven Indian cities are afflicted with lead poisoning. The situation is grave.

There are surely some bright spots in India. It is still the largest parliamentary democracy in the world. Moreover, since 1991 large-scale capital has been invested in India, and a new software computer industry has developed in Mumbai, Hyderabad, Bangalore, and elsewhere. This is due in large part to the removal of burdensome governmental regulations and the opening up of a free market for foreign capital. Indian computer specialists are now regarded among the best in the world. As a result of this and other industrial developments, a growing middle class of some 250 million people is emerging. Yet for every step forward, the growth of population drains resources and impedes any appreciable advance in the standard of living. Mumbai's pollution is enormous—there are few catalytic converters on automobiles and taxis and unbelievable traffic jams fill the air with unbreathable smog. With open sewers everywhere in evidence, health standards, particularly for children, are difficult to maintain. Indeed, at the Centre where we met, nearby swamps were infested with mosquitoes, and many Western delegates were fearful of contracting malaria, filariasis, and other diseases.

Nonetheless, our Indian colleagues—representing at least a dozen humanist, secular, rationalist, skeptical, and atheist groups on the subcontinent, and hundreds of thousands, even millions, of supporters throughout India—are dedicated to the improvement of the living conditions of the poor. They are keenly aware of India's problems, and they have resolved to do something about it. They are especially distressed by the religious superstitions that permeate Indian culture, the intolerable repression of women, and the continuance of the caste system, in spite of efforts to prohibit it. They are alarmed by the resurgence of Muslim and Hindu fundamentalism. The Hindu Bharatiya Janata Party, which has grown in strength, has attempted to modify the secular constitution inaugurated by Nehru, the first prime minister of India, and has exacerbated the nuclear-arms race with Pakistan. Intense religious hatred and intolerance, especially between Hindus, Muslims, and Sikhs, have led to communal riots. Indeed, while we were in India the media reported there were violent attacks on Christians in the state of Gujarat.

Generally the humanists of India have taken as their top priority the need for a basic cultural renaissance in which education has the highest priority. This includes the need to cultivate an appreciation for critical thinking and science, the values of individual freedom and autonomy, self-determination and self-respect. Humanists believe that, if India is to enter fully into the modern world, each individual needs to improve his or her own condition in life. Indians need to take responsibility for their own destiny. But if they are to succeed, the rest of the world, I submit, has an obligation to help them by providing the tools. The distinguished French astrophysicist Jean-Claude Pecker felt pessimistic about the enormity of the problem and expressed some reservations about what we in the humanist world can do to help. In my address to the Congress I argued for the need for courage and determination, not despair or nihilism, and I was pleased by the positive response that this evinced from the delegates present.

An Ethic of Caring

I submit that neo-humanists need to defend the ethical principle that *we have a responsibility to care about each and every person in the planetary community*. We cannot and should not abandon our fellow human beings in Asia, Africa, and Latin America. Given this ethical principle intrinsic to the global community, there are a number of practical programs of action that follow. High on the list is the need to support family-planning efforts, to improve nutrition and health, to advance programs of modern education, to protect the environment, and to encourage foreign capital investments in new industries. Many in the West have been rightly concerned about the nuclear bombs that India and Pakistan have tested. The real bomb, in my view, that we should be concerned about, is *the population time bomb*; and the neo-humanist worldwide secular coalition, wherever possible, should cooperate in attempting to defuse it. We should do this not only because it is in the interest of the people who live in those countries, but it is in our own long-range self-interest to help secure a safe, healthy, inhabitable planet. The humanist approach must focus on the needs of the individual families as perhaps the best way to stem population growth and also improve the health and standard of living of ordinary people.

25

Reflections on the
New Left Students' Movement

The New Left students' movement played a vital role on American university and college campuses more than three decades ago. The rebellion began with the free-speech movement in Berkeley in 1964 and was brought to increased intensity by protests against the Vietnam War—from the Democratic National Convention in Chicago to the student riots in Paris in 1968. It became even more violent as Nixon took office, and in 1970–71 with the Cambodian incursions. It was tied up with the emergence of the so-called New Left, Black Power, demands for open admissions and the legalization of drugs, and widespread calls for fundamental structural reform of the universities, and indeed of American society at large. The Students' Movement more or less petered out by 1972.

This is a good time to reflect on that dramatic period in Higher Education and what lessons it holds for us today. We now have enough distance so that we can reflect on its meaning; though its reverberations are still being felt today.

Delivered at the New York State meeting of the National Association of Scholars for a conference on "Academic Freedom in Perspective: A Conference at Canisius College," held on April 26–26, 1997 at Canisius College, Buffalo, New York. This was the twenty-fifth anniversary of the end of the Students' Movement.

I will focus on events at the State University of New York at Buffalo, as symptomatic of the period, especially since I was directly involved in what occurred. But my reflections, I submit, may be generalized. The University of Buffalo (UB) was founded in 1846 as a private institution under the chancellorship of former U.S. President Millard Fillmore. In 1962 it merged with the newly founded State University of New York to become one of its four major university centers. SUNY eventually encompassed 64 campuses and became the largest university in the nation. New York State had many distinguished private institutions, but no public university. It was the intention of Governor Nelson Rockefeller to create a great university system, competing with the University of California and other state universities. SUNY at Buffalo was heralded as the Berkeley of the East. In 1968 ground was broken for a spanking new campus on a large parcel of land in Amherst. It would be, we were told, the largest single and most expensive university center ever built at one time, with plans for 40,000 students. Martin Meyerson, formerly of Berkeley, was appointed in 1966 as the new president succeeding Clifford Furnas. (Incidentally, this was the same year that I arrived at UB's Philosophy Department.)

Meyerson had great educational plans—to completely remake the university, breaking it into seven faculties and twenty experimental colleges, and designing a new curriculum "relevant" to the problems of the day. He attracted to his administration educational innovators such as Warren Bennis and Eric Larrabee and several internationally known faculty stars, such as Roger Creeley, Dwight MacDonald, John Barth, Sir John Eccles, Leslie Fiedler, Lukas Foss, and Ludwig von Bertalanffy. As part of his plan, traditional requirements were to be abandoned, and students in various colleges graded themselves. Bennis described the new curriculum "as a streetcar named desire" where students could take what they wanted and at their own pace. Meyerson's plans were never fully implemented, for the main UB campus on Main Street was torn asunder by disruption and destruction, and as this occurred faculty opposition intensified to his proposals (the "old guard" they were called by the Meyerson administration). Although hundreds of American universities and colleges became embroiled in controversy during the Students' Movement, SUNY at Buffalo had the distinction, at one time at least, of being the most violent. According to the *National Review* (June 2, 1970), a journal I usually don't quote:

> ... with the possible exception of Cornell, no university east of the Mississippi has been so racked by turmoil as SUNY at Buffalo. During the past academic year there was a riot a week, complete with arson, fire bombings, and ... on at least one occasion sniper fire .... The grand finale came on March 15th, when 45

faculty members . . . sat in the office of President Martin Meyerson to demand the removal of 400 Buffalo policemen from campus.[1]

This was written shortly before the shootings at Kent State, but it was clear that Buffalo was host to one of the most explosive rebellions in the nation.

It is hard to re-create the turmoil that engulfed the campus at that time, and also to explain *why* it occurred with such ferocity. In one sense, the ferment on the UB campus may be traced back to the demands of its own Free Speech Movement, in 1962 and 1964, when Oswald Moseley, a fascist, and Herbert Apthecker, a communist, were invited to speak, despite strong protests from the community and members of the legislature. Town and gown often were at odds in Buffalo, particularly about the nature of the university. Having just emerged from the McCarthy period, many conservatives already considered UB to be a den of communist subversives. University officials consistently defended the right of invited speakers to hold forth on campus, even if controversial.

But it was the Vietnam War that brought the Students' Movement to a fever pitch. At first there was student opposition to Selective Service exams being given on campus, for many students resisted going to Vietnam. As the revolution developed, there were demonstrations against allowing the Dow Chemical Corporation (the maker of Napalm) to recruit job applicants on campus, as did other major corporations; there were demands that ROTC be thrown off campus, and that Themis, a U.S. Naval Research-supported project, be terminated.

A key part of the growing revolution was the fact that UB became the magnet for all sorts of revolutionary groups. These were the days of the hippie counterculture. In the Philosophy Department, for example, several graduate students showed up who were avowed Marxist-Leninists and/or Maoists (Robert Cohn, Terry Keegan, etc.); they truly believed that a new ideological dawn was emerging. Many of these students were convinced that Ho Chi Minh, father of North Vietnam, was an "agrarian democrat" who merely wished to return land to the peasants and to be free of colonial domination by France and the U.S.; and there was considerable sympathy for this view among some liberal faculty members. Many of the leading radicals of the day—Tom Hayden, Rennie Davis, Abbie Hoffman, and Jerry Rubin—descended on the campus to keep the pot boiling; and Herbert Marcuse, the spiritual leader of the student revolution at one point spoke to a vast throng in Clark Gym, preaching a new day in which students, blacks, and women would lead an uprising and create a new society. The universities would point the way, he claimed, but they could only do so by becoming instruments of social change; and by being intolerant of "repressive tolerance." In this all-out struggle, the universities had to be politicized. The main opponents of the movement, apparently, were the liberals on campus, those committed to traditional academic freedom and free inquiry, for they were considered to be defenders of the Establishment. (Interestingly, I had taken a course with Herbert Marcuse as a graduate student at Columbia University. He was dapper in the dress suits he wore to class every session, very polished and polite. We thought of him as a competent Hegelian scholar. His sudden transformation into the ideological leader of the Students' Movement surprised everyone, including Marcuse himself.)

The student revolution at SUNY at Buffalo, from 1968–1971, was sparked by a hard core of 40 to 50 militants; they could attract some 200–300 supporters, and some faculty sympathizers, to their meetings; and on provocative issues they could bring out 1,000 to 2,000 people and more— though the vast majority of faculty and students were opposed to their tactics. There were weekly, even daily, demonstrations of one sort or another.

The key issue at that time, for those who cherished academic freedom and wished to maintain the integrity of the university, was the failure of many faculty and administrators to distinguish between dissent and disruption. Those of us who had vociferously criticized McCarthyism of the right when it appeared on many campuses in the 1950s, were appalled by a new form of McCarthyism of the left, which now went unchallenged. The faculty was predominantly liberal or moderately conservative. It believed deeply in free speech and the right to criticize. But the militant students went beyond these parameters. They staged teach-ins, which became sit-ins; and they blocked entrances to classrooms and offices, refused to let people enter, and they often disrupted faculty meetings. At the height of the rebellion there was an estimated $300,000 in property damage, many files were trashed, windows smashed, cars overturned, 1,000 to 2,000 rare books were set afire in Lockwood Library, and strikes were initiated to shut down the university. Well over 100 people, including students and police, were bloodied at various riots.

What appalled those of us who cherished academic freedom was the impact that these demonstrations had on the very idea of a university. This included *lernfreiheit* (the right of students to learn) and *lehrfreiheit* (the right of professors to teach) as central to the university. This was graphically illustrated, for example, when the classrooms of professors were disrupted. Lionel Abel, the famous critic, and Selig Adler, distinguished historian, had ammonia thrown in their classrooms, and they along with their students were forced to flee.

In my own case, my classes were invaded on several occasions. Baseball bats and clubs were rattled against walls and windows, and my lectures interrupted. Indeed, public meetings where I was invited to speak were disrupted by the Students for a Democratic Society and later by Lyndon LaRouche's U.S. Labor Party. I received abusive phone calls and hate mail for years and was even threatened with death. One reason for this was that I was neither a hawk nor a dove in regard to Vietnam, but an *owl*. I didn't think that the U.S. should become involved in a land war in Asia; on the other hand, I considered Ho Chi

Minh to be a ruthless Stalinist and had no illusion about his "democratic credentials," and I made my views well known. But no doubt the most important reason for efforts to intimidate and harass me was the fact that I had organized a moderate liberal-conservative coalition of a thousand faculty in SUNY statewide, and I also founded a chapter of the newly established Universities for Rational Alternatives at the University at Buffalo (UCRA). As a student of Sidney Hook, I worked closely with him in attempting to provide some opposition to the disruptions of university campuses nationwide. By then, hundreds of campuses were in the throes of confrontation. UCRA attracted distinguished faculty to its cause, including Charles Frankel, Jacques Barzun, John Bunzel, Oscar Handlin, W. V. Quine, and Bruno Bettelheim among others. Our task was to defend the "vital center" so essential to the open society and the university itself.

The issues seemed to us to be clear. Did the students or anyone else have the right to intimidate and harass students and faculty or to prevent them from speaking or meeting their classes? Unfortunately, all too many faculty and administrators caved in during this period. Sidney Hook remarked that he was shocked by the failure of nerve displayed by faculty, who currying favor with students, were fearful of applying sanctions for their disgraceful behavior. Many faculty were opposed to the war and they were sensitive to the attacks on the "Academic Establishment." They thus capitulated to student demands, and they declined to take any action to protect those who were being disrupted. In the past, the assaults on academic freedom seemed to come from right-wing forces allied with the state or church or powerful economic interests. To have it come from the left seemed to make a moral difference to some of them. As men and women of good will, they believed that the students had some just grievances, and they sought to negotiate a compromise. They were surprised to discover that concessions to intimidation and disruption often led to an escalation of demands and that people who wished to negotiate in good faith were shouted down.

Martin Meyerson, a well-meaning idealist, took a leave of absence during the high-point of confrontation. An acting president, Peter Regan, a member of the medical faculty, was placed in charge. Unaccustomed to warlike conditions, in which classes and buildings were barricaded and damaged, he was uncertain as to what to do. At one point, from February twentieth to March 8th, 1970, matters had become so bad that the liberal-conservative coalition of faculty that I led petitioned the administration to bring the Buffalo police on campus to restore some semblance of civility. The twenty-man campus police force was unable to do so. We urged that those students who were responsible for the mayhem be held accountable for their actions and be suspended from school. Finally, on Sunday, March 8th, 1970, Regan agreed to summon the Buffalo Police Department—and hundreds appeared in force on campus. Although they were able to restore order, this provoked further student protests and violence, at which time the Faculty Senate, horrified by the confrontation, urged that the police be removed. Many faculty members thought that the bringing of police on campus was ill-timed and a form of overkill.

The UCRA maintained that if sanctions for misbehavior had been imposed earlier, much of the subsequent destruction could have been avoided. Their opponents believed that the university should be a sanctuary for reasoned debate (we agreed), but that this meant that the police should *never* be called. The UCRA held that the campus should not be immune to the laws everywhere applicable in society. If a rapist were loose on campus, one would clearly call for police protection. If people were being attacked and property destroyed, why should not the same standards apply?

In subsequent days some 45 members of the faculty (predominantly junior) sat in at the president's office at Hayes Hall to register their disagreement with the Administration's policies. Some of my colleagues in the Philosophy Department were involved. The sit-in was in direct violation of a court order that the Administration had secured prohibiting the occupation of buildings. These faculty members were arrested. This aroused tremendous national press attention. The faculty members maintained that their "moral consciences" impelled them to violate the court injunction against sit-ins, and therefore to become "civilly disobedient." I thought that President Regan should at least have met with them. Nevertheless, they broke the law. They were subsequently charged and convicted, though many months later the charges were dismissed.

During this period, one particularly explosive situation occurred when a student mob broke into a Faculty Senate meeting, cursing and shouting, and forced the proceedings to be suspended. There were demands for "power to the people," which meant equal votes for students in faculty meetings. Many of the militants who entered were outsiders, who had never before been seen on campus. Many years later it was revealed that *agents provocateurs* had infiltrated the Students' Movement, apparently to inflame the radicals, and turn public opinion against the students' revolution. "Tommy the Red," who was a student militant, was allegedly an undercover agent.

During this period, I chaired a meeting in New York City at the Ethical Society; the topic was "In Defense of Academic Freedom." The invited speakers were Sidney Hook; Albert Shanker, and Jules Kolodny, president and vice president of the Teacher's Union; Harold Taylor, president of Sarah Lawrence College, who sympathized with the Students' Movement; and Edgar Friedenberg, well-known sociologist, who was the darling of the New Left at UB. The meeting was interrupted by a group called the Crazies, bedecked in red, white. and blue. They tried to break up the meeting, placing the head of a pig before Edgar Friedenberg on the podium. The audience was shocked. We called the New York City Police Department. After the Crazies left, I asked for reactions from the panel. Both Edgar Friedenberg and Harold Lawrence defended the disruptions, saying that "the students were trying to tell us something." Sidney Hook strongly condemned the intruders, likening them to Nazi storm troopers and Stalinist rogues. Years later, during the Senate hearings conducted by Senator Church, it was revealed that the Crazies worked for Cointelprol, an FBI undercover group, whose purpose was to arouse the public against the anti-Vietnam War movement.

UCRA made several recommendations to calm the situation on campuses, often to no avail. First, we maintained that the university should not be politicized, and that it should not be compelled as a corporate body to take ideological stands, other than to defend the integrity of the university, academic freedom and excellence, and uphold the values of the democratic society. Second, we recommended that faculty and administrators should be prepared to discuss with responsible student groups any issue, providing the discourse was in a rational forum. Third, students and faculty had the right to dissent, to protest, and to make their views known. Fourth, those who disrupted the academic process or prevented people from speaking should be suspended after due-process hearings. Sanctions had to be imposed. These should be spelled out beforehand. Fifth, if violence occurred and peace and order could not be restored by the campus police—always the first resort—then the university should call upon municipal police for assistance—the last resort. It is estimated that of the hundreds of campuses engulfed in protests, some 55 percent did call the municipal police to help quell the violence. Sixth, the courts should be used when necessary to guarantee due process and protect the rights of all concerned.

To argue for the above position at that time was considered to be "reactionary" by student and faculty radicals. I was bitterly castigated, considered a "right-wing fascist," a "CIA agent," a "lackey of Kissinger, Nixon, and Rockefeller"—though I was a Hubert Humphrey Democrat, perhaps an even worse offense at that time for some.

In my view, anyone who violated court injunctions against the occupation of buildings must be prepared to suffer the legal consequences (as did Thoreau and Martin Luther King). Those who defended civil disobedience on campus appealed to their "moral conscience" as a justification for their behavior. But if *they* could flout the law with impunity, would they extend the same rights to those with whom they disagreed? Writing in *Dissent* in 1970, I said in an article on the "Misuses of Civil Disobedience"[2] that if the Left was willing to tolerate civil disruption, then at what point would they respect those on the Right in the future who might wish to do the same? If people objected to abortions on moral grounds, did this give them the right to "block clinics where abortions may be legally performed?" Little did I know when I wrote that this would occur using the same appeal to moral conscience. Is the "moral conscience" of a Timothy McVeigh, based on an ideology of anti-government racism, sufficient justification for blowing up a building in Oklahoma City and killing and injuring innocent people? The response to this is that, in a democratic community, the rules of the game should apply to everyone; and the same thing is true on university campuses—one cannot take the law into one's own hands without suffering the consequences. I grant that under certain conditions civil disobedience may have a profound moral message, but on the condition that it is nonviolent.

In Conclusion

We have come a long way since the late 60s and early 70s. The New Left collapsed on campuses. In its wake emerged Right-Wing fundamentalists expressing equally strong moral convictions—though thankfully they did not take their protests to the campuses. Paradoxically, in the 1980s I had been vociferously attacked by right-wing fundamentalists for being a "wicked secular humanist." I much preferred this to being considered a "reactionary."

One important result that came out of that period is that universities and colleges everywhere enacted codes of conduct similar to those recommended by the UCRA. The traditional bastion of academic freedom, the AAUP I might add, waffled terribly on this issue. The faculties had been polarized and the AAUP reflected that division.

In retrospect, of course, there were *positive* contributions of the student movement. By criticizing the authoritarian character of many universities, an often recalcitrant professoriate was forced to extend some degree of student governance, participation, and consultation in the educational process. Moreover, universities were opened up to more minorities and women in admissions and appointment to faculties. It is essential that our democratic society be inclusive—though performance and admission should be judged by merit, not quotas. One negative fall-out from the student revolution is that the university suffered, in my view, a great loss of prestige in society at large; and there has been a drastic cut in public financial support, which we are still suffering. Last, the student movement also contributed to the end of the Vietnam War for those who opposed it; though whether it was that or the bombings in Cambodia that stimulated the peace talks is still debatable.

Since that period, colleges and universities have been engulfed by successive waves of intellectual assault: multiculturalism, radical feminism, Afrocentrism, deconstructionism, postmodernism, and continued attacks on the possibility of scientific objectivity and reason. In one sense these are continuous with the countercultural romantic protests of the 60s and 70s. There has also been a decline in standards of excellence on many campuses—though perhaps this is due to the vast number of students now attending colleges and universities, which are no longer bastions of a privileged elite, but involve wide sectors of our population.

Unfortunately, the university has become less vital in the dissemination of knowledge than before. In this regard, the mass media have replaced institutions of higher education. Universities and colleges are today beholden to the corporate economy and the intense demands for specialization and professionalization; and in the process the idea that the vital mission of the university is to keep alive intellectual inquiry and æsthetic creativity, a repository of wisdom, and a place where new and vital ideas are debated, has declined. With the emergence of the cyber age, a culture based upon books seems to be challenged as never before.

Universities and colleges have a significant role to play in our society. The life of the mind is surely not the sole mission of the university; it has other functions to fulfill for society; but at the very least, we need to continue to defend academic freedom and the rational exchange of ideas as vital presuppositions of a liberal education. We must be prepared to defend anew the integrity of the university from the tyranny of fads and fashions. The university stands as a key bastion of intellectual freedom, an essential principal of Western civilization, even though today many in the university are prepared to assault the canon of Western literature, from which the very idea of free inquiry emerged. This is a serious challenge to which those of us who are committed to academic freedom are called upon again to respond.

Sources

Siggelkow, Richard A. *Dissent and Disruption: A University under Siege*. Amherst, N.Y.: Prometheus Books, 1991. Siggelkow was vice president for student affairs all during this period. He gives a blow-by-blow account from one who was sympathetic to the student movement at that time, and has since modified his views.

Hook, Sidney, ed. *In Defense of Academic Freedom*. New York: Bobbs-Merrill Co., 1971. This describes the UCRA perspective, written at the height of the confrontations, with articles about many campuses. See especially my article, "Inside the Buffalo Commune, or, How to Destroy a University," on the situation at SUNY at Buffalo, pp. 220–224.

---

1. *National Review* (June 2, 1970), p. 560.

2. Paul Kurtz, "The Misuses of Civil Disobedience," *Dissent* (January/February 1970).

26

New Direction for Liberalism

Richard Rorty, regarded by many to be America's leading philosopher, argues for the need for a new liberal orientation—one that focuses primarily on economic and political reform rather than cultural issues, a participatory leftist movement rather than a mocking, spectatorial Left.

Rorty is responsible more than anyone for the current revival of American Pragmatism, especially the philosophy of John Dewey; though he has also not been unsympathetic to postmodernism (and he supports the abandonment of Dewey's reliance on scientific methodology). In *Achieving Our Country*,[1] Rorty advises us to return to the optimistic and reformist Left of the first two-thirds of the twentieth century, and he heralds the democratic and progressive philosophy of hope of both Dewey and Walt Whitman and the national pride in America that they exhibited. Dewey and Whitman attempted to secularize American life, and they expressed the values of liberal humanism in doing so. Rorty uses the term *reformist Left* (I think that the use of the term *Left* at this late date is unfortunate) to include all those Americans, liberals and leftists, who worked within the framework of constitutional democracy to improve the lot of ordinary working families and to protect the weak from the strong. These include people as diverse as Eugene Debs and Woodrow Wilson, Jane Addams and Angela Davis, John L. Lewis and Eleanor Roosevelt, A. Phillip Randolph, Jr., and

Originally published in *Free Inquiry* 19, no. 2 (Spring 1999), pp. 62–63.

Walter Reuther, Arthur Schlessinger, Robert Reich, and Jesse Jackson. These reformers thought that the struggle for social justice was essential to America's moral identity.

The reformist Left was rejected, says Rorty, somewhere around 1964 by the "New Left," which gave up on the system and abandoned any effort at genuine political and economic reform. It despaired of America, refused to work with the labor movement, and opposed the anticommunist agenda of Cold War liberals. Rorty applauds the protests of the students' movement, which helped to bring an end to the Vietnam War. But he identifies himself with the anti-Stalinism of Sidney Hook, Lionel Trilling, and Norman Thomas and the kind of social democracy that they defended.

The New Left's main program of action turned from political to cultural reform—especially in the universities—where they focused on feminism, African-American studies, gay rights, and multiculturalism. This politics of "identity," "recognition," and "difference" is concerned more with removing stigma than greed or inequality. The cultural Left wishes to blot out "humiliation" from social life, and in this it has been extraordinarily effective in gaining public support—even though the right wing sneers at what it considers to be "politically correct behavior." This is a misnomer, for what the cultural Left has defended (sometimes as a fetish) is moral and social acceptance of those who have been rejected or ignored on the basis of gender, sexual orientation, race, or ethnicity.

Rorty agrees with these accomplishments, but he deplores the fact that the cultural Left has cut all ties with the reformist-liberal Left and has thus retreated from the field before the onslaught of conservative forces. The central issue today, he says, is the urgent need to turn back to the battle for reform. For inequality and insecurity grow as global conglomerates downsize and export jobs overseas, and the gap between rich and poor is widened. We have developed in the United States, he says, a highly educated, cosmopolitan "overclass"—twenty-five percent of the population—which thrives under present conditions; yet people from the bottom and middle rungs and their children are being squeezed out of the system. We need to reestablish the American dream for them and restore its vision of hope and progress; but we can only do that by embarking upon economic and political reform, within the framework of the market economy.

The forces on the Right oppose redistribution politics, progressive taxation, governmental regulation of corporations, etc., for they believe that the free market can do no wrong. Rorty disagrees with their appraisal. He wishes to reinvigorate the democratic system (corrupted by campaign contributions) and restore social equity.

Many will welcome Rorty's advice and will agree that liberals and Leftists need a new agenda. What Rorty leaves out of his equation, in my view, is the growth of the religious Right and its role in the culture wars, and the fact that one cannot retreat from this front. The contrast in America today is not simply differences on economic policies—*laissez-faire* versus social democratic economics—but profound differences about the moral framework implicit in American democracy. Dewey espoused humanistic and secular values and an experimental and scientific approach to morality. He said that we need to revise inherited absolute standards where desirable in the light of new situations and altered circumstances. Humanist morality has been embraced by both the cultural Left and reformist liberals; this led to the legalization of abortion, the growth of the right-to-die movement, sexual freedom, the right to privacy, etc. Much of this is still bitterly opposed by the religious Right, which focuses on moral "sin" and "virtue" and ignores the social context. Humanistic morality presupposes a naturalistic framework. At the very least it seeks to bypass intense ideological-religious differences and to negotiate disagreements, appealing to the democratic civic virtues of rational dialogue and tolerance and trying to find some common ground for all factions.

At the present juncture it is unclear whether a new reformist agenda will succeed in joining disparate forces of different cultural persuasions (religious and nonreligious) into a common effort. Will the "new spirituality" now so pervasive in the public square erode the separation principle and continue to embroil America in cultural battles and prevent a united front?

The need to realize the American ideal of unlimited opportunity for all is still inspiring. Yet at the same time liberal neo-humanists believe that we need a basic reevaluation of our values, often held hostage to religious dogmas of the past and inappropriate to the postindustrial information global society that is emerging. The cultural Left is to be indicted—as Rorty so effectively argues—because its agenda was too narrow in scope. So we must go on to other frontiers. Yet at the same time we should not abandon a cultural reformation—drawing upon reason, science, and critical thinking—which many humanists feel is likewise necessary if we are to transform America into a more democratic and inclusive society. Indeed, if we retreat on the cultural front we may never achieve the other worthy goals that Rorty so eminently extols.

---

1. Richard Rorty, *Achieving Our Country: Leftist Thought in Twentieth-Century America* (Cambridge, Mass: Harvard University Press, 1998).

Part Four

Humanism Writ Large

27

The Evolution of Contemporary Humanism

Humanism and Science

The intimate relationship between humanism and science is rather unique in this post-postmodern world. Contemporary humanism, unlike most other philosophical, literary, ideological or religious movements, entails an essential commitment to the scientific outlook. This had not always been the case. In classical civilization, the precursors of humanism were the philosophers—Protagoras, Socrates, Aristotle, Epicurus, Carneades, and others. They attempted to develop a theoretical/philosophical outlook of nature, emphasized the ethics of reason, and believed that the good life was achievable through the realization of human nature. During the Renaissance the great humanists—such as Gianozzo Manelli, Marsilia Ficino, and Pico della Mirandola—were largely literary and/or philosophical authors, who called for a return to the classics, as an antidote to medieval religiosity, and heralded earthly pleasures, the dignity of

Paper read on Tuesday, June 24, 1997, at a conference on "The Moral and Scientific Arts: The Huxleys in Context," at Westminster College, Oxford, England. This conference was a celebration of the Huxleys on the 110th anniversary of the birth of Sir Julian Huxley, first president of the International Humanist and Ethical Union.

Man, and his capacity for freedom. With Desiderius Erasmus, they defended religious tolerance.

It is only in the modern period, beginning in the sixteenth and seventeenth centuries, when the scientific revolution began to sweep the classical-philosophical-theological systems, that an appreciation of science emerged. From Copernicus and Newton to the *philosophes* of the Enlightenment, great confidence was expressed in the scientific view of nature and the conviction that science could contribute enormously to human progress. Thus there has been a gradual evolution of humanism to its present position at the dawn of the twenty-first century. Humanism, perhaps better called *naturalistic* or *secular humanism*, considers scientific inquiry to be the most powerful instrument that we have for unlocking the secrets of nature and a model to be used in other domains of human conduct. In no small way it was Charles Darwin and those who promoted a Darwinian view of human evolution that have contributed most to the naturalisic humanist world view that emerged full-blown in the twentieth century.

T. H. Huxley

The brilliant Huxley family, like the Jameses in America (William, Henry, etc.) were impressive in talent and achievement. Both Thomas Henry Huxley (1825–1895) and Sir Julian Huxley (1887–1975) were strong proponents of a Darwinian conception of nature in their own day, thus contributing to the evolution of humanism. Aldous Huxley, brother of Julian and a famous novelist, was not part of this effort.

I will begin with T. H. Huxley. Two aspects of his work bear special attention, first, his position on agnosticism and second, his defense of Darwinism.

The term "agnosticism" is so widely used today that it is surprising to learn that it was first introduced a little more than a century ago by T. H. Huxley. Unfortunately, the meaning of that term has been stretched beyond Huxley's original intention. According to *Webster's Dictionary*, an agnostic is "one who holds the view that any ultimate reality (a god) is unknown and probably unknowable." According to the *Catholic Encyclopedia*, "an agnostic is not an atheist. An atheist denies the existence of God; an agnostic professes ignorance about His existence. For the latter, God may exist, but reasons cannot neither prove nor disprove it."[1]

Huxley hardly meant these interpretations of his term. He coined "agnosticism" as early as 1869 at a meeting of the Metaphysical Society. In his essay, "Agnosticism" (1895), he tells us why he introduced the term. When he had reached intellectual maturity, he asked himself if he were an atheist, theist, pantheist, materialist, idealist, Christian, or freethinker—he found that he was most sympathetic to the latter. The other denominations, said Huxley, were quite certain that they had reached a "gnosis"; i.e., they had solved the problem of existence, which Huxley was quite sure that he had not.[2] Huxley said that he invented the term "agnostic" as antithetical to the "gnostic" of church history, who claims to know so much.

Agnosticism, he tells us in his essay, "Agnosticism and Christianity,"[3] is not a negative creed; except that it is committed to the validity of the following principle: "That it is wrong for a man to say that he is certain of the objective truth of any proposition, unless he can produce evidence which logically justifies that certainty." This principle, he tells us, is both ethical and intellectual and it is justified by its success. The application of the above principle "results in denial of, or the suspension of judgement concerning, a number of propositions" held by ecclesiastical gnostics—such as the existence of God and a variety of dogmatic miraculous claims. Huxley explicitly denies that he is speaking of anything as "unknowable" *per se*, though on many questions, we have to suspend judgment if there is insufficient evidence. For Huxley, a person ought not to assert that a proposition is true unless he can provide adequate evidence to support it. Conversely, he rejects the view of the faithful that holds that "there are propositions which men *ought* to believe in without logically satisfactory evidence."

Huxley's principle, it seems to me, is eminently reasonable. In one sense, it is the culmination of an entire line of epistemological inquiry in modern philosophy—from Descartes down to the present—an attempt to find objective methods by which we can test our beliefs. There is an extreme version of the principle, defended by W. K. Clifford, a writer who was a contemporary of Huxley. In his essay, written in 1887, "The Ethics of Belief," Clifford states, "that it is wrong always, everywhere, and for anyone, to believe anything upon insufficient evidence."[4] Given the practical demands and contingencies of life, it is often difficult to apply this to all aspects of conduct, where one often has to make choices and frame beliefs on the best available evidence, although this may be fragmentary. Bertrand Russell's formulation of a similar principle is no doubt less sweeping. Russell states a doctrine that he says appears to be "highly paradoxical and subversive," namely, "that it is undesirable to believe a proposition when there is no ground whatsoever for supposing it true."[5] For Charles Peirce, the father of American pragmatism, the best way to fix belief and resolve doubt is by using "the method of science." This is most in accord with the real world, and far superior, comparatively, with all other methods.

Although we may not agree technically on all of the criteria of adequacy, nonetheless naturalist humanists, at least today, draw upon Huxley's principle, for they believe that there are *some* standards of adequacy. This principle, however, perhaps should not be equated with "agnosticism," given the confusion to which the term has led.

Another term that was widely used at the turn of the century many considered preferable to "agnosticism." I am here referring to "rationalism." In the statement issued at the founding of the Rationalist Press Association (in 1899), we read, "Rationalism may be defended as the mental attitude which unreservedly accepts the supremacy of reason and aims at establishing a system of philosophy and ethics verifiable by experience and independent of all arbitrary assumptions and authority."[6] According to the statement, the "spirit of rationalism" is the chief feature distinguishing modern from medieval life and thought. The rationalist statement goes on to say that rationalism is closely allied to modern science and critical research. According to the statement, "the physical sciences are . . . the most consistent embodiment of rationalism." What we need, it advises, is to extend the spirit of rationalism to other areas of ordinary life, including ethics and religion. Unfortunately, many people are willing to use rationalism in selected fields, but they will resist extending it to areas such as religious doctrines.

The term "rationalism" today likewise is somewhat dated. It cannot, of course, be identified with the rationalist school of philosophy, which emphasizes formal logic, deduction, and coherence as tests of knowledge, but needs to be supplemented by empiricism and include the tests of evidence, observation, and experience. Perhaps *reason* is a more inclusive term, insofar as it attempts to incorporate both rationalism and empiricism. Many naturalistic or secular humanists have used the phrase *methods of scientific inquiry* to describe the principle. This is appealing, given the tremendous progress that scientific inquiry has made in domains that were considered unthinkable a century ago. The methods of scientific inquiry are continuous with the processes of reason and experience that we use in practical life to test our beliefs. Some maintain that the generic term *critical thinking* best describes what scientists use and that this is continuous with the tests of common sense.

The appeal to scientific methodology is not without its sharp critics. I suppose that the fate of any term is to suffer criticism at the hands of its detractors. Postmodernists deny that scientific objectivity is possible and maintain that science is only one mythic narrative among others.

Given the tremendous leap forward of contemporary science in field after field, I don't see how this nihilistic abandonment of objective methods is credible, since the ultimate tests of its methodology are its experimental and practical consequences.

Contemporary humanism is closely allied with "the spirit of scientific inquiry" in the sense that, as nearly as possible, we should accept the following normative methodological principle: All claims to knowledge should be corroborated by the best evidence or reasons available that can be brought to support them; if some beliefs are unable to meet these tests, then we should be reluctant to accept them. This means that our beliefs should, in principle, be considered to be hypotheses, not final or absolute, and that their truth values are proportional to the evidential grounds appealed to support them. I think that this is what T. H. Huxley had in mind, and it is a cardinal principle of naturalistic or secular humanism, as distinct from supernatural theism.

The Darwinian Revolution

A key element in the evolution of contemporary humanism is that it draws primarily upon the sciences to frame its interpretations of nature. In this regard, Charles Darwin plays a key role, for he demonstrated how scientific inquiry could explain the origin of species. Darwin offered, for the first time, a credible alternative to creationist accounts of human origins. T. H. Huxley assumed a central role in the exposition and promotion of Darwinism. Indeed, he was often called "the bulldog of Darwinism." When the publication of Darwin's *Origin of Species* in 1859 led to immediate controversies, it was T. H. Huxley who acted as his chief public proponent, rather than Darwin himself, who was reticent about entering to personal controversies. The attack on Darwinism by Bishop Samuel Wilberforce at Oxford in 1860 at the meetings of the British Association for the Advancement of Science opened the door to Huxley's famous response. Wilberforce and other divines considered the new evolutionary theory to be "dangerous," but the good Bishop made a fatal blunder by inquiring about Huxley's "simian ancestry." When Huxley was called upon to reply, he responded:

> If ... the question is put to me, Would I rather have a miserable ape for a grandfather or a man highly endowed by nature and possessed of great means of influence, and yet who employs these faculties and that influence for the mere purpose of introducing ridicule into a grave scientific discussion—I unhesitatingly affirm my preference for the ape.

This paved the way for a fair hearing of Darwin's theory. It was, in a sense, a clear declaration of the autonomy of scientific inquiry in biology, without theological restrictions. Thus, the Darwinian revolution (like the earlier Copernican revolution) was upon us, and we have been feeling its reverberations ever since. Regretfully, it is only in that backwater of Western civilization, the deep American heartland, that creationist Biblomania still has its militant advocates.

Naturalistic humanism, as I said, draws upon the sciences, not upon revelation, poetry, intuition, or metaphysical speculation for its *weltanschauung*. This not only applies to the life sciences, but to the natural and social sciences as well. Indeed, one might ask, Where would astronomy, physics, and geology be without the evolutionary model? Contemporary theories of cosmology have extended our idea of the universe far beyond what was imagined during the Newtonian era. Since Hubble, we recognize that there are billions and billions of galaxies in a rapidly expanding universe, and that the evolution of the human species is only a small part of the continuing evolutionary processes discerned throughout the vastness of space. This marks a sharp break with the ancient and medieval view that the universe is a fixed, unchanging, perfect, and eternal system.

Julian Huxley

Julian Huxley, grandson of T. H., was likewise a strong proponent of evolution. He described his humanism as evolutionary. "Evolutionary humanism," he said, "was compatible with science." "Modern humanism must be scientific, because the method of science is the most efficient method yet invented by humanity to getting at the truth."[7]

May I quote Julian Huxley from his statement, "Evolutionary Humanism as a World-Unifying Philosophy," written in 1952:

> It seems clear that any civilization needs some over-all framework of thought and some central driving force of ideas, if it is to be powerful and progressive. It also seems clear that our western civilization lacks any such simple framework or driving force. . . .

> To my mind, the only basis on which this new framework or driving force can be built is that of *Evolutionary Humanism.*

> In the last few decades, science has, for the first time, reached the position in which we can frame a general theory of evolution—i.e., one which will cover not only biological evolution, but also inorganic and stellar evolution on the one hand and human and social evolution on the other.

> In the light of such a general doctrine of Evolution, man appears as the highest product of evolution to date, and also as the only element capable of furthering evolutionary progress. (When I say the only element, I mean, of course, the only element of the universe of which we have knowledge: It is possible that similar potentially progressive elements exist in other galaxies.)

> The full implications of the acceptance of these two facts are tremendous, both for the individual and his own development, and for society and its relation with the individual. There are implications in regard to population, human rights, education, art, conservation, planning, world government,—and indeed every aspect of human activity, and the ideas can have enormous driving force as well as being capable of development into a coherent and all-embracing intellectual framework.

> It will be the task of Humanists to develop these implications to the full in the next few years.[8]

Huxley considered humanism to be the religion of the future, though it was a religion without revelation. Although he rejected belief in God, he still wished to use the term "religious." This usage was current in American humanist circles at that time, influenced by Unitarianism. Huxley had lived and taught in the United States for many years. In his commemorative address, delivered at the University of Chicago in 1959, the centenary celebration of Darwin's *Origin of Species*, Huxley made it clear that this emergent religion of humanism would be based upon knowledge, and "instead of worshipping supernatural rulers, it will sanctify the highest manifestations of human nature."[9]

Huxley applied the term "religion" broadly to refer to any form of belief, including beliefs as disparate as communism, fascism, astrology, and numerology. By "religion" he meant "an organized system of ideas and emotions which relates man to his destiny, over and beyond the practical affairs of everyday."[10]

I think that it only confuses meanings to call everything a religion, and I think that it was a mistake for the proponents and opponents of "religious humanism," particularly in the United States, to do so. That is why the term *secular* has been applied to humanism by many American humanists, to ensure that it is seen as both naturalistic and nonreligious.

In any case, Huxley felt keenly that human evolution was transcending its purely biological phase, and that it had become psycho-social-cultural in dimension. The human species can control the direction of evolution, he said, for we may intervene in natural processes and thus determine to some extent who and what we will become. For example, society can keep alive handicapped persons who otherwise might have died in the struggle for survival, and they are able to reproduce; though Huxley, like others of his day, advocated eugenic policies to improve the genetic stock. Since Huxley's death, biogenetic engineering has given us vast new powers to manipulate our genetic inheritance.

Huxley was the first president of UNESCO (his appointment was vigorously opposed by conservative forces in the United States) and also the first president of the International Humanist and Ethical Union. He was very much committed to a liberal humanitarian concern for improvement of the human civilization. He was, for example, concerned with solving the population problem and disparities in wealth between the have and have-not nations. Huxley thought that the humanist movement could play a vital role in formulating a new creed which scientific and historical knowledge now made possible.

... There are large numbers of people all over the world who, dissatisfied with supernaturalism or with purely political creeds ... are potential humanists in believing that we must rely on the resources of human nature and their full utilization. If we do not reach some general agreement on a humanist creed and on one capable of inspiring to action and endurance, as well as merely satisfying intellectualist scruples; these men and women will remain disunited and ineffective.[11]

Failure of Nerve

Unfortunately, there has been a widespread change of emphasis and mood since then. The postmodern world is no longer confident that tomorrow will be better than today, that scientific progress is inevitable, and/or that humanism can provide sufficient nourishment for the soul. There is a longing to return to spirituality. One aspect of this paradigm shift has occurred among many evolution scientists themselves. Many Darwinians (including Sir Julian) considered the human species in some way "higher" than other forms of life, and they believed that a kind of progressive improvement of human institutions and ideals was intrinsic to the evolutionary process. Recently, however, evolutionists, such as Stephen Jay Gould, have expressed a dissenting viewpoint. We are told that the human species is not necessarily the "highest." Other very complex finely tuned species have become extinct. The same thing may happen to the human species. The Burgess shale in Canada shows a great number of exotic species that totally disappeared during the Cambrian period 530–535 million years ago. Should the human species, like the sabre-toothed tiger, dinosaurs, and millions of other species, become extinct, no one, besides ourselves, would grieve our passing from the scene. Whether the human species survives depends upon contingent events, such as the impact of meteors and asteroids, or an invasion by extraterrestrials. Lady Luck will play a role on the stage of life.

With the collapse of liberal socialist ideals has come the abandonment of any notion that history is progressive. We are skeptical of utopias. Many claim to be realists, perhaps even cynics. Since the human species has no fixed essence and no ultimate purpose, human beings are condemned, to paraphrase Sartre, to create who and what they will be at any moment in the future, and we are not certain that the future will not be awful.

There is a positive dimension to this that humanists should not overlook. Our destiny is tied up with our plans and projects, ideals and values. What these are and how or whether they will be achieved depends upon us, not nature; and if we are truly alone as a species; then we are responsible for our own destinies. This may be awesome and burdensome to many. But it can be an opportunity for humanists. Theists read purpose and design into nature; humanists can find no evidence for this solace. On the contrary, we constantly are confronted with new opportunities and challenges. Whether we seize them or choose to withdraw is an option we always face. Yet confronting brute reality is too difficult for many or most men and women. Thus, they are all too willing to postulate unseen realms beyond death to which they can flee and be rescued. They willingly take a transcendental leap. The failure of nerve is grown in the soil of existential despair; and it is out of this that spiritualistic, religious, and ideological fantasies sprout; and these are accelerated by the escape from reason. The spiritual opiates imbibed are often consumed in order to numb our sense of reality and to make life bearable—for those who lack the courage to face the universe for what it is and is not. This applies not only to my own death or that of my loved ones, but to the possible death of the human species on this planet. In the past, we could always be sustained by the view that we had a responsibility to future generations, and that, at the very least, what we do will be appreciated by posterity and by the civilizations of the future. This unwillingness to face the fact that evolution does not guarantee a future for the human species, let alone a bright one, perhaps explains why deceptive fundamentalist creeds are so rampant, and why new paranormal cults of unreason today flourish everywhere—except perhaps the British Isles—all promising escape to eternity and immortality.

Wanted: A Vision of the Future

I have thus far discussed only two aspects of the modern humanist agenda: its reliance upon scientific methodology and the scientific/evolutionary outlook. I have not dealt with perhaps the most important aspect of its agenda, which we urgently need to address. What I have in mind is the application of humanism to the normative domain of ethical and social life. Much has already been written by humanists about ethical values: we cherish individual autonomy and freedom, we encourage creativity, we seek a joyful life here and now, and this includes pleasure, creative expression, sexual love, friends and family, the life of mind and the arts, all part of a meaningful existence. We also wish to help bring into being a democratic world community, in which the principles of justice and the rights of diverse individuals and groups are respected.

But do we need *something more*? Not much has been written about our need to create a *viable vision of the future* that is affirmative and constructive, especially in response to the possible pessmistic appraisals of evolution. Living in a post-Darwinian age, we now see all too clearly that neither God nor Evolution offers any secure haven for the human species. Human population growth continues at a breath-taking pace, technological innovation transforms our planet, depletes our resources, and the information revolution radically alters the economic, political, and social systems of the past. What we need perhaps more than anything else are positive ideals about our future. We need to paint a realistic and naturalistic, though ideal, image of a possible future for humankind. This will no doubt be pluralistic, and change as time goes on; our images of the future need to inspire devotion and dedication, motivation and commitment, and to infuse life with a deep sense of meaning and purpose. We live today in market-driven consumer-oriented societies, often banal and vulgar, propelled by the need to produce and consume more and more goods and services without rhyme or reason. With the collapse of many of the liberal ideals that prevailed in the late nineteenth and twentieth centuries, there is a vast vacuum, and the only forces seeking to fill it are either orthodox theological doctrines spawned in the nomadic and agricultural age of past civilizations, or New Age spiritualist and paranormal creeds fed by science-fiction imagination run riot. We need to ask, Can humanism provide a dramatic and inspiring viable alternative?

That is the great challenge we face. We must try to meet it if we are not to be overwhelmed by new passionate ideological-theological dogmas waiting in the wings to overcome us all. Either we help develop an exciting vision of tomorrow, which human beings will find sufficiently attractive, and stimulating, or humanism will be deemed irrelevant by future generations and will be vanquished by those who promise something more.

---

1. Gordon Stein, *An Anthology of Atheism and Rationalism* (Amherst, N.Y.: Prometheus Books, 1980), p. 53.

2. See Thomas Henry Huxley, *Agnosticism and Christianity and Other Essays* (Amherst, N.Y.: Prometheus Books, 1992), p. 162.

3. Ibid., p. 193.

4. W. K. Clifford, *The Ethics of Belief and Other Essays* (London: Watts, 1947).

5. *The Bertrand Russell Sceptical Essays* (London: Allen & Unwin, 1928).

6. Gordon Stein, *An Anthology of Atheism and Rationalism*, op. cit., p. 315.

7. Julian Huxley, *Evolutionary Humanism* (Amherst, N.Y.: Prometheus Books, 1982); *The Humanist* (1952) no. 4, p. 171.

8. Julian Huxley, "Evolutionary Humanism as a World-Unifying Philosophy," *The Humanist* 9, no. 2 (July 1949), pp. 57–58.

9. Julian Huxley, "The Humanist Frame," in *Evolutionary Humanism*, op. cit., p. 88.

10. *The Humanist* (1952) no. 5, p. 202.

11. Julian Huxley, "Evolutionary Humanist II," *The Humanist* (1952), no. 6.

28

The Humanist Prospect

Britain and World Humanism

We are gathered here in London on an historic occasion—to inaugurate the new headquarters of the International Humanist and Ethical Union. Nineteen ninety-seven marks the forty-fifth anniversary of the founding of the IHEU. We are grateful for the support that our Dutch colleagues provided for the IHEU, which was headquartered since 1952 in the Netherlands. For a variety of strategic reasons it seemed appropriate to reach out to new frontiers, beyond Northern Europe or North America. This could mean a great leap forward for the world humanist movement.

Britain was one of the original sponsoring countries founding the IHEU. These included the American Ethical Union, the American Humanist Association, the Humanist Association of Holland, the Vienna Ethical Society, and the English Ethical Union (precursor of the British Humanist Association). They were joined by other groups from Belgium, Germany, and India. The first President of the Congress was Sir Julian Huxley. There were several resolutions adopted at the first Congress and a Statement of Principles and Purposes. The

Read at the inauguration of the new IHEU headquarters in London, England, June 1997.

most important resolution that passed on the closing day of the Congress was the decision to found the IHEU and to incorporate the Union in New York State. May I read from the remarks of Edwin H. Wilson, an American delegate:

> Passed unanimously by the voting delegates present, the act was greeted by cheers from the whole Congress of 250 persons. It was the historic moment in which Humanism became an organized world movement.[1]

Thus we got off to an auspicious start. We have had our ups and downs. The past decade, however, has been the period of our greatest growth. Today we number almost 100 organizations in 35 countries. We can have a great future if we resolve to work together as we enter the twenty-first century. We have a responsibility to the world community to see that we will succeed, as we are the *only* world body representing hundreds of millions of nonbelievers who share our humanist ideals and values.

Why move to Britain? Great Britain was one of the great colonial sea powers. Its vast exploration contributed in no small way to the development of the modern world—from Asia and Africa to Australia and North America. At its heyday the sun never set on the British Empire. Colonialism has all but collapsed today; though for well or for woe, English has become the chief language of commerce, the Internet, scientific and cultural communication worldwide, much to the chagrin of the French and others.

If I may wax autobiographical. Like so many in America, I consider Britain to be my second homeland. I first visited London in 1944 as a young GI, age nineteen—during the height of the Buzzbomb attack—prior to joining the Allied forces in Europe. I returned in late 1945, still in the American Army, to study at a red-brick university at Shrivenham for three months—where I was first introduced to philosophy. And I have been back at least two dozen times since them.

But more, I have visited all parts of the Commonwealth over the years—North America, Canada, and the Caribbean, Nassau and Barbados, India, South Africa, Zimbabwe, Zambia, and Australia, and I have been impressed by the powerful influence of Britain throughout the world.

The British Isles have exported many seminal ideas and institutions in its history. Its great literary figures from Chaucer and Shakespeare to its modern poets and novelists have been read everywhere. And its philosophers from Bacon and Locke to Hume and Mill have encouraged empiricism and a healthy skepticism. Britain's scientists (from Newton to Farraday and Darwin) have contributed to the development of modern science; its statesmen helped develop parliamentary democratic institutions and an appreciation for the free market of ideas; and it was in Manchester and Birmingham that the industrial revolution, applying technology to industry, first occurred.

It is time, I submit, for the British Isles again to take the lead—this time in promoting humanism. Humanism, we believe, is the most viable, scientific, ethical, and philosophical point of view applicable to the world community, for it seeks to find some common ground in ideals and values beyond narrow ethnic, nationalistic, racial, or religious chauvinism.

The relocation of the IHEU to London could be a vital part of a new global humanism. It can provide a significant alternative to the "divine hand" of rampant market libertarianism on the one hand, and primitive fundamentalism or the new cults of unreason on the other. Will humanists in these islands again play a vital role in helping us to build a humanist planetary community—based on science and reason, committed to democratic values, yet bold and energetic in the defense of the humanist outlook? Granted that America may be the only superpower, but America, like Rome, has always looked to Britain as its Athenian inspiration. Will our colleagues and friends in the humanist movement respond to the challenge or will you retreat in indecision and hesitation? One reason why Britain is so important for world humanism is that you are among the *least* religious of folk on this planet (unlike America); yet you have managed to have achieved a reasonably cultivated and meaningful life as a society.

The Courage to Become

In my talk this afternoon I wish to focus on the significance of the virtue of *courage* to the humanist stance—not simply scientific reason and experience, which we've always emphasized; or indeed caring and compassion, which we have perhaps underemphasized—but courage as a central value in the humanism of the future.

I expect to travel to Edinburgh tomorrow to view a new a statue of David Hume to be erected as a memorial to his memory. Many commentators consider David Hume, though he was Scottish, to have been the most important philosopher that the British Isles have ever produced. Hume was surely the greatest of the skeptics. He attempted to develop rigorous methods of empirical observation for testing belief claims, and this led to a devastating critique of metaphysics and theology. Hume died on August 25th, 1776, and it is a sad commentary that there was no proper recognition for him in Scotland. In reading the life of Hume in the great biography by Ernest Campbell Mossner,[2] we note that the University of Edinburgh refused to appoint him to the faculty because of his heretical views on religion.[3]

James Boswell reported on his visit to Hume, in his last days as he awaited death. Boswell was dismayed to discover that Hume was not fearful of death, but accepted it with equanimity. He apparently died of cancer of the bowels or liver at the age of 65. He knew he was dying and accepted it cheerfully. Hume's courage in facing death is an inspiration for humanists who likewise lack any belief in salvation or redemption.

I am reminded here, of another great skeptic and atheist, namely the comedian W. C. Fields, who on his deathbed was caught reading the Bible. And when confronted, someone asked him, "W. C., why are you reading the Bible? Does this mean that you're going to make peace with your maker?" Fields's alleged reply was "Hell no. I'm looking for loopholes."

The *courage to be* (in Paul Tillich's language) is not enough; what we need is the *courage to become*, that is, the fortitude to create the conditions under which our goals and plans can be fulfilled. Every day presents new challenges for human choice and persistence.

Humanists are often assailed by the nay-sayers. Unable to accept their own finitude, religious believers are willing to barter their lives for fake eschatological promises. Classical monotheistic religions emphasize immortality, which is promised by Jesus, Moses, Muhammad and other prophets. The ultimate virtue for these religions is subservience to the will of God. Indeed, the terms "Muslim" and "Islam" mean obedience and dependence, not independence and autonomy.

What this suggests, then, is that for the humanist a key value is existential courage; that is, the willingness to face the universe for what it is, and an acceptance of our own finitude. For the humanist, we need to create the best life here and now by drawing upon our own powers and resources.

The centrality of the *courage to become* needs to be all the more emphasized today in this age of evolution. For humanists, there are no teleological goals discernible in nature, neither divine nor evolutionary; what happens depends on a wide variety of contingent factors. As a species we have some power to redirect the course of our own evolution—for example, by means of biogenetic research. The recent possibility of cloning animals provides additional positive powers to human beings. Incidentally, I deplore the attempt to censor scientific inquiry. Much of the great opposition to cloning emanates from religious sources. The Pope has replaced Bishop Wilberforce. It is difficult to see why—especially if we were to take the immaculate conception and the virgin birth as true. Was Jesus asexually reproduced as a clone of Mary, or someone else?

What this all means is that the human species is now responsible in part for its own destiny. How and in what form we will survive in the future depends upon natural processes and chance, but it also depends on what we choose to do or not do. We have the capacity, because of our creative intelligence, to create a better world and to enhance the welfare of the human species. The great issue is how these immense powers now being untapped by science and technology will be used. Will biogenetic engineering contribute to human happiness, or will it lead to a totalitarian, "brave new world"—as Aldous Huxley feared? What is the prospect for the human species on the planet earth?

These questions surely are of central concern for the international humanist movement. We are surrounded by doomsday forecasts of Armageddon, from those on the theological right, who think the end days are near, to those on the theological left, who think that resource depletion, nuclear proliferation, environmental pollution, and the population explosion are intractable problems. In answer to the extremists, is not the wisest alternative to use our pooled intelligence as best we can, fulfilling humanist values? Perhaps not all problems can be solved in any perfect, utopian way; nonetheless, melioristic intelligence can perhaps most effectively achieve the best results.

Let us think back four and a half decades, at the founding of the IHEU. We were then at the height of the Cold War, when Leninism-Stalinism had a strong influence and many people feared a nuclear holocaust. If we go back still a decade earlier, we were in the midst of the Second World War, a war waged against barbaric and genocidal fascism. Yet the human species has managed to survive in spite of earlier gloomsday forecasts. There are no doubt grave problems in the world today, especially in Africa and the developing world. Still, enormous progress continues to be made; for example, in India a new middle class is developing and the green revolution has led, at least for the present, to the end of famine. China is rapidly developing as part of the community of nations—we hope that it will democratize. Each generation faces new challenges. But the underlying humanist virtue is still existential courage, the recognition that we can build a humanistic world rooted in naturalistic premises, and that we can forge new ideals and values appropriate to the human condition.

It is this approach that contrasts with the messianic theological doctrines that surround us. The humanist prospect, I submit, is good. We can help ameliorate the human condition and contribute to more people enjoying wholesome, healthy, happy lives—provided we exercise intelligence, and express some caring concern for others under conditions of freedom and democracy. But it also depends on whether we can summon the courage of our convictions to continue to work for such high ideals.

The humanist message on the current world context is rather important and unique. It is a message that we earnestly hope our British humanist cousins will help us take to the rest of the world.

---

1. *The Humanist* (1952), no. 5, p. 231.

2. Ernest Campbell Mossner, *The Life of David Hume* (Austin: University of Texas Press, 1954).

3. Interestingly, Hume's major attacks on religion in one sense were withheld until after his death. He entrusted to his friend, Adam Smith, one of the great intellectual figures of the modern world, his *Dialogues Concerning Natural Religion*, and also the publication of his two famous essays, "On Immortality" and "On Suicide," which it was deemed prudent to publish *after* his death.

29

The Infomedia Revolution

I wish to take this opportunity to deal with the question, Where does humanism stand at the present juncture—at the beginning of the new millennium—an arbitrary dividing line no doubt, yet of considerable intellectual fascination. We may ask, Is humanism reaching an end, as so many critics today predict; or is it at a promising new beginning in the unfolding infomedia cyber-age. The latter, I submit, but only if we seize the opportunities that are emerging.

I wish to be clear at the offset as to what I mean by humanism. I am here referring to *naturalistic* or *secular humanism*, which is (1) nontheistic, i.e., denies the existence of God and immortality, and provides new meaning to human life; (2) believes in the possibility of objective knowledge and encourages the continued development of science and technology to understand and to cope with nature and the use of reason to solve human problems; (3) expresses a new humanistic ethic that is responsive to human interests and

An earlier version of this paper was delivered as "Humanism and the Information Revolution" at "Humanist Visions of European Integration," a European Humanist Federation international conference at the University of Warsaw, Poland, on September 28, 1996. The present version was delivered as "The Infomedia Revolution: Opportunities for Global Humanism," at the International Humanist and Ethical Union World Congress, held in Mexico City in November 1996. First published in *New Humanist* 111, no. 4 (December 1996), pp. 3–6.

needs; (4) is committed to democracy, human rights, the separation of church and state, and the building of a world community; and last but not least, (5) is optimistic about the human prospect and affirms our ability to control future events and to ameliorate the human condition.

Assaults on Humanism

Let me begin by stating the negative case of those who believe that we have reached "the end of the secular century" (Irving Kristol, Richard John Neuhaus, Paul Johnson, and other religious and conservative pundits), and that "spirituality" (old and new) will again come to dominate the world. These critics believe that a basic paradigm shift (to use the language of the late Thomas Kuhn) is or has occurred. Michael Novak believes that secular humanism has reached the end of its five-century hegemony, and that a new spiritual age is about to open up.

Two main intellectual developments have led to this appraisal. First, the virtual collapse of Marxism, and second the widespread attacks on the Enlightenment and the rejection of modernity. If at the end of the nineteenth century socialist and Enlightenment ideals had a powerful appeal to intellectuals, at the end of the twentieth century this is no longer the case. In my view, Marx was a seminal thinker of the first rank. That his philosophical views were transformed into a totalitarian and terrorist state ideology by Leninism and Stalinism was one of the great tragedies of modern times. I will not here detail all of the factors that led to the collapse of Marxism. Our colleagues in Eastern Europe no doubt have their own interpretations of what happened.

Although Marx was a trenchant critic of nineteenth-century capitalism, he did not and could not foresee the dynamic new forces that were to emerge in the twentieth century, and his recommendations about what to do were often mistaken. History in my view is contingent and often unpredictable, and to expect that Marx would be not only an astute analyst of social trends but an infallible prophet was to endow him with superhuman qualities. Speaking as both a social democrat *and* libertarian (who believes in the vital role of the free market), I believe that the failure to fully appreciate the importance of political democracy, as Karl Popper and Sidney Hook have pointed out, was a cardinal error of the Marxists: This means a defense of the open society, civil liberties, a free press, dissent, the legal right of opposition, majority rule, due process, and the rule of law. If socialism means anything it must include an appreciation for democratic values, human rights and freedoms. To violate these in the name of a utopian end is to contradict the basic principles of humanism. Nor did Marx or the Marxists fully appreciate the explosive character of free-market entrepreneurial economies, which were able to innovate and to develop new products, far greater than any centralized planning boards. Marxist-Leninist economies were simply unable to produce the goods and services that they promised to the people; they were inefficient and bureaucratic. In my view, another failure of Marxism—particularly its Leninist variety—was the inability to anticipate the emergence of information technologies. Marxism-Leninism was predicated on the industrial model and the heavy industries of the nineteenth and early twentieth centuries, but these have long since been outdistanced in postindustrial societies of the cyber-age. If we refer to Marx and Engels's "sociological interpretation of history," it is the expansion of the *forces* of production—especially advanced technologies and the capital investments to develop and market them—and not the relationships of production or the so-called "class structure" that has been the dynamic factor in social change in affluent Western-style democratic societies. This also applies to the agricultural revolution in the twentieth century geared to high technology, which is far more efficient than communes or collectives that are based on earlier industrial models.

In no small measure, anticlerical secularism at the end of the nineteenth and early twentieth centuries was accelerated because of its alliance with socialist movements. With the collapse of socialist ideals, secularism has been weakened, and fundamentalist and conservative voices have questioned the very idea of the secular state. This confrontation is occurring everywhere—North and South America, Europe, the Middle East, and Asia. Today we are challenged on all sides by those who wish to bridge the separation of church and state and feel emboldened to do so. This is in spite of the growth of political democracy throughout the world.

A second intellectual movement that has emerged to challenge humanism is postmodernism, a rather esoteric but significant movement. Drawing on Heidegger, French philosophers Derrida, Foucault, Lyotard, and others have launched a major attack on modernity and the Enlightenment, and this has had a profound impact on the Academy, especially on the humanities and the social sciences. The fact that Heidegger was identified with Nazism and that he had attacked humanism is scandalous. Yet a whole legion of postmodernist authors have drunk deeply at the Heideggerian well. This is particularly the case in America today, where literary criticism has become poststructural, political science postbehavioral, sociology postpositivist, and philosophy postanalytic. Of crucial significance is the fact that postmodernists have attacked science, denying its objectivity. They have criticized our ability to understand and master causal relationships or even the capacity of language to describe or represent the external world. Science, they maintain, is one narrative among others, no more true than other mythic systems. They have derided rational inquiry as a prelude to reform, and have rejected the development of free and autonomous individuals—both ideals of which are fundamental to humanism.

Postmodernists have also disavowed any idea of the progressive improvement of the human condition, which they maintain is an illusion. They bemoan the pervasive influence of technology—while they use it to etch out their ideas on word processors, or listen to stereophonic music, or hop about the world on jets, have heart-bypass surgery, or use antibiotics. Postmodernists appear to express an undue pessimism about social reform; they are overly subjective, even nihilistic. No doubt many of their critiques of consumer-style capitalist economies are well-taken: the massification of tastes, the mindless pursuit of gain, the deracination of persons, the banality of values. Foucault's criticisms of insane asylums, the prison system, and the maltreatment of homosexuals, have had a responsive hearing. But with these criticisms has come a deflation of confidence in the power of human beings to guide their own destinies by rational means. Humanists throughout the world—Jürgen Habermas in Germany, post-Deweyan pragmatic humanists in America, and Luc Ferry and Alain Renaut in France, for example—have denied that the Enlightenment project is over. Still, many philosophers of science today talk about the crisis in epistemology. Paul Feyerabend maintained there are no objective methods of science and hence no reliable knowledge upon which we can frame our judgments. And even the new Humanist University in Utrecht is pervaded by postmodernist views. Can the secular and democratic humanist ideals which grew out of the Enlightenment survive the destruction of confidence in reason and science, education, and progress?—asks Richard Rorty. This is a question that humanists need to respond to at the present juncture.

The collapse of Marxism and the growth of postmodernism have contributed to the emergence, as we all are aware, of still a third force, the new or old "spirituality." This is anti-intellectual, anti-modernist, and even pre-modernist in outlook. It includes fundamentalisms of all sorts—Islamic, Roman Catholic, Protestant, Judaic, and Hindu; but it also includes the growth of newer cults of unreason and belief in the New Age. What I have in mind here is the worldwide fascination with claims of the paranormal—psychics, faith healers, alternative medicines, extraterrestrial abductions, near-death experiences, reincarnation, etc.

If Friedrich Nietzsche could proclaim at the end of the nineteenth century that "God is dead," we are not so certain that this applies at the end of the twentieth century. We were fortunately able to see the destruction of two virulent European ideological movements in the twentieth century—fascism and Stalinism. We may ask, will we be able to prevail over the revival of religious ideologies and paranormal faiths, which likewise threaten our humanistic values? The recrudescence of ancient religious dogmas has led in no small measure to the emergence of old ethnic rivalries and nationalistic hatreds—of which Yugoslavia and Bosnia are the most brutal example. These conflicts are based on chauvinistic loyalties and prejudices, which are beyond all reason.

Interestingly, they are fed by postmodernist concerns with multiculturalism and the abandonment of any effort to develop universal values that transcend ethnic boundaries or extreme cultural relativism.

The Challenge of the Global Information Age

Several additional objective factors have emerged recently, which enormously complicate any analysis of the present situation. Freemarket economies are now global in reach, and they are growing by leaps and bounds. In this process huge conglomerates have developed, transcending national frontiers, and they are often more powerful than the national states in which they do business. Although competition for markets is fierce, there is a concentration of power in fewer and fewer corporate hands. Marxists may derive some satisfaction from these developments, which might seem to verify their predictions. The trends discerned in the nineteenth century by Marx have only been exacerbated in the twentieth. What was unforeseen by Marxists, however, was that new corporations proliferate and entirely new industries spring up almost overnight: the computer industry, telecommunications, biotechnology and the emergence of nanotechnology are some recent illustrations. Supporters of mergers and acquisitions welcome the trend, claiming that the economies of scale require it, and that efficiency, productivity, lower prices, and innovation are the result. Critics maintain that there are dangers in this unrestrained growth, that dominant centers of transnational corporate and economic power have emerged, that the constant downsizing of the labor force and the disappearance of local and regional companies, threaten the well-being of democratic societies.

I do not believe that traditional Marxist or even liberal democratic analyses—both spawned in the nineteenth century—will help us very much in providing guidelines of how to cope with the new global economy and the infomedia revolution. We need fresh thinking applicable to the new social realities. This is particularly the case for democratic humanism, which presupposes an educated citizenry, comprised of autonomous individuals, who are be able to make reflective choices. John Stuart Mill's defense of liberty assumed a free market of ideas, where an informed public opinion would develop, able to decide the main policies and the chief officials to carry them out. Mill hoped that diversity of taste and opinion would allow individuality, uniqueness and creativity to flourish, and hence contribute to the common good.

Unfortunately, the worldwide growth of infomedia conglomerates in the cyber-age now challenges this premise. The growth of the mass infomedia have no doubt been a great boon to literacy and education. The impact is Asia, Africa, and Latin America has been incalculable, confronting old ideas and values with new ones, and bringing the back waters of humanity into the modern age. At the same time the commercial media, focusing on advertising rather than information, have undermined the level of taste and appreciation in affluent societies, and especially the capacity for critical thinking.

The medium not only conveys the message, but defines it (as Marshall McLuhan pointed out). In ancient society, neither Socrates, Jesus, nor Muhammad wrote anything down, and an oral tradition sought to capture the power of vocal expression, gesture, and sign. It was Plato and Xenophon, the authors of the gospel fictions of the New Testament, and the disciples of Muhammad who translated oral messages into written words and symbols and penned the Koran. The invention of the printing press by Gutenberg led to the Protestant Reformation (where each person should read and judge the Bible for himself) and subsequently to the democratic revolutions of the eighteenth century. What shall we say about the transforming effect of the computer screen and the Internet on the next generation, let alone the corrupting influence of TV, radio, and movies? Are we at the beginning of the end of the age of books, and what does this portend for the humanist message?

I should point out that democratic humanists have objected vigorously to totalitarian societies where the state has a monopoly of the means of expression and communication. Today Western democracies are becoming more narrow in their viewpoints, limiting creativity and the quest for truth, because the oligopolic infomedia tend to blot out critical and radical dissent and to emphasize pop culture. Here the infomedia goliaths homogenize, distort, and suppress the message. They are responsible in no small part for the "dumbing down" of America. The picture is not entirely bleak, and it is still possible to publish dissenting magazines and books, form associations, appear on radio and television. So there is still some diversity, but it is becoming increasingly difficult to express alternative viewpoints. The outlook that prevails in the mass media is a vague kind of religiosity or spirituality, at least in the United States. There is also a growing antiscientific attitude. The enemy is often seen as the mad scientist who is akin to Dr. Frankenstein. There is an inflated fascination with the paranormal universe, and science-fiction fantasy captures the imagination. In the present context, even the old-time religious miracles—angels, weeping statues, the Virgin Mary—have all come back with a vengeance. (Interestingly, the appearance of the Virgin Mary at Medjugorjie in Bosnia did not help that strife-ridden country.) Positively, the mass media have encouraged more liberal attitudes toward repressive human sexuality and there has been a loosening of the grip of doctrinaire religion. Nonetheless TV is a moral wasteland, full of violence and vulgarity, sensationalism and banality.

A new development that is overtaking us rapidly is the development of the Internet. The best and the brightest minds are surfing the WorldWide Web daily, not only receiving e-mail, but making use of the storehouse of information that is now available. The Internet provides a new free market of ideas that is open to diversity. It is instantaneous and transnational. People in San Francisco, Berlin, Warsaw, London, Beijing, Singapore, and Jakarta can talk to each other. What an incredible tool, far eclipsing the telegraph, short-wave radio, and telephone. A new and exciting dimension has thus been added to the global community. This new technological force of production is transforming world culture by creating for the first time a worldwide network of human beings participating in dialogue. Is it a cacophany of discordant voices—or does it hold forth the promise of developing a genuine planetary community?

What should be the response of secular humanists to this ongoing infomedia revolution—which some have heralded as a pivotal turning point not unlike the industrial revolution? And how shall we respond to the nay-sayers—postmodernist and fundamentalists—who have given up on the prospects for constructive reform? Since I believe that the scientific and technological revolution cannot be turned back or shut down, those societies that encourage scientific and technological developments will thrive. Those societies that nourish an antiscientific state of mind—such as the postmodernists in the Academy and the fundamentalists at large—will stagnate and decline.

The information age provides an unparalleled opportunity for humanism to reach hundreds of millions of people on this planet and to provide a viable alternative to the orthodoxies of the past and the banalities of the present. Whether it will be able to marshall the resources to respond is the great challenge that it will have to face in the twenty-first century.

30

Science and Reason in an Irrational World

The Growth of the Irrational

As we enter the new millennium, we can speculate about what is likely to occur in the future. Humanists especially ask, "What is the prospect for humanism?" Given the collapse of communism, many people in post-Marxist Russia have apparently become cynical about anyone who proposes idealistic visions of the future.

I submit that we as humans constantly need to think about our futures. Surely we cannot abandon our commitment to ideals, though to be viable these need to be constantly revised in the light of concrete realities.

What the future will be like, however, is often unpredictable, for it depends upon a plurality of scenarios that people may propose, and it depends in part on what we decide to do. No one can predict with precision the future course of human civilization; for totally unexpected events may intervene. The *contingent*

The inaugural address read at the opening of the new Center for Inquiry at Moscow State University, at a conference on "Science and Common Sense in Russia: Crisis or New Possibilities?" sponsored by the Russian Humanist Society, the International Academy of Humanism, and the Department of Philosophy of the Moscow State University, in October 1997. Originally published in the Russian journal, *Common Sense*, no. 5 (1997), pp. 6–15.

is a real factor in history. Hegel and Marx believed that there were dialectical "laws of history," and that on the basis of these, we could forecast in broad outline what was likely to occur. Although we can extrapolate from the present, and some trends are discernible, and no one can foretell with certainty what will happen next year, let alone the next decade. For example, who can say which charismatic individuals, heroic or despotic, will emerge, or what new movements will captivate humankind? Nor can we forecast natural catastrophes. The role of chance in human history often undermines even the best-laid plans and most confident forecasts. Life is precarious and what will occur often depends on a series of unrelated events. Regretfully, what is considered unthinkable in one age may even come to pass in the next.

Think back retrospectively to the year 1900. Who could have then imagined that a small group of Bolshevik revolutionaries would topple the Czarist regime and assume power in the largest country of the world? Could anyone have predicted that the revolution would subsequently be betrayed by Stalin, and that the leading idealists of the revolution would be devoured by him? Who indeed could have predicted only a decade ago that communism would suddenly collapse in Russia and Eastern Europe?

Again, who could have envisioned in 1900 the present worldwide religious revival? If one looks back to the turn of the century, most social historians and Marxists confidently believed that traditional religions would die out as people became more affluent and better educated. It was widely held that science would undermine superstition and that modern life would become more secularized. Although secularization has increased, religion has not declined. Indeed, fundamentalist religions, rather than disappearing, are growing in various parts of the globe. Islam, Hinduism, and Protestant fundamentalism are on the upsweep. Evangelical missionaries are spreading the gospel in North and South America, Africa, Asia, and Eastern Europe. The Roman Catholic Church (although losing ground in Western Europe due to the growth of secularism and humanism) has become more militant in its dogmas and more influential in the third world.

This religious revival is especially troubling in the United States, whose constitution is based on the separation of church and state. All of the major political leaders today—left and right—profess their religious piety, and no one will admit to being an agnostic or atheist. Indeed, neo-conservative pundits sing praises to the resurgence of the Old-Time Religion. Concomitant with this is the emergence of "New Age" paranormal religions, a concoction of strange beliefs. The paranormal age has revived the ancient craft of astrology. Astrologers cast their horoscopes based upon the time and place of a person's birth; yet scientific examinations of their claims have found no empirical basis for their prognostications.

Also proliferating on the contemporary scene are various sects—Hare Krishna, Reverend Moon, Scientology, Urantia, Jehovah's Witnesses, Seventh-Day Adventists, the Mormons, etc. In the USA and Europe bizarre space-age gurus have appeared, proclaiming revelations from nowhere. These have attracted impressionable, often well-educated people—in some cases it has led to mass suicides.

Tribal warfare and ethnic cleansing have provoked outright genocide. In Israel and Palestine, fanatic Muslims strap explosives to their bodies and blow themselves to kingdom come. Orthodox Jews insist that they are the Chosen People of the Old Testament, entitled to sacred ground. Devout Muslims citing the Koran insist that Palestine is theirs. And fundamentalist evangelicals await the Second Coming of Jesus Christ.

Russia is now open to these cults of unreason—paranormal and spiritual, ancient and postmodern. Perhaps you have asked, How shall we cope with these new forms of irrationalism? May I suggest that unless your educators, philosophers, and scientists develop wise strategies to cope with these phenomena, you will most likely be overtaken in time by these revival movements.

The complication in the present situation is that both the economy and the media of information have become global. No one nation can solve its internal economic problems by itself, for it is dependent on trade and exchange with other nations. But perhaps more decisively, information is now global: the Internet, radio, television, cinema, fax, e-mail, satellites, mean that whatever happens in any corner of the planet can be known instantly everywhere. Increasingly, the mass media, often controlled by vast conglomerates, are replacing the schools and universities in many parts of the world as the main source of education, and this has become an age of misinformation. The mass media tend to blend science fiction with religious fantasy, and this is sold to gullible consumers worldwide in magazines and books, TV programs and movies. Often, sensationalism and the lowest common denominator captures public consciousness.

The Role of Critical Thinking

What does secular and scientific humanism have to say in this context? It is essential, I submit, that we seek to raise the level of education and information and the standards of taste. We say that the best therapy against nonsense, deception, and self-deception is the cultivation of reflective thinking. Indeed, the chief reliance that we have for exposing irrational claims is by developing within the public an appreciation for thinking skills and for the importance of science to society. Interestingly, the infomedia age in which we now live depends upon the development of new technologies, and there is a constant competitive race among corporations to improve upon them. Since this depends upon scientific research, science and technology has become the primary force of production in postindustrial information societies. Those countries that do not encourage scientific research and technological innovation will not be able to compete or develop within the world economic system. Increasingly, prosperity is dependent on the emergence of new industries. Equally important is the recognition that democratic societies presuppose an educated citizenry, capable of reaching wise decisions about the public weal.

Secular humanism is consonant with the open democratic society, for it is committed to using the *methods of reflective inquiry* in all fields of human endeavor. This implies that we will resist all efforts to limit freedom of inquiry or to say that some areas of human conduct or nature are beyond the range of investigation. Ecclesiastical, economic, and political authorities have invariably sought to defend the sacred cows of society, to proclaim that they are so vital to the fabric of social life that they should not be examined. To do so, they fear, would shake the foundations of the social order. Freethinkers have insisted that it is wrong to define orthodoxy, legislate belief, claim that a system is eternally fixed, or that it has reached its ultimate formulation. All efforts in human history to prevent inquiry by appealing to authority have failed. Thus, we have a right to inquire, to accept or not accept that something is the case. Yet defenders of the dogma, whether religious or ideological, have sought to brand such inquiries as heretical, and they have sought to prevent the creative mind from exercising its talents.

Incidentally, I do not think that efforts to ban the new cults or sects, as a recent law enacted in Russia, will be effective. They will only fester underground. The best remedy is criticism. This is precisely what the Center for Inquiry proposes to do—to examine paranormal and religious claims and provide critiques for the general public. I don't see how a democratic society can censor the promulgation of ideas. One may hate the views expressed by new irrational cults, but the best response cannot be to prohibit but to refute them on the battleground of ideas.

We may ask, How should we test truth claims? Secular humanists have emphasized the importance of developing objective methods of inquiry for doing so. Modern scientists and philosophers ever since Galileo have searched for objective methods. Beginning in the sixteenth century the scientific revolution sought to use the hypothetico-deductive method for testing hypotheses and theories: these need to be rationally coherent, grounded in evidence, and verified by predictions drawn from them. Such standards of justification are intersubjective in the sense that they are corroborated by a community of inquirers. No theories are beyond revision. They should be open to modification in the light of new discoveries. Thus, skeptical doubt is part of the quest for knowledge. Skepticism need not be negative; it can be constructive and positive; and as such it is essential to the process of appraising claims to truth. These methods have been enormously effective in science, enabling us to extend the frontiers of knowledge.

The methods of scientific inquiry are not esoteric, nor open only to the initiated. Anyone who has the requisite talent and training can understand and use them. They are continuous with common sense and the ordinary processes of reflective behavior drawn upon in everyday life. We need to use reason to cope with problems encountered in life, and we do so by examining the facts of the case, and we test our beliefs by reference to their consequential results in practice. Perhaps the generic term which best describes their use is *critical thinking*. Immanuel Kant held that formal concepts are empty unless they are given perceptual content, and I may add unless they are also judged by their impact on the world.

The real challenge is how far critical and/or scientific thinking can be extended. Most defenders of religious dogma believe that scientific inquiry is limited and that there are "two truths." My response is that it is unwise to restrict the range of inquiry *a priori*. The question concerning the limits of science can best be resolved by the hard work of scientific researchers as they try to break new ground. Many or most people unfortunately abandon the methods of science and prefer to resort to feeling, passion, emotion, faith, revelation, intuition, tradition, or authority to justify their beliefs.

A key point that I need to emphasize is that critical inquiry especially needs to be applied to religious and paranormal claims. Most of the traditional religions are shrouded in history and cloaked by mystery. But the Old and New Testaments and the Koran need to be objectively examined by the methods of critical inquiry. Skepticism is the best antidote to those who claim to have a special road to truth or a monopoly of virtue. This applies to both priests and politicians. Critical thinking is not infallible—and mistakes are often made—but it does provide some checks on those who would impose their brand of truth on everyone else. This appeal to reason is, of course, familiar in Western philosophy. "The unexamined life is not worth living," said Socrates. The "method of intelligence," observed John Dewey, in the last analysis, is the most reliable safeguard that we have that a democratic society will be able to function well. Policies should be based on reason and persuasion, not power; dialogue and debate, not coercion.

There are often competing claims to truth; and in these situations it is difficult for the average person to decide who is right and who is wrong. In totalitarian societies, the state seeks to dictate a set of doctrines, and these are inculcated in the young. Education becomes indoctrination; truth is instilled by means of propaganda. In theocratic societies the articles of faith are proclaimed, and unbelievers or apostates are condemned. When an entire population is instructed to accept a set of precepts without question, dogma rules, the inquiring mind is stifled, and duplicity and hypocrisy are the result. When suddenly freed from the straitjacket of official doctrines, such individuals are often thrown into a quandary. They may either be ripe for another dogma to fill the vacuum or they may become so cynical and resentful that they will accept nothing as true.

Critical thinking is so important to both the individual and the social good that secular humanists and skeptics have urged basic curricular reform in education. We need to provide courses in critical thinking, on the elementary and secondary level, in the colleges, and universities. I am not here referring to the teaching of formal logic *per se*, but applied or practical logic. This means that we should not simply seek to teach students what to think, but *how* to think, which is far more basic to the educated mind. We also need to raise an appreciation for critical thinking and the methods of science in the public at large. Unfortunately, most people interpret science by its results, ignoring the fact that it is primarily a process of inquiry.

We are facing a worldwide challenge today, for the mass media have virtually replaced the schools and universities as the main source of knowledge. Unfortunately, they are, in capitalist-consumer societies, more often than not concerned with entertainment not information, ratings rather than quality, profit instead of education. In totalitarian societies, the great problem was that the state or party determined the kind of propaganda that would be disseminated by the media, allowing little room for dissent. We face a growing crisis in Western democratic societies today because of the concentration of media control by huge transnational conglomerates. These begin to narrow the range of ideas. If democracy is to function, then we need diversity of opinion and the capacity for critical skepticism. The new technology has created a global village, it also has provided us with the problem of access: How open will the media be to the scientific outlook and critical thinking?

A key issue today for many individuals in mass culture concerns alienation. Individuals often feel isolated and estranged and their daily existence is devoid of meaning. The existential questions are thus vital. In totalitarian or authoritarian societies, the individual is smothered by the collective. In consumer-oriented societies, the range of choices is expanded, but these are often banal and vulgar, as tastes are conditioned by advertisers and hucksters. In this framework, unsuspecting consumers are all too often unable to evaluate critically religious faiths or the cults of unreason offered to them. These doctrines are invariably mired in metaphysical and spiritual quagmire. They invoke uncorroborated claims of historic revelations. They postulate supernatural realms that transcend the categories of logic and experience. The ancient religions emerged in prescientific, preliterate, rural, or nomadic societies. Unable to face tragedy or death, believers bartered their souls for promises of salvation or immortality. Individuals who are unable to think critically have little immunity against infection, and are easy prey to irrational appeals. The danger in a democracy is that those who cannot think for themselves eventually may be prone to follow a dictator on a white horse who makes extravagant ideological or theological promises.

Scientific Naturalism and Ethical Humanism

What do humanists have to say about "the meaning of life"? People ask, What is reality and how do I fit into the scheme of things? We respond that the most reliable source of knowledge about nature is provided by scientific inquiry. The rapidly developing fields of science—the natural, biological, social, and behavioral—have in the past four centuries expanded our knowledge of the universe enormously. What they tell is that the objects and events that we encounter in the universe may be explained in terms of natural causes. The most reliable interpretation of nature is *scientific naturalism*. This form of naturalism is a nonreductive kind of materialism. Nature is basically physical-chemical at root, though there are levels of organization. There is no basis, as far as we can tell, for a "spiritual" universe.

The frontiers of astronomy are extending our knowledge in a dramatic way. Our planet and solar system are part of a vast expanding universe of billions and billions of galaxies. The human species exists within the biosphere and is continuous with nature. It has not been created by divine *fiat*, but is a result of a long process of evolution, in which adaptation, survival of the fittest, chance genetic mutations, differential reproduction, and other factors play a role. The Darwinian revolution has thus dethroned man from the center of an anthropomorphic universe. Contrary to religious doctrine, there is no dualism between mind and body, and no evidence for a separable immortal soul.

Present-day secular humanists believe that science, reason, and education are essential for the future progress of humankind, and that we ought not to abandon this agenda. We are surrounded by pessimists and nihilists who have given up on our capacity to solve our problems. Today postmodernist philosophers attack science and reason and they have lost confidence in the ability of men and women to improve the human condition.

What is basic for secular humanism, I submit, is its existential perspective. For it provides a response to the question of the meaning of life. If God is dead, then Humans are alive; and the great question we face is *how* we ought to live and live well. Clearly, we need to ensure the principles of social justice, but over and beyond this remains the question of the place of the individual in the universe. If there is no divine purpose or design discernible in nature, then the option for each individual is to live a full life as a free person. Life has no meaning *per se*, it provides us with opportunities. Its meanings are discovered in our plans and projects. That is why the courage to persist in spite of adversity and to *become*, in our own terms, is become is vital for every person. A person's life is like a work of art; it is up to the individual to paint his own canvas, to create his or her own perspective, and to give his own meaning to life. We should not abandon our rights as free persons to the demands of the church, the collective, or the state.

It is at this point that, I think, ethical guidance becomes central to our concerns. Although we need reason and science to evaluate claims to truth, we are also engaged in action. Philosophy historically was "the love of wisdom," but what we need is the *practice of wisdom*. That is why I have introduced the term *eupraxsophy*. But by wisdom I do not mean abstract philosophical wisdom, but knowledge based upon the sciences. Thus, secular humanism is a eupraxsophy that draws on science, philosophy, and ethics, but it is primarily concerned with applying this wisdom to life as lived.

Secular humanists believe that we can achieve the good life within a naturalistic perspective. Dostoevsky, in *Crime and Punishment*, was mistaken when he said that "if God is dead, all things are possible." I say that if humans are alive and freed from the chains of illusion, then we need to demonstrate that an ethical life can be realized.

The standard of good that we seek is happiness for every individual in society. But by that I mean that society ought to afford, wherever it can, the opportunities for individuals to fulfill their own unique capacities, creative talents, and visions of the good life. It is up to each individual to achieve happiness in his or her own terms. What one seeks is a meaningful life of joyful exuberance, in which we can satisfy our needs and realize our interests and aspirations, and these vary from individual to individual. I am here talking about an ethics of ends (teleological), in which the goal is the maximization of personal happiness. Such an emphasis on individual happiness need not be subjective nor capricious. There are a set of criteria of excellences—balance, self-restraint, rational order—which it is possible to apply. Basic to the ethics of humanism is the idea that individuals should be accorded a maximum degree of autonomy, consonant with the public good and the rights of others. For the secular humanist this means that we ought to seek the good life here and now without worrying about eternal salvation.

But we also require an ethics of principles (deontological). Namely, there are some general or universal moral principles that apply in our relationship to others and are so important that they cannot be sacrificed at that altar of expediency. There is or should be a means-end continuum. I believe that there are a discernible set of "common moral decencies." These transcend the limits of cultural relativity and are the common possession of humankind—such as the principles of integrity, trustworthiness, benevolence, and fairness.[1] There are also a set of basic human rights that provide a universal framework of moral standards within a system of global ethics.[2]

The question often raised is whether or not the ethical choices we make are amenable to rational control. There is a historic philosophical literature—from Aristotle to Spinoza, Kant, Mill, and Dewey—which affirms that there are standards of reason. I submit that critical thinking applies to ethical conduct. Although our values are relative to our individual and social interests and needs, they may be modified in the light of cognitive inquiry.

It is essential that moral education be taught in the schools. We need to develop in our children character, good habits, and principles of moral conduct. Children need to respect the common moral decencies and the rights of others. They need to tolerate differences of opinion and diversity in lifestyles. They need to develop the art of rational negotiation and compromise. But if children are to develop as moral beings, they need to actualize their capacities for reflective behavior. Moral choices should be based upon a process of inquiry. In the last analysis, this method is the most reliable way to deal with the concrete moral dilemmas that we encounter in life. The most effective method for solving moral problems is by deliberating about our alternatives and evaluating their consequences. Critical thinking thus is relevant not only to factual matters within science, but to normative questions as well. Here we seek to formulate the wisest decisions on a comparative scale of value. It is difficult to find moral absolutes in life. Where we face a conflict of goods and rights, we should seek to maximize that which is most appropriate, on balance, within the situation.

The ethics of humanism, I reiterate, is not concerned solely with individual moral choice. Since we live in communities, we must be concerned with principles of social justice. Humanists have argued for an open society in which individual freedom of choice is encouraged. Such a society seeks to maximize the opportunities for individual autonomy. Humanists have been in the forefront of those who have defended women's rights—including the right to a career, reproductive freedom, birth control, and abortion. They have defended the rights of homosexuals—the view that the state should not regulate conduct between consenting adults. And they have supported the right to die with dignity and euthanasia. These presuppose the right to privacy.

Humanists have also been in the vanguard defending democracy, including civil liberties, a free press, due process of law, and the legal right to criticize and oppose government policies without fear of recrimination. These discussion are no doubt familiar in Russia as you have begun to develop democratic institutions similar to those in other democratic societies in the world.

We are seeking to develop a secular ethical alternative to the prevailing religious doctrines of the day. Religions, unfortunately, are sectarian insofar as they identify human beings by creed, ethnicity, or nationality. Humanism wishes to overcome the limits of narrow religious parochialism and to go beyond national, racial, or ethnic differences. Humanism offers a global ethics that is universal. It wishes to transcend the chauvinistic creeds that divide humanity.

Thus, humanists seek to build a world community based on commonly shared ethical values.

On the world scene today, humanism competes with supernatural religious faiths for the minds and hearts of men and women. It rejects religious doctrines, whether ancient or New Age, because they are empirically false, logically inconsistent, and irrelevant to the global postindustrial information age that is now developing.

In order to achieve more secular and humanistic societies, it is important that we help to bring about a genuine *cultural renaissance*. We do not concentrate primarily on political and economic reform, though this is important; for we think that there are *deeper* needs that have been overlooked. Thus, we wish to address the basic existential questions that individuals ask— Who am I? How do I fit into the universe? What may I hope for? How can I achieve a good life for myself and my fellow human beings? In this regard, we wish to emphasize the importance of cultivating the method of intelligence at all levels of society. This method, if consistently applied, would mean a radical cultural transformation of society.

The humanist movement is a worldwide voluntary association of free individuals. It does not depend upon official government approval. In being committed to the ethics of rationality, it hopes to fulfill a secular and humanist agenda. This involves building democratic societies, in which individuals are free to develop their own lives by using their own resources and intelligence. It recommends that we work together cooperatively, as citizens of the world, in order to build a genuine global community.

Concluding Post-Marxist Postscript

By way of conclusion, I wish to make some final remarks about the continuing importance of the work of Marx, and to suggest some basis for convergence between naturalistic and secular humanism and Marxism. I do not claim to be a Marxist scholar, but I have studied Marx and have reflected upon his work for almost half a century.

Let me make some ten brief points, without elaborate argument:

First, both naturalistic and secular humanism and Marxism are heirs to the ideals of the Enlightenment. Both believe that no deity will save us, but that we must save ourselves; that is, they reject traditional supernatural theologies of salvation. They share a similar nonreductive materialism. And they draw upon evolutionary hypotheses to explain the development of the human species. Both express some optimism about the ability of humans to understand nature and to use reason to guide our future. Both wish to use the best scientific knowledge to improve the human condition. They wish to relate ideas to *praxis*, abstract thought to concrete pragmatic consequences.

Second, Marx was truly one of the great philosophers of the nineteenth century. Marx has been unfairly discredited in most parts of the world. The tragedy of Marxism, in my view, is that Marx was transformed into an infallible prophet by many of his disciples. Marxism was based on nineteenth-century science and this left insufficient room for the scientific discoveries of the twentieth century. Unfortunately, Marx's thought became dogma that had to be accepted without dissent. More importantly, his philosophy became the official philosophy of many countries, including the former Soviet Union, and as such was enforced by state power; so Marxism withered because it was not critically discussed and revised.

Third, in my view, Marx should be read for his insightful analyses of nineteenth-century capitalist society, and his explanation of previous historical epochs, if not for his recommendations of how to transcend the limits of capitalist societies. The economic interpretation of history should be taken as a tool of analysis, not an iron-clad universal law. In particular, factors in the superstructure may at times be more decisive (as Engels recognized) than those in the substructure of society.

Fourth, the basic difference between those naturalistic humanists who were social democrats and those Marxists who were Leninists, between Mensheviks and Bolsheviks, was on the use of violence and terror to achieve ideological ends, rather than democratic persuasion. For democratic socialists or democratic libertarians, democracy comes first, and this means an open society, a free press, civil liberties, free elections, the legal right of opposition, due process of law, the right of voluntary associations, and limitations on state power. Politics should not be viewed simply as part of the superstructure or an appendage of economic control. Political democracy must be taken as a precondition of any just society, and as a guarantee against the abuse of state power.

Fifth, no one realized how difficult it was for state planning boards to plan for an entire economy, nor the dynamic character of market forces, entrepreneurship and innovation. However, untrammeled market forces cannot satisfy all public needs, as economic libertarians believe, but must be regulated by a social concern. The competitive character of the free market leads to efficiency, and it is able to stimulate the introduction of new products and the creation of new industries. It is the consumer rather than the commissar who can best decide where the shoe pinches and which shoes to be manufactured.

Sixth, what nineteenth-century Marxism failed to envision was the rapid emergence of a postindustrial mode of production, namely information and knowledge. In my view, one of the primary reasons communism collapsed was that it was based on the nineteenth-century view of industrial production and did not envision a new society, beyond national frontiers and based upon information and services rather than manufactured products.

Seventh, in my view, Marx's analysis of the tendency of nineteenth-century capitalism to develop monopolies and trusts still applies to capitalism in the twentieth and twenty-first centuries, where we are witness to corporate mergers and the growth of conglomerates and oligopolies. These international megacorporations have become huge centers of power, and it is difficult for any one nation to regulate them. They are particularly dangerous where they control the media of information. No one knows quite how to regulate them. The most viable solution, I think, is to keep the competitive marketplace open, but to supplement it to fulfill unmet social needs. In the last analysis, the global economy can best be regulated by the development of global institutions and an international federal system of democratic law.

Eighth, the dynamic factor of economic and social change has become technology; but this depends upon new scientific discoveries. Thus, using a Marxist analysis, I would say that the forces of production that have been developed by a society seem to be more decisive than the relationships of production. Classes were meaningful in the medieval and industrial mode; they are less so in an information society, where one develops a whole cadre of skilled professionals with technical knowledge. It is essential to encourage scientific research as a powerful stimulus to economic growth and development. This can best be done, in my judgment, where conditions of free scientific research prevail.

Ninth, ethics is not simply a reflection of economic classes or the mode of production, but is autonomous as a field of inquiry. We need to introduce and develop ethical principles that transcend multicultural relativity. Humanism provides a global system of ethics that allows us to do that. It focuses on human rights and commonly shared values. Our ethical systems have emerged from ancient, rural, and agricultural societies, and they were continued even in urban and capitalist societies. We need a new post-postmodern global ethics relevant to the information age.

Tenth, no one envisioned the persistence of ancient chauvinistic religious, ethnic, national, and racial loyalties in the industrial and postindustrial age. These loyalties grew out of the historically isolated populations living in geographical proximity. We should recognize that the human species shares a common heritage. We are all citizens of our common planetary habitat. We need to transcend ancient religious and national boundaries and build a new world community. We are, as it were, cosmopolitans, transnationalists. We need to work cooperatively to deal with the problems of the twenty-first century. I think that the ethics of humanism can do that. It would emphasize the importance of international contact, travel, tourism, immigration and emigration, intermarriage and miscegenation. But above all, it would emphasize the need to develop a new identity beyond our ancient identities, as citizens of the world community. Although Marxist dogma is dead the philosophical outlook of Marx is still relevant to the future. Both Marxism and naturalistic secular humanism are concerned with improving the human condition. Neither is wedded to the ancient loyalties of the past. Both wish to use reason in order to create a new world. In the above analysis, I have pointed out some basis for a convergence of these two schools of philosophy and some ground for cooperation and even reunion.

---

1. For a fuller discussion of my ethical theory, see Paul Kurtz, *Forbidden Fruit: The Ethics of Humanism* (Amherst, N.Y.: Prometheus Books, 1988). The full list of common moral decencies consists of truthfulness, promise-keeping, sincerity, honesty, fidelity, dependability, goodwill, nonmalfeasance as applied to persons, nonmalfeasance as applied to private and public property, sexual consent, beneficence, gratitude, accountability, justice, tolerance, cooperation.

2. In *Forbidden Fruit* I list the following basic universal rights: (1) the right to life: security and protection of one's person, defense from external aggression, freedom from endangerment by the state; (2) the right to personal liberty: freedom of movement and residence, freedom from involuntary servitude or slavery, freedom of thought and conscience, freedom of speech and expression, moral freedom, privacy; (3) the right to health care: adequate medical treatment, informed consent, voluntary euthanasia; (4) freedom from want: basic economic needs, right to work, care for the elderly, right to leisure and relaxation; (5) economic rights: the right to own property, public property, the right to organize, protection from fraud; (6) intellectual and cultural freedom: free inquiry, the right to learn, the right to cultural enrichment; (7) moral equality: equal opportunity, equal access, no discrimination; (8) equal protection of the law: the right to a fair trial, the right to judicial protection, the right to humane treatment, the rule of law; (9) the right to democratic participation in government: the right to vote, the legal right of opposition, civil liberties, the right of assembly and association, the separation of church and state; (10) the rights of marriage, family, and children: the right to marriage, the right to divorce, the right to bear children, the rights of motherhood and fatherhood, parental rights, the rights of the child.

31

Do the Arts Convey Knowledge?

Many Humanist Agendas

Many recent critics of the humanist movement—including humanists themselves—argue that humanists have overemphasized the purely cerebral aspects of humanism that focus on scientific knowledge and philosophy. They maintain that humanists must redirect their focus. We must appeal to the *whole* person, including the poetic imagination, feelings, and emotions. We need to nourish the æsthetic response more than we have.

Humanists are almost unique on the contemporary scene, defending reason and science and criticizing irrational cults and myths, at a time when so few are doing so. Nevertheless, I agree with this basic thrust: we need to use the arts to express humanist attitudes. We need to explore literature, poetry, music, the visual arts, sculpture, dance, the theater, and the cinema—to mention only a few

Opening remarks for an Institute for Inquiry workshop on "Humanism and the Arts," given on Saturday, September 17, 1994, in Cincinnati, Ohio. Later read at the Humanist Institute Conference, "Living as a Humanist," in January 1995. First published as "Humanism and the Arts: Does Art Convey Knowledge?" in Robert Tapp, ed., *Living as Humanists: Essays from the Humanist Institute*, Vol. 10 (1996) of "Humanism Today" (Albuquerque, N. Mex: North American Committee for Humanism [NACH], 1999, pp. 153–164).

of the arts. This includes the need to recapture the imagination, to use fiction, narrative, and fantasy to dramatize the humanist outlook and humanist values. Thus a case can be made for revivifying humanism by relating it more closely to the arts.

Something similar, however, has been said about many other fields of human interest. When I grew up in the 1930s and 40s the great focus was on ideology. Activists said that humanism was mere abstract cant unless it related its general ethical principles to concrete political praxis. They urged us to get into the struggle for social justice, freedom, and equality. We had to take sides, they admonished us, on the basic economic and political issues of our time. Thus some humanists became democratic socialists, revolutionaries, or radicals, others conservatives, liberals, or more recently, libertarians.

Still other humanists have maintained that the real frontier of humanism should be primarily in the field of education and that we needed to teach moral education and how to think. Some went further and wished to reform the schools fundamentally and relate them to the solution of social problems. Other humanists have argued that humanism was indelibly related to democracy and that defending human rights and freedoms, the secular state, and the separation of church and state was the key frontier of humanism. Humanistic psychologists of the last generation—Carl Rogers, Erich Fromm, A. H. Maslow—have emphasized ways of developing self-actualization, self-respect, and creative growth. For other humanists, sexual freedom, the emancipation from repressive social and ecclesiastical institutions, and self-determination were central to human liberation. Religious humanists have argued that humanism is first and foremost a nontheistic religion, that it ought to perform the same function as churches and temples, that humanists ought to build secular communities, aping religiosity, and that humanists need a clergy to perform ceremonies and celebrations. Some humanists have said that humanism should be primarily humanitarian, that it needs to help build a world community, be concerned primarily with peace, hunger, and overpopulation, and to focus on the welfare of humanity as a whole. Thus there have been many agendas of what humanist ought or ought not to undertake.

Perhaps we should go still further and seek to relate humanism to other aspects of human interest. We can imagine someone saying: Let's tap the tremendous enthusiasm for competitive sports and involve humanists in these ventures. Or again, some may even wish to relate humanism to cuisine in order to attract the human pallet: fine wines and cheeses, bourguignon and bouillabaisse. Some humanists might say that we need to make humanism entertaining and untap the vast potential of the mass media.

No doubt many or most of these recommendations are valid: for they all contribute in multifarious ways to the ability of humanism to enhance the good life, the just society, and human happiness. Thus, if we are to succeed in fulfilling our aims, humanism should be concerned with the arts, politics, economics, education, ethics, the rites of passage, the sciences, philosophy, the media, and all of the diverse forms of human interest.

The Measure of Life

The problem, we may argue, may be in attempting to remake humanism into *one* thing exclusively. Perhaps we should be pluralistic and allow every form of humanism within the mansion of humanism. The question is then raised: Is anything *distinctive* to humanism *per se*?

Every generation seeks to define and redefine humanism in its own terms. B. F. Skinner defined a humanist as one who is "concerned for the future of mankind." Sidney Hook defined a humanist as one "who relies on the arts of intelligence to defend, enlarge, and enhance ... human freedom." Marvin Zimmerman differed and equated "humanism with atheism." Harold Blackham, the British humanist, called it "a concept of Man." And Corliss Lamont labeled humanism as "a philosophy or way of life."[1]

If I were asked what I think is central to the humanist outlook, or ought to be, I would say that *humanism offers a unique answer to the question: "What is the meaning of life?"* This response entails a scientific, ethical, and æsthetic dimension. We first need to define humanism negatively by what it rejects. Clearly, secular humanism, as I use it, does not interpret nature in supernatural terms, for we can find no evidence for a divine origin or purpose; nor does it think that the human species is fulfilling some transcendental plan of salvation. Humanism thus rejects the liturgy of sin and redemption. But more importantly humanism has an affirmative statement to make that is in sharp contrast with salvational supernatural doctrines that still prevail; namely, that humanism emphasizes *the fulfillment and enrichment of this life here and now as the primary good.*

The meaning of life is a question that is pondered by any person who confronts disappointment, failure, disease, or death, who contemplates his own finitude; or conversely is moved by adventure, exploration, and the achievement motive.

Humanism draws upon the sciences, philosophy, ethics, education, and the arts to answer the meaning question. Humanism provides us with a *eupraxsophy*; that is, a cosmic outlook, nontheistic and atheistic in focus, and this is based primarily on scientific knowledge, *sophia* or wisdom, and an ethical life stance or *eupraxis*, on how to achieve the good life. In both regards, it draws upon science and philosophy to provide a rational interpretation of nature and some practical wisdom in one's ethical life: and that is the distinctive message. Humanism abandons any fixation on otherworldly spiritual notions; it emphasizes our own responsibility for who and what we are; and it affirms that the universe does not possess a hidden divine plan, but that it presents us with opportunities. Life has no *a priori* meaning *per se*, but it can be abundant and meaningful; for we encounter challenges and options and we can live life exuberantly; we can expand our horizons of appreciation and enjoyment as free individuals and we can share the riches of experiences with others in the community.

The Role of the Fine Arts

One may ask, How do the arts fit into this humanistic eupraxsophy? This depends in one sense on our definition of the term "art." Let us begin by defining what I mean by "art." In its primary sense, art is related to *techné*, the Greek word meaning "art, skill, craft." Aristotle related this to a means-end process.[2] Things happen, said Aristotle, either "by nature" or "by art." In an artistic mode of production, the skilled technician has a purpose in mind and he adapts and molds materials to fulfill this end. If he is to succeed in his task, he needs to develop his expertise. There is a kind of craftsmanship and intelligence at work in the practice of his art. Whether a ship builder or weaver, he applies his practical know-how, virtuosity, and talent in fashioning objects that he is creating, and he draws upon general principles which he applies to concrete cases.

In the modern world technology is the most sophisticated application of *techné* and the applied sciences. It draws up general principles from the theoretical sciences, which it adapts to concrete cases. Thus inventors, architects, designers, and engineers build bridges and construct cities, shopping malls and university campuses, sports cars and transistor radios, steam engines and computers. They apply their intelligence to create objects for human use. The technological arts are functional; and if they are successful, consumers will applaud their efforts and flock to purchase their wares.

The critics of humanism who indict it for ignoring the arts do not mean the technological or practical arts, but the *fine arts:* music and song, poetry and literature, the theater, fiction and painting, sculpture and architecture. The artist here creates art objects, which, if critics and connoisseurs judge to be of high quality, may be collected and be put into art museums. Wealthy patrons collect work of art, which they hope will become valuable in time. I recently visited the new Richelieu wing of the Louvre, which contained the finest sculpture from ancient Egypt, Greece, and Rome through the Renaissance and modern period, including works by Maillol, Rodin, and Brancusi. Great musical compositions become part of the repertoire of philharmonic orchestras performed on special occasions—from Mozart to Bartok and Hindemith. And great plays become the repertoire of the theater, especially Shakespeare at Stratford, Molière in Paris, and even George Bernard Shaw in Niagara-on-the-Lake.

John Dewey, in *Art as Experience*,[3] made the point, however, that we should not divorce art from life, for there is not a sharp dividing line between the fine and practical arts. We need to integrate art and æsthetic enjoyment into all aspects of life. An architect who conceives of a building has a utilitarian function in mind for the structure; but if given the opportunity, it should be a thing of beauty, pleasing to the eye—the magnificent Parthenon was home to Athena, the Greek goddess, and had a central role in the civic life of the Athenians. The great Pyramids were burial tombs for dead pharaohs seeking everlasting life, and the Arc du Triomphe was a tribute to victory. The fine jewelry, vases, portraits, furniture, and antiques now exhibited in art museums were used to adorn men and women and/or decorate places where they lived and assembled. Many or most works of art were created for multiple uses and also enjoyment, depending on the particular art. Today, works of art are photographed and musical performances or plays are replicated on records, tapes, or CDs and distributed to countless millions of homes and offices, and the printing press has made great literature accessible to all. Moreover, the concept of what is "artistic" has been properly extended to include fashion and perfume, floral arrangements, interior decoration, electronic music, classical automobiles, sports and parades; *indeed a "work of art" applies to almost any creation of the human imagination that is thought to be pleasing or beautiful.* Thus art needs to be integrated into social and cultural life. It is not the esoteric possession of elite critics, collectors, and connoisseurs.

What is the main purpose of art? In a primary sense, the artist-craftsman is bringing into being something new; and in doing so, expresses feelings and ideas, attitudes and values, and attempts to communicate them by means of the object thus created. If the artist is successful, the work will arouse similar feelings, ideas, and values in others.

Santayana thought that beauty was "pleasure objectified"; that is, it was defined in terms of the pleasure it aroused,[4] depending on the work. What we encounter is engrossing, exciting, lively (or conversely, dull and wooden), and it stimulates feelings and imagination. It may even be cathartic, as Aristotle thought: great tragedies, such as *Oedipus Rex* were able to purge our emotions. Powerful dramas may even have a moral lesson—as what befalls a great person due to a defect of character. Comedy may provoke laughter and wit and poke fun at the ironies of life. The uniquely *æsthetic dimension*, I submit, arouses feelings, attitudes and engender moods—mystery, fear, love, hate, humor. Thus it *exists in the realm of imagination and emotion*.

Humans cannot be defined simply as rational animals because they seek to know and understand, but also as active, creative makers and doers. As æsthetic beings they enter into nature, not simply to imitate it, but to bring into being something new. They are or can become artists and craftsmen—Promethean figures seeking to build new worlds, creating new vistas as products of their dreams and aspirations, imagination, and inspiration. Artists spin out tales of fiction; but these may one day become real in human culture, as science fiction demonstrates. Prophets spawn myths and parables in order to fulfill religious, moral, and æsthetic functions. The point again is that the æsthetic object cannot be abstracted from the deeper utilitarian processes of life.

Nonetheless, the fine arts have different functions from the technical arts: and that is to arouse mood and enhance enjoyment. In one sense different arts have different functions, yet works of art are intrinsically enjoyable for their own sake. They are not primarily instrumental, nor made to fulfill utilitarian functions: The manufacturer of a urinal has a specific function or use for the object; but the purpose of a work of fine art is to be delightful in its own terms and not for an extrinsic use. A beautiful woman is pleasing to look at, but that surely is not her primary function as a human being; but it is for a statue of her.

Art and Knowledge

Let me raise the further question: what is the relationship of the fine arts to knowledge? This is an important issue for contemporary secular humanism because it focuses on the methods of science and reason as the most effective way of developing reliable knowledge. Does art provide us with another form of truth which we cannot get in any other way?

There are two major theories of the relationship of art to knowledge that I wish to state and reject:

The first is the *Platonic theory* of art—that art provides us with an intuition of universal ideas and that the work of art gives us eternal truths. This presupposes a metaphysical theory that is highly dubious: the existence of a realm of ideal forms—for which I can find no evidence. It is a reification of items of thought. On the contrary, the artist is dealing with the mundane world, not some spiritual or mystical realm laid up in heaven. Plato thought the artist was mad, and so he banished him from the state.

The second is the *representational theory* that maintains that art is supposed to represent realities in nature and are "true" insofar as they depict or describe what's out there. This generalized account of art misses the central æsthetic dimension of mood and feeling, and it is too literal in interpretation. It does apply to some portraits or statues that were commissioned by aristocrats and wealthy patrons before the advent of photography or cinematography, for these may render a good likeness of the person. But this theory fails to account for modern painting and sculpture, which takes us into a new world of possibilities and gives free reign to the creative imagination. What do Picasso or Jackson Pollack represent? They seem to distort reality; but nonetheless they are exciting for they have created new metaphors of the imagination. How does the representational theory account for music? What do the late quartets of

Beethoven or a symphony by Shostakovich mean beyond the music itself, which is able to arouse powerful feelings. The demand for a didactic interpretation thus misses the main point.

But surely some forms of literature: novels, plays, historical romances, even if fiction—may capture the essential characteristics of life, the pathos of tragedy or the humorous qualities of some human situations. Granted, but not in a strictly literal or descriptive sense, for it is the consummate union of passionate feelings with intellectual insights, emotion and cognition, form and content, that makes a fine novel or play so moving; and it is the æsthetic component that is able to arouse our feelings.

The salient point is that great art is worthwhile *for its own sake:* it is pleasing or engrossing to the eyes, interesting to the ears, able to arouse both the senses and the mind.

Dewey has used the word "consumatory" and A. H. Maslow "peak experience" to interpret an æsthetic experience and to distinguish it from humdrum daily life; for it has special sensuous qualities. It is like an orgasm, or glass of fine wine, or a fragrant lilac; for it stands out. If it is attractive and stunning it contributes to the beauty of life. In this sense, art *celebrates life.* It is evocative and expressive. It enables us to savor its taste, bouquet, and fragrance, and to delight in the sensuous immediacies and qualities of experience, and it helps bring life to fruition. This applies to the eloquent renderings of the tragic aspects of the human condition as well as the mundane and comic.

Does art convey knowledge? My response to that is yes and no, depending on the art; but not uniquely so.

First, art forms are relative to cultures and the modes of expression may vary from generation to generation: Inca pottery, Chinese opera, the Spanish bullfight, baroque religious chants, are localized in their nuances. Yet they may communicate nigh universal ideas or values common to the human condition and cut across societies and epochs; death and defeat, betrayal and cowardice, bravery and endurance, stupidity and comedy are perennial under whatever sky.

Second, the border lines between descriptive knowledge, historical narrative and art in literature or the theater, for example, may be difficult to demarcate. Obviously a great novelist, essayist, or dramatist is able to convey knowledge, and his message may be powerfully rendered. But is it knowledge that we cannot get in any other way? I doubt it. To abstract the message in didactic rendition may lose the total æsthetic effect, as in the Neil Simon comedy *Brighton Beach* or Thomas Mann's *Buddenbrooks.* Yet some forms of art are deceptive. What is the truth of a painting of Jesus on the cross or Mary and the Infant so richly depicted in medieval art?

On the other hand, the classical paintings, *The Rape of the Sabine Women,* or *The Last Day of Socrates,* may give us a pretty good idea of what went on. Thus the arts do communicate information and understanding. But often this is subjective, and although it may be emotionally powerful, is it always "true," or does it have value? The Nazis during the height of Hitler's power would parade 100,000 SS troops, dressed in black, with torch lights and drums on Unter der Linden in Berlin, singing the Horstwessel song. This inspired millions of Germans, as they watched the æsthetic spectacle. But it also engendered fear and loathing in many who viewed it. There is good and bad art on both sides of the barricades. The fundamentalist may be moved by the organ and the choir, or the devout Catholic by the magnificent cathedral and the pomp and splendor of the Mass, or the humanist by naturalistic art. We may disagree politically with many of the finest playwrights of our time; for example, Bertolt Brecht. Yet we can be moved by the drama. We can enjoy a Wagnerian opera even though his exaltation of the gods is based on pure fantasy. Many postmodernists claim there are no objective standards for judging truth claims in any fields of endeavor. What does that say about truth and falsity? Are there any criteria for judging; or is it simply a question of subjective taste and caprice?

These are large-order questions. I have argued that humanism, secular humanism in particular, is committed to a method of inquiry and that there are objective standards for deriving and testing claims to truth: evidence, experimental predictions, reasons, logical validity. Such claims must be replicated by a community of inquirers. Hypotheses are not absolute truths, but fallible and open to modification. The controlled use of scientific methods has been the most effective way we have for developing reliable knowledge. They apply not simply to empirical fact but to value judgments. They are not esoteric, but continuous with the method of reason and intelligence that we use in ordinary life.

But what about the arts? Some of them seek to convey knowledge, and we can dispute or agree with the "message." But this is perhaps not their primary function. The purpose of art is to heighten the senses, raise the level of taste and appreciation, expand the dimensions of experience.

We are not simply intellectual creatures. We wish to make love, to enjoy a gourmet dinner, to jog in the park, to cheer lustily at a ball game, to engage in spirited conversation with our friends, to play bridge or tennis, travel to exotic places, struggle with others to build a better world, and to enjoy the arts. The arts are so vital because they help to make life worth living. Music, poetry, literature, paintings, dance, and the theater are among our richest joys. Indeed, for the humanist the æsthetic dimension of life is perhaps the most eloquent expression of human creativity. The fine arts contribute immeasurably to the good life and that is why we cherish them.

Thus humanism needs to untap the poetic metaphors of the creative human imagination and to use these to dramatize humanist ideals in æsthetic form. Art does not substitute subjective intuition for knowledge claims justified by reason and experiment; it is not a replacement for objective methods of inquiry. It simply adds an eloquent dimension to experience by rendering humanist truths and humanist values in æsthetic form. And as such it can help to inspire intensity of conviction and devotion to commitment. It is thus able to make humanism both intellectually true and æsthetically satisfying. As such, art has a powerful role to play in life. It is thus intrinsic to the fullest expression of humanist eupraxsophy.

---

1. See Paul Kurtz, ed., *The Humanist Alternative: Some Definitions of Humanism* (Buffalo, New York: Prometheus Books; London: Pemberton Books, 1973).

2. Aristotle, *Poetica.*

3. John Dewey, *Art as Experience* (New York: Minton, Balch & Co., 1934).

4. George Santayana, *The Sense of Beauty* (New York: Scribners, 1896).

Selected List of Publications by Paul Kurtz

Prepared by Ranjit Sandhu

This seven-year bibliography supplements the bibliography that appeared in *Toward a New Enlightenment: The Philosophy of Paul Kurtz*, edited by Vern L. Bullough and Timothy J. Madigan (New Brunswick, N.J.: Transaction Publishers, 1994). It contains publications from 1993 through 2000.

Books

1. Co-editor, with Timothy J. Madigan. *Challenges to the Enlightenment: In Defense of Reason and Science.* Amherst, N.Y.: Prometheus Books, 1994.

2. *The Courage to Become: The Virtues of Humanism.* Westport, Conn.: Praeger Publishers, an imprint of Greenwood Publishing Group, 1997.

3. *Humanist Manifesto 2000: A Call for a New Planetary Humanism* (drafted by Paul Kurtz). Amherst, N.Y.: Prometheus Books, 1999.

* * * * *

4. *Leben ohne Religion: Eupraxophie.* A German translation of *Living without Religion: Eupraxophy.* Tr. by Arnher E. Lenz. Neustadt am Rübenberge: Angelika Lenz Verlag, 1993.

5. *Запретный Плод: Этика гуманизма.* A Russian translation of *Forbidden Fruit: The Ethics of Humanism.* Tr. by E. A. Kuvakina. Moscow: Gnozis, 1993.

6. *Valakkappetta Kani — Part I, Valakkappetta Kani — Part II,* and *Manushyavakasangalum Swakaryathayum.* A Malayalam translation of *Forbidden Fruit: The Ethics of Humanism,* in three volumes. Tr. by G. Jayan. New Delhi: Indian Atheist Publishers, 1995.

7. *Sandelhavadathinte Prasakthi* and *Yesuvum Mosayum.* A Malayalam translation, in two volumes, of *The Transcendental Temptation: A Critique of Religion and the Paranormal.* Tr. by G. Jayan. New Delhi: Indian Atheist Publishers, 1997.

8. *Zakázané ovocie: etika humanizmu.* A Slovakian translation of *Forbidden Fruit: The Ethics of Humanism.* Tr. by Rastislav Škoda. Bratislava: Prometheus Society of Slovakia, 1998.

9. *Verbotene Früchte: Ethik des Humanismus.* A German translation of *Forbidden Fruit: The Ethics of Humanism.* Tr. by Arnher E. Lenz. Neustadt am Rübenberge: Angelika Lenz Verlag, 1998.

10. *Zakazany Owoc: Etyka humanizmu.* A Polish translation of *Forbidden Fruit: The Ethics of Humanism,* tr. by Tadeusz Chawziuk. Issued as vol. 3 of a "Biblioteka *Bez Dogmatu.*" Warsaw, Poland: Instytut Wydawniczy "Ksiʃka i Prasa," 2000.

11. *Искушение потусторонним.* A Russian translation of *The Transcendental Temptation: A Critique of Religion and the Paranormal.* Tr. by Valeri0 A. Kuvakin. Moscow: Akademicheski0 Proekt, 1999.

Articles or Chapters in Books; Monographs; Encyclopedia Entries

1. *Humanism, Spirituality, and Esotericism: A Debate between Paul Kurtz and Fons Elders.* A booklet published by the Council for Democratic and Secular Humanism (now known as the Council for Secular Humanism) in 1994. It is a transcription of a debate between Paul Kurtz and Fons Elders, held in Berlin on Thursday, July 29, 1993, at a European Humanist Congress on "Democracy—Human Rights—Humanism: The Future Ethics of the 21st Century." An abridgment appeared as "A Debate on Humanism, Spirituality and Esotericism," in Fons Elders, ed. *Humanism Toward the Third Millennium II* (Brussels: VUB University Press, 1996), pp. 145–167. Quotes from the debate appeared in *Humanist: Magasin for Kultur–Og Livssynsdebatt* (Netherlands) no. 5 (1993), p. 16.

2. "Overview: Humanism and the Idea of Freedom." In George D. Smith, Jr., ed., *Religion, Feminism, and Freedom of Conscience: A Mormon/Humanist Dialogue.* Salt Lake City, Utah: Signature Books; Amherst, N.Y.: Prometheus Books, 1994, pp. xvii–xxiii.

3. "Two Sources of Unreason in Democratic Societies: The Paranormal and Religion." In Paul R. Gross and Norman Levitt, eds., *The Flight from Science and Reason: Annals of the New York Academy of Sciences,* vol. 775 (1996), pp. 500–501. An excerpt appeared in *Pique: Newsletter of the Secular Humanist Society of New York* (September 1998), pp. 3–4.

4. "Skepticism and the Paranormal." In Gordon Stein, ed., *The Encyclopedia of the Paranormal.* Amherst, N.Y.: Prometheus Books, 1996, pp. 684–701.

5. "Reason and the Courage to Become." In Eustoquio Molina, Alberto Carreras, and Jesús Puertas, eds., *Evolucionismo y racionalismo,* Zaragoza: Institución «Fernando el Católico», Universidad de Zaragoza, 1998, pp. 189–200.

6. "Our Responsibility to Humanity as a Whole." In Indumati Parikh, ed., *14th IHEU World Congress, Mumbai, India, 1999: Report.* Mumbai, India: Centre for the Study of Social Change, 1999, pp. 15–21.

7. "Two Senses of Secular and Secularism." In M. A. Rane, ed., *V. M. Tarkunde 90: A Restless Crusader for Human Freedoms.* Mumbai, India: Indian Radical Humanist Association, Mumbai Branch, 1999, pp. 15–20.

8. "Sidney Hook. 1902–1989. American Political Philosopher and Educator." *Encyclopedia Americana.* Available to schools online at go.grolier.com. Danbury, Conn.: Grolier, Inc., March 2000.

9. "Preface." In Isaac Asimov, *The Roving Mind.* 2nd ed. Amherst, N.Y.: Prometheus Books, 1997.

Articles in Magazines, Newspapers, and Journals

1. "Notes from the Editor: Has a Third World War, with Islam, Begun? / Galileo and Papal Fallibility / Gays and Lesbians in the Military." *Free Inquiry* 13, no. 2 (Spring 1993). "Galileo and Papal Fallibility" later appeared as "Il caso Galileo e la fallibilità papale" in *La nuova ragione* (Rome) 4, no. 1 (January-March 1993). "Has a Third World War, with Islam, Begun?" also ran in *The Secularist* (Pune, India) no. 142 (June-August 1993), pp. 91–93, 95; and in *New Quest* (published by the Indian Association for Cultural Freedom), no. 101 (September–October 1993), pp. 306–308.

2. "Exploring the Television Wasteland." *Skeptical Inquirer* 17, no. 3 (Summer 1993), pp. 350–354.

3. "Notes from the Editor. The Need for Free Inquiry into Religious Foundations. Academic Freedom at Brigham Young University. Ethnic Cleansing or "Religious Purification"? Spanish Freethought. The Movement Toward a Polish Theocracy." *Free Inquiry* 13, no. 3 (Summer 1993),
pp. 4–6.

4. "A Key Meeting in Madrid: Building Humanism in the Spanish-Speaking World." *International Humanist News* 1, no. 2 (July 1993), p. 1. This article was later reprinted as "Humanism in the Spanish-Speaking World" in *The Secularist* (Pune, India) no. 144 (November–December 1993), pp. 132–133.

5. "Letter from Berlin." *Free Inquiry* 13, no. 4 (Fall 1993), pp. 4–5. A report on the first Congress of the European Humanist Federation, July 25–30, 1993, Berlin.

6. "An Affirmative View of Celebrations." Part of a symposium on "Should Secular Humanists Celebrate the Rites of Passage?" *Free Inquiry* 13, no. 4 (Fall 1993), pp. 14–15.

7. "Advice to Young Lovers About to Be Wed." *Free Inquiry* 13, no. 4 (Fall 1993), p. 15.

8. "Introduction: Faith Healing Revisited." Introduction to a symposium on "Faith Healing: Miracle or Mirage?" *Free Inquiry* 14, no. 1 (Winter 1993/1994), p. 4.

9. "Are We Approaching the End of the Age of Books? Prometheus at Twenty-Five." *Free Inquiry* 14, no. 1 (Winter 1993/1994), pp. 25–28.

10. "The Growth of Antiscience." *Skeptical Inquirer* 18, no. 3 (Spring 1994), pp. 255–263. This article later appeared as "The Antiscience Problem" in Kendrick Frazier, ed., *Encounters with the Paranormal*, Amherst, N.Y.: Prometheus Books, 1998, pp. 65–73.

11. "Ode to Football." *Free Inquiry* 14, no. 2 (Spring 1994), pp. 38–39.

12. "Target Islamic Culture." *International Humanist News* 2, no. 1 (March 1994), p. 10.

13. "Some Lessons for Humanists." *Free Inquiry* 14, no. 3 (Summer 1994), pp. 12–13.

14. "Milestones: World War II: Fifty Years Later. International Humanism. Children of Mixed Marriages. Secular Memorial Ceremonies. Secular Humanism and Crime." *Free Inquiry* 14, no. 4 (Fall 1994), pp. 5–6.

15. "Notes from the Editor. The Culture Wars Intensify. Two Senses of Freedom. Revising History Texts. Is the Pope a Humanist?" *Free Inquiry* 15, no. 1 (Winter 1994/1995), pp. 4–6.

16. "New Departure for the Skeptical Inquirer." *Skeptical Inquirer* 19, no. 1 (January/February 1995), pp. 3–4, 62. With photo.

17. "The Cairo Conference: A Hopeful Sign." Part of a section on "Secularism and Enlightenment in Islamic Countries." *Free Inquiry* 15, no. 2 (Spring 1995), pp. 36–38. With photos.

18. "Is John Beloff an Absolute Paranormalist?" *Skeptical Inquirer* 19, no. 3 (May/June 1995), p. 28. This was a response to John Beloff's article, "The Skeptical Position: Is It Tenable?" in *Skeptical Inquirer* 19, no. 3 (May/June 1995), pp. 19–24.

19. "Agenda for the Humanist Movement in the Twenty-First Century." *Free Inquiry* 15, no. 3 (Summer 1995), pp. 8–12.

20. "Remembering World War II: Racial Superiority and 'Ethnic Cleansing' Revisited." *Free Inquiry* 15, no. 3 (Summer 1995), p. 19.

21. "Notes from the Editor. Pro Ecclesia et Commercia: The Disneyfication of America / Will the Twenty-First Century Be 'The Religious Century'? / The "Religious Equality" Amendment / Jewish Intermarriage / Islamic Intolerance." *Free Inquiry* 15, no. 4 (Fall 1995), pp. 5–8.

22. "In Retrospect: Corliss Lamont 1902–1995." *Free Inquiry* 15, no. 4 (Fall 1995), pp. 8–9.

23. With others. "In Defense of Freedom of Conscience: A Cooperative Baptist/Secular Humanist Declaration." *Free Inquiry* 16, no. 1 (Winter 1995/1996), pp. 4–7. Later published in Paul D. Simmons, ed., *Freedom of Conscience: A Baptist/Humanist Dialogue.* Amherst, N.Y.: Prometheus Books, 2000.

24. "History Shows You Can Lead an Ethical Life without Religion." *The Charlotte Observer* (Monday, February 12, 1996), p. 9A.

25. "The Common Moral Decencies Don't Depend on Faith." *Free Inquiry* 16, no. 2 (Spring 1996), pp. 5, 7. Part of a debate with John M. Frame entitled "Do We Need God to Be Moral?" *Free Inquiry* 16, no. 3 (Summer 1996), pp. 3, 60.

26. "Response from the Editor." *Free Inquiry* 16, no. 3 (Summer 1996), p. 61. A reply to the criticisms of Tom Flynn's article, "The Case for Affirmative Secularism."

27. "Bonnie Bullough 1927–1996." *Free Inquiry* 16, no. 3 (Summer 1996), p. 15.

28. "The Survival of Humankind Is the Basic Humanist Value: A[n] Interview with Svetozar Stojanovi}." *Free Inquiry* 16, no. 3 (Summer 1996), pp. 49–54.

29. "The Future Course of Humanism." *New Humanist* (Great Britain) 111, no. 2 (June 1996), pp. 2–5. It was later republished in *The Atheist* (July 1996), pp. 8–10 (part 1).

30. "From the Chairman. CSICOP at Twenty." *Skeptical Inquirer* 20, no. 4 (July/August 1996), pp. 5–8. Originally delivered as the opening address at the First World Skeptics Congress, "Science in the Age of (Mis)Information," June 20–23, 1996, Amherst Campus, State University of New York at Buffalo, Amherst, New York.

31. "Neospiritualismus, Religion und das Paranormale" (tr. by Fabian Lischka). *Skeptiker: Parawissenschaften unter der Lupe* (Germany) 9, no. 3 (1996), pp. 80–87.

32. "Introduction: Beyond Religion." *Free Inquiry* 16, no. 4 (Fall 1996), pp. 4–6. Introduction to a section on "Defining Humanism: The Battle Continues."

33. "Gordon Stein 1941–1996." *Free Inquiry* 16, no. 4 (Fall 1996), p. 45.

34. "The Infomedia Revolution: Opportunities for Global Humanism." *New Humanist* 111, no. 4 (December 1996), pp. 3–6. This speech was summarized in *Free Mind* 39, no. 4 (July/August 1996), pp. 1–2. The article later appeared in *Free Inquiry* 17, no. 1 (Winter 1996/97), pp. 34–37; as "Humanizm a rewolucja w info-mediach" in *Bez Dogmatu: Kwartalnik Kulturalno-Polityczny*, no. 31 (Winter [1996–]1997), pp. 13–15; as "Гуманизм и революция в средствах массовой информациё" in *рубеже вековл научно-публицистиуеский журнал*, no. 4 (October–

December 1996), pp. 43–47 (translated by Mariny Shinkarenko); and as "Humanism and the Information Revolution" in *The Secularist: Journal of the Indian Secular Society*, no. 163 (January–February 1997), pp. 5–11, 15.

35. "The Darkened Cosmos: A Tribute to Carl Sagan." Tributes by Kendrick Frazier, Richard Dawkins, Arthur C. Clarke, Martin Gardner, David Morrison, James Randi, Jill Tarter, Paul Kurtz, Alan Hale, Christopher Chyba, Leon M. Lederman, Clifford A. Pickover, John Allen Paulos, Chip Denman, Shawn Carlson, Nicholas Humphrey, Daniel R. Alonso, Javier E. Armentia, Barry Williams, Swedish Skeptics, Michael D. Sofka, Mark Boslough, and Colin Groves. *Skeptical Inquirer* 21, no. 2 (March/April 1997), pp. 5–15. The tributes by Kendrick Frazier (uncredited), Richard Dawkins, and Paul Kurtz later appeared in "The Darkened Cosmos: A Tribute to Carl Sagan," *The Modern Rationalist* 22, no. 6 (June 1997), pp. 9–12.

36. With Jan Willem Nienhuys and Ranjit Sandhu. "Is the 'Mars Effect' Genuine?" *Journal of Scientific Exploration* 11, no. 1 (Spring 1997), pp. 19–39. This was a response to Suitbert Ertel and Kenneth Irving, "Biased Data Selection in Mars Effect Research," *Journal of Scientific Exploration* 11, no. 1 (Spring 1997), pp. 1–18.

37. "Notes from the Editor. Surviving Bypass and Enjoying the Exuberant Life: A Personal Account / Open-Heart Surgery / Existential Reflections / The Virtues of Humanism / Secular Humanism in American Society." *Free Inquiry* 17, no. 2 (Spring 1997), pp. 10–13.

38. "The Need to Reach Out." *Free Inquiry* 17, no. 3 (Summer 1997), p. 5.

39. "Declaration in Defense of Cloning and the Integrity of Scientific Research." *Free Inquiry* 17, no. 3 (Summer 1997), pp. 11–12. Drafted by Paul Kurtz and others. Signed by 30 members of the International Academy of Humanism. This generated an article: Karla Haworth. "Group Issues Statement Supporting Cloning." *Chronicle of Higher Education* (May 30, 1997).

40. "UFO-Mythology: The Escape to Oblivion." *Skeptical Inquirer* 21, no. 4 (July/August 1997), pp. 12–14. An abridgment was later published as "Perspective on the Media: A Marriage Made in Heaven's Gate," *The Los Angeles Times* (Monday, May 19, 1997), p. B5, cols. 3–5; "Mass Consumption of Pseudoscience Incites 'Transcendental' Tragedies," *Tacoma* [Washington] *News Tribune* (Wednesday, May 21, 1997); "A Marriage Made in Heaven's Gate," *Kalispell* [Montana] *Inter Lake* (Wednesday, May 21, 1997); "A Marriage Made in Heaven's Gate," *Las Vegas Review-Journal* (Wednesday, May 21, 1997); "Modern Mythology? Who Is to Blame When Reality Begins to Rival Science Fiction?" *Winter Haven* [Florida] *News Chief* (Thursday, May 22, 1997); "Why Do 'Space Aliens' Find So Many Willing Believers on Earth?" *Sacramento Bee* (Friday, May 23, 1997); "In the Debate: With Goofy 'Science' All Around, It's Small Wonder Deluded Souls Try to Head Skyward to a UFO," *The*

Buffalo News (Friday, May 23, 1997), p. C2, cols. 4–5; "A Marriage Made in Heaven's Gate: UFO Mythology," *Minnesota Star-Tribune* (Friday, May 23, 1997); "Beware These Brain-Eating Monsters," *Pittsburgh Post-Gazette* (Sunday, May 25, 1997); "Media Give Sci-Fi an Authentic Ring," *Madison Capital Times* (Monday, May 26, 1997); and "Stairway to Heaven's Gate: Mass Media Must Share Blame for Spreading UFO Myths," *Sunday* [Wilmington, N.C.] *Star-News* (Sunday, June 15, 1997).

41. "The Evolution of Humanism." *New Humanist: The Quarterly Journal of the Rationalist Press Association* 112, no. 2 (August 1997), pp. 5–7.

42. "Cosmic Humanism for the Space Age." *Free Inquiry* 17, no. 4 (Fall 1997), pp. 5, 55.

43. "Science and Reason in an Irrational World." *International Humanist News* 5, nos. 3–4 (December 1997), pp. 8–9. A translation by Tatyana Zeliknoi was published as "Наука и разим в иррациолъном мире," *Здравый смысл: журнал скептикове оптимистов и гуманистов*, no. 5 (1997), pp. 6–15.

44. "Is Secular Humanism a Religion?" *The Harbinger* 16, no. 6 (December 9–31, 1997), pp. 1, 4, 17, 20, 23.

45. "Secular Humanism in the New Russia." *Free Inquiry* 18, no. 1 (Winter 1997/98), pp. 5, 56. A translation by Jean Dierickx appeared as "L'humanisme laïque dans la nouvelle Russie," *Espace libertés: Magazine du Centre d'Action Laïque* (Belgium) no. 263 (August–September 1998), pp. 16–17.

46. "Where Are the Secularists? The Battles of the Past for a Secular Society Must Be Waged All Over Again." *Free Inquiry* 18, no. 1 (Winter 1997/1998), pp. 16–17. A revised version of this article appeared as "In Defense of Secularism," *Las Vegas Review–Journal–Sun*, March 15, 1998.

47. "First Things First: Toward a Minimal Definition of Humanism." *Philo* 1, no. 1 (Spring/Summer 1998), pp. 5–14. A translation by Aleksandra Kruzlova appeared as "Сначала о главном: к минимальному определению гуманизма," *Здравый смысл: журнал скептикове оптимистов и гуманистов* (Russia), no. 11 ([June] 1999), pp. 22–33.

48. "Efforts to Build a Center for Inquiry in Southland Proceeding Rapidly." *Friends of the Center for Inquiry–West Newsletter: The Newsletter for Skeptics and Humanists in Southern California* 1, no. 2 (January 1998), pp. 1, 2, 7.

49. "On the Barricades: Oligopolic Control of America / Desecularizing Universities and Colleges / The Pope in Cuba." *Free Inquiry* 18, no. 2 (Spring 1998), pp. 5, 56.

50. "Darwin Re-Crucified: Why Are So Many Afraid of Naturalism?" *Free Inquiry* 18, no. 2 (Spring 1998), pp. 15–17.

51. "As a Few Companies Control Information, the World Risks a Dangerous Control of Ideas." *The Buffalo News* (Tuesday, May 26, 1998). The article also appeared as "Secular Humanists *vs.* the Global Mediacracy." *Free Inquiry* 18, no. 3 (Summer 1998), pp. 5, 57–59. An addendum to this article appeared as "Legal Recourse," ibid., p. 59.

52. "The New Skepticism: A Worldwide Movement." *Skeptical Briefs: Newsletter of the Committee for the Scientific Investigation of Claims of the Paranormal* 8, no. 2 (June 1998), pp. 1–3, 9–11; *The Skeptic* [Australia] 18, no. 2 (Winter 1998), pp. 23–28. Translated into Spanish as as "El nuevo escépticismo: un movimiento mundial" (tr. by Iñaki Camiruaga) in *El escéptico: La revista para el fomento de la razón y la ciencia* 1998, no. 1 (June), pp. 50–59. Translated into Italian as "Il nuovo scetticismo: Un movimento mondiale," *Scienza & paranormale: Rivista di indagine critica sul paranormale* 7, no. 23 (January/February 1999), pp. 46–48 [part 1]; 7, no. 24 (March/April 1999), pp. 46–48 [part 2].

53. "Humanist Politics: The Need for a New Coalition." *Free Inquiry* 18, no. 4 (Fall 1998), pp. 5, 60.

54. "The McCarthyites of Virtue." *Free Inquiry* 19, no. 1 (Winter 1998/1999), pp. 5, 61.

55. "Beyond Humanist Manifesto II." *The Humanist* 58, no. 5 (September/October 1998), pp. 25–33.

56. "Fears of the Apocalypse." *Skeptical Inquirer* 23, no. 1 (January/February 1999), pp. 20–24.

57. "New Russian Initiative to Defend Science and Reason." *Skeptical Inquirer* 23, no. 1 (January/February 1999), p. 33.

58. "India's Population Time Bomb" and "An Urgent Appeal for Funds." *Free Inquiry* 19, no. 2 (Spring 1999), pp. 5, 57–59. An abridgment of these two items also appeared in *The Irish Humanist: Quarterly Journal of the Association of Irish Humanists*, no. 21 (April–June 1999), pp. 6–7.

59. "Confronting the 'Corporate Mystique.'" *Free Inquiry* 19, no. 3 (Summer 1999), pp. 5, 54–56.

60. "Why Do People Believe or Disbelieve?" *Free Inquiry* 19, no. 3 (Summer 1999), pp. 23–27.

61. "Should the *Skeptical Inquirer* Investigate Religion?" *Skeptical Inquirer* 23, no. 4 (July/August 1999), pp. 24–28.

62. "Humanism and the Arts: Does Art Convey Knowledge?" In Robert Tapp, ed., *Living as Humanists: Essays from the Humanist Institute*, Vol. 10 (1996) of "Humanism Today." Albuquerque, N. Mex: North American Committee for Humanism (NACH), 1999, pp. 153–164.

63. "Humanist Manifesto 2000: A Call for a New Planetary Humanism." *Free Inquiry* 19, no. 4 (Fall 1999). Translated into German, Spanish, Russian,

Norwegian, Swedish, Arabic, Hindi. Excerpted in *The Syracuse* (N.Y.) *Herald-American* (January 2, 2000).

64. "Triumphalist Trends of '90s a Prelude to Global 21st Century." *The Buffalo News* (December 26, 1999), pp. H1, H4.

65. "On Entering the Third Decade: Personal Reflections." *Free Inquiry* 20, no. 1 (Spring 2000), pp. 28–38.

Book Reviews

1. "The Churching and Unchurching of America." A review of Roger Finke and Rodney Stark, *The Churching of America, 1776–1990: Winners and Losers in Our Religious Economy. Free Inquiry* 13, no. 3 (Summer 1993), pp. 55–56.

2. "Academic Antiscience." A review of Paul R. Gross and Norman Levitt, *Higher Superstition: The Academic Left and Its Quarrels with Science. Free Inquiry* 14, no. 4 (Fall 1994), p. 60.

3. "The New Wave: French Humanism." A review of Mark Lilla, ed., *New French Thought: Political Philosophy. Free Inquiry* 15, no. 1 (Winter 1994/1995), pp. 57–58.

4. "Reflections on the Cult of Lenin." A review of Dmitri Volkogonov, *Lenin: A New Biography. Free Inquiry* 15, no. 2 (Spring 1995), pp. 52–54.

5. "Who Is a Jew? Rising above the Ancient Loyalties." A review of Alan M. Dershowitz, *The Vanishing American Jew: In Search of Jewish Identity for the Next Century*, and Paul Wexler, *The Ashkenazic Jews: A Slavo-Turkic People in Search of a Jewish Identity. Free Inquiry* 17, no. 3 (Summer 1997), pp. 54–57.

6. "The Relevance of Sidney Hook Today: A Good Interpretation of Hook's Work Still Awaits." A review of Christopher Phelps, *Young Sidney Hook: Marxist and Pragmatist. Free Inquiry* 18, no. 4 (Fall 1998), pp. 61–63.

7. "Can the Sciences Be Unified?" A review of Edward O. Wilson, *Consilience: The Unity of Knowledge.* In *Skeptical Inquirer* 22, no. 4 (July/August 1998), pp. 47–49. A translation by Bohdan Dhwede|czuk appeared as "Czy mo⌐na zjednoczy nauki?," *Bez Dogmatu: Kwartalnik kulturalno-polityczny* (Warsaw, Poland) no. 38 (Fall 1998), pp. 22–24.

Miscellaneous

1. "Birthday Greetings." *The Ethical Record* (London, England) 98, no. 2 (February 1993).

2. "The Proposed Center for Inquiry Library." *Skeptical Inquirer* 17, no. 3 (Spring 1993).

3. "The Center for Inquiry Library: The Freethought and Secular Humanist Collection." *Free Inquiry* 13, no. 2 (Spring 1993).

4. Letter to the Editor ("A Disdain for Political Theology"). *The Wall Street Journal* (April 15, 1993), p. A15.

5. "Letters." *Measure: In Defense of Academic Freedom and Integrity* (University Centers for Rational Alternatives, New York), no. 117 (June 1993). A critique of Nino Langiulli's "When It Came to 'That' at the University of Cincinnati" and E. Michael Jones's "Jane's Affliction: PC From the Inside," both of which appeared in *Measure*, no. 114 (March 1993).

6. "What They Said . . . " *The New Zealand Rationalist & Humanist* (Autumn 1997), pp. 13–14. Excerpts from letters of acceptance from various personages who were elected Honorary Associates of the enlarged New Zealand Association of Rationalists and Humanists.

Index